Brian Solomon's
RAILWAY
Guide to Europe

KALMBACH BOOKS

Kalmbach Books
21027 Crossroads Circle
Waukesha, Wisconsin 53186
www.KalmbachHobbyStore.com

Published in 2018
22 21 20 19 18   1 2 3 4 5

Manufactured in China

ISBN: 978-1-62700-477-0
EISBN: 978-1-62700-478-7

Editor: Randy Rehberg
Book Design: Tom Ford

Unless noted, photographs were taken by the author.

Library of Congress Control Number: 2017934278

Contents

Preface.. 4

Acknowledgments 6

Introduction... 7

Map of Europe 16

Part 1: Great Britain & Ireland

Great Britain 18

Ireland 60

Part 2: Central Europe

Germany.. 94

France 138

Belgium.. 176

Luxembourg 198

The Netherlands.. 204

Part 3: Alpine Countries

Switzerland 220

Austria 264

Italy.. 294

Part 4: Scandinavia

Finland... 330

Sweden and Norway.. 344

Part 5: Iberia

Portugal.. 356

Spain 376

Part 6: Eastern Europe

Czech Republic.. 386

Slovakia.. 402

Hungary 410

Preface

Over the last 20 years, I've spent months every year exploring, studying, and photographing railways across Europe. I've found something new and fascinating at each bend in the line, at every new station, and at every new city I visit. There's an incomparable thrill to arrive in an unexplored city by train. As the brakes are applied and the train comes to a halt, you'll see a place for the first time. All across Europe are hundreds of old cities and towns imbued with history, filled with interesting architecture, sumptuous scents, and interesting things to see and do.

This is my guidebook, and with it, I hope to advise and encourage you in your travels. Although it covers a wide scope of railways and places from Ireland to eastern Europe and Iberia to Scandinavia, it isn't intended as a comprehensive guide. Rather, I've focused on the places that I've found to be most interesting and most worthy of revisiting.

My travels have covered far more ground than I could possibly illustrate in a book this size. I've traveled alone and with friends; with a plan and without; by train, by automobile, in planes, and on ships. I've walked streets in dozens of cities by day and by night. I hope that my experiences will encourage you to travel and explore.

I also hope to entertain and inform you. I want to encourage you to visit the places I've been, but also to push your limits and explore new places too. I offer practical advice on how to buy the best

tickets, and offer suggestions on how to plan your journey. I suggest some itineraries and places to visit. In some instances, I urge caution since not all railways offer the same level of service and not all trains provide wonderful experiences.

Europe and European railways have undergone many changes since I first visited in the mid-1990s, and Europe continues to change. So while I've made every effort to provide up-to-date information and keep the book current, over time it inevitably will become dated: prices will change and railways will adjust their schedules. Some routes may close or passenger services withdrawn, while new lines will open and new trains will be introduced. The impressive new high-speed train introduced today may seem old hat after a few years. The fascinating antique equipment still in service right now will eventually be withdrawn.

I've tried to offer useful tips and hints based on personal experience and fill gaps left by other guidebooks. I've detailed a variety of public transit systems, specified how to buy tickets or passes, and which are the best to buy. Often when traveling, I've arrived in a city and found the details of the transportation system opaque or overly complex, so hopefully, I've made that easier for you.

For each country, I offer a little history and context, supply some nuts and bolts on how to travel and buy tickets, profile interesting destinations, and highlight interesting railway lines. Many of the routes I've selected are noted for their scenic splendor, engineering wonders, or exemplary trains. Yet other journeys are more functional. Not all railways in Europe feature stunning scenery. The high-speed journey from Brussels to Paris is admittedly a bit bland, yet being whisked along at 186 mph (300km/h) is a thrill, and the train is a practical, pleasant way to travel between these two cities. Likewise, a journey down the West Coast Main Line in Britain may not make many travelers' top-ten railway trips, but it can still be part of a great railway adventure. Some readers may be shocked to learn that not all Swiss railways terminate atop a snow-crested peak (and that some reach these peaks below ground).

I've taken most of the photos in this book, while some have been supplied by my fellow travelers. By and large, I've aimed at using images that show how things appear today. In some instances, I've included older or historic images to add breadth or because an older photo provides an angle or perspective that I feel is better than what I've been able to see in more recent times.

The Internet offers wonderful tools to assist with planning. Years ago, I'd plan my trips using a Thomas Cook guide, and buy my tickets through travel agencies or wait in lines at a foreign station to try to find someone that spoke enough English to sell me what I needed. I recall being shouted at in Milan by an unhelpful agent who blasted me and declared my journey impossible. (All I wanted was a ticket to the French border station at Modane.) In another instance, I arrived at a remote French town hoping to ride a branch line, only to find that it had suspended service. In a similar instance in Poland, when I looked for my train, a kind railwayman advised me with the dreaded word *autobus*.

Happily today, you can get excellent and up-to-the-minute schedule information online using your phone. Often, you can check and compare ticket prices weeks in advance. In many instances, you can buy your tickets electronically. You still need to be smart about making your plans and this is where this book can help. I've provided dozens of useful web addresses and listed helpful mobile apps, while suggesting caution when these tools prove difficult or fall short.

It helps to plan, but today's tools also allow for a great degree of spontaneous travel. You might find a cheap seat on a train you hadn't plan to ride and visit some distant town you'd never even heard of. What about a hotel? Book it online from the train! Enjoy your trip. Push the boundaries of railway travel. Bring along your family and friends, or maybe you'll make some new friends as you go. I have.

Brian Solomon
Dublin, Ireland
September 2017

Acknowledgments

This book represents more than 20 years of railway exploration and study, and during that time, I've met dozens of people who have aided me in my travels. Furthermore, I've researched and prepared many other books and articles relating to European railways, which have contributed to the content of this book. I often travel with friends who participate in planning the trips and arranging tickets, accommodations, and special tours. Without their help, this book would not have been possible.

I've spent hundreds of hours in the library of the Irish Railway Record Society in Dublin reading about railways, so special thanks to the members who gave me advice on places to visit and travel tips on European railways.

Colm O'Callaghan, Barry Carse, John Clery, Diarmaid Collins, Tony Cooke, Donncha Cronin, Jim Deegan of Railtours Ireland First Class, Hugh Dempsey, Dom Dominick, Paul and Sarah Dowd, Oliver Doyle, Noel Enright, Donal Flynn, Ken Fox, Lar Griffin, Mark Healy, Mark Hodge, Eamon Jones, William Malone, Tommy Martin, Kevin Meanie, Jay Monaghan, Paul Quinlan, Sean Twohig, and Michael Walsh are among my many Irish friends that aided my travels in the Republic.

Thanks to everyone at the Railway Preservation Society of Ireland for their help during steam trips and tours.

Members of the Modern Railway Society of Ireland hosted me in Belfast and assisted with my photography of NI Railways.

Gerry Conmy, Stephen Hirsch, Denis McCabe, Norman McAdams, and Dan Smith are among my Irish friends that traveled with me across Europe while providing advice for further travel and tips on railway history, operations, and technology.

Michael Stewart provided tours of Belfast and Derry.

Dan and Tony Renehan encouraged me to visit the Festiniog Railway in Wales and offered expert opinions on steam locomotives.

Dave Murphy offered suggestions on traveling in Finland and Estonia.

David Hegarty and Hassard Stacpoole for extensive travels in Ireland and the UK.

Honer Travers traveled with me in Ireland, Northern Ireland, and Italy, plus provided text on the Downpatrick and County Down Railway.

Colin Horan traveled with me in Belgium, France, Germany, Holland, Ireland, and Luxembourg and took me on a tour of Train World in Brussels.

Peter Rigney and Anthony Bools assisted with travels in Italy.

Jack May and Walter E. Zullig offered advice and perspective on places to visit.

Tessa Bold traveled with me in Germany, Sweden and the UK.

Alan Reekie provided detailed tours of Brussels.

Special thanks to Markku Pulkinnen, Petri and Pietu Tuovinen, Asko Räsänen, Mikko Tikkanen, Matti Mäntyvaara, Saki K. Salo, and Juhani Katajisto for Scandinavian adventures.

Mauno Pajunen assisted with visits in Belgium, Finland, and France.

M. Ross Valentine and John Gruber traveled with me in Germany and Poland.

Bonnie Gruber supplied photos of Norway.

Chris Guss supplied photos of Scandinavia.

Tim Doherty traveled with me in Austria, Czech Republic, Germany, Ireland, and Slovakia and provided insight on visits to Italy and London Paddington Station.

Colin Garratt hosted me on visits to Leicestershire and offered advice on photographing British railways.

Tom Hoover and I explored railways around Leeds and the Settle & Carlisle.

Alistair Mearns offered advice on Scottish railways.

Thanks to my brother Seán Solomon and Isabelle Dijols for visits in Paris.

My father Richard J. Solomon introduced me to European railways, suggested itineraries, supplied photos, traveled with me on several occasions across Europe and proofread the text.

Special thanks to Brian Schmidt at *Trains* magazine for suggesting this project and making the necessary introductions, and to Kalmbach Books editor Randy Rehberg and the production team for their input and advice and seeing this project to completion.

Introduction

In addition to domestic service, SNCF high-speed trains connect French cities with those in neighboring countries. A modern TGV glides through Esslingen, Germany, on a spring evening.

Europe's comprehensive, varied, colorful, and efficient railways offer visitors endless opportunities to explore. Railways range from intensively operated networks, such as those in Great Britain, Holland, and Germany, where trains operate every few minutes on core routes, to lightly traveled rural lines in Finland, Portugal, and western Ireland. Railway travel is an excellent way to visit destinations without needing to negotiate the complexities, claustrophobic constraints, and unpleasantness associated with airlines and airports or dealing with stress, navigational nightmares, and complications of driving on European roads.

European railways are as varied as the nations and communities that they serve. They include some of the world's fastest intercity ground transportation, such as the famous French high-speed lines that whisk passengers along at speeds sometimes in excess of 200 mph. They also feature meandering lines, among them historic preserved railways like the Welsh narrow gauges and rustic Swiss rack railways.

Railway travel allows passengers to comfortably take in a rolling panorama of historic landscapes with castles, churches, quaint villages, river valleys, and towering mountain peaks, as well as complex urban tapestries. You can see beautiful scenery, gaze in wonder at the chaos of morning rush hour, or enjoy a meal served to your seat as you fly along the ground at tremendous speed.

What is difficult to comprehend, let alone appreciate, is the vast scope of European railways. Europe as a whole, including countries within and outside the European Union, is connected by more than 216,000 railway route miles (348,000km), with considerable portions of this network consisting of heavily built electrified double-track. Germany alone operates more than 20,000 route miles (32,187km). Not all railways are passenger lines, and some routes are exclusively used for the movement of freight, yet most major railways carry passenger trains.

Across much of central Europe, passenger services on main routes operate on regular interval timetables. On some busy lines, there may be 10 or more trains each way per hour. Britain, which introduced the railway to the world in the 1820s, has one of the most intensely operated networks. To earn an appreciation for this, during the evening rush hour, stand at the end of a railway platform at London's Clapham Junction—which boasts Britain's busiest railway intersection—and watch up to six trains closing in on the station simultaneously and the floods of passengers disgorged and absorbed by these trains.

RAILWAY EVOLUTION

Europe's railways have undergone continual changes reflecting demographics, evolving travel patterns, competition with nonrail transport, and varying degrees of political support and investment, not to mention the introduction of new types of trains, new technology, and new railway operators.

Among the changes are those spurred by the European Union including directives for functional separation between infrastructure and operations regarding traditional state-owned railway companies. Coincident with this has been a liberalization of operations that has facilitated a growing number of new train operators and increased competition on some major routes. This has made for greater variety of trains, and in some situations has lowered the price of travel; yet for some journeys, it has made traveling more compli-cated, especially in regards to ticketing and choosing the best trains to travel on.

Over the last 40 years, the styles of railway equipment have changed. Historically, most European state-run railways procured trains that were custom-designed for their individ-ual systems, which resulted in a disparity of train designs between the different countries (especially regarding equipment assigned to domestic services). In recent years, tendering and purchasing requirements—combined with the rapid consolidation of railway equip-ment manufacturers into a few multinational builders—has streamlined the variety of trains on the move. Today railway operators select equipment from only a few families of standardized trains.

Italian-designed tilting Pendolino trains now operate in intercity service everywhere from the Iberian Peninsula to Russia, and from Great Britain to the Balkans. Swiss-made Stadler railcars are found across Europe and have even penetrated the North American market. Did that new German electric seem remarkably familiar? That's because the now-standard Siemens Vectron is essentially the same as Amtrak's Siemens-built Cities Sprinters employed on the Northeast Corridor in the United States.

In general, European railways have been moving away from traditional locomotive-hauled passenger trains in favor of fixed-consist, self-propelled trains. These may be in the form of diesel- or electric-powered multiple units, railcars, or semi-permanently coupled consists with power cars on one or both ends. While multiple units of various types have worked in suburban services for more than a century, today they are becoming increasingly common for all types of service, including long-distance trains.

Coinciding with these changes has been the shift to modern high-speed trains such as the French TGV, Spanish AVE, and German ICE in place of older conventional trains on slower intercity schedules. The growing dominance of significantly faster high-speed rail services (often operating on an hourly frequency or better), combined with modal competition from low-cost airlines such as Ryan Air, have resulted in a dramatic decline in international overnight sleeping-car services. While there

Germany's InterCity Express trains operate in domestic and international services on both dedicated high-speed lines and conventional routes. An ICE train pauses for passengers at Jenback, Austria.

are still some overnight trains, and these remain well patronized in eastern Europe and Scandinavia, overall sleeping-car travel has been in decline in recent years.

The interior configurations of trains have evolved. The once-standard side-corridor carriages, with enclosed compartments and seats facing one another, have gradually given way to various central corridor, open-carriage seating arrangements. Two-by-two seating is common in second class, with one-by-two seating often employed in first class. In some situations, seating is airline style (seats back to front), while in others, a central table is positioned between groups of two or four seats.

PLANNING

The European network enables travelers to explore myriad routes while connecting the dots on their journey. However, to make the most of your individual railway experience, you often need to employ some clever strategies in planning your railway travel. Each European nation has its own railway network, and each has its own peculiarities

when it comes to operations, scheduling, planning systems, ticketing, and station access. And international services have their own considerations.

Planning is different than it used to be. Paper timetables are virtually obsolete, and many railways no longer issue timetables. Instead, online trip planners, mobile apps for smart phones and tablets, plus other inter-active tools are readily available. On the plus side, you can often get up-to-the-minute scheduling information, ticket prices, and seat availability. However, these systems aren't perfect. While many railways offer English-language options, not all European railways have had the same degree of success with their Internet tools, and navigating them takes patience. Current web addresses and apps are provided for each railway in this book.

Deutsche Bahn (Germany Railways) offers one of the easiest and most useful websites for planning. Not only does it provide detailed train scheduling information across Germany, but the website also covers the rest of Europe as well. One of its most helpful features are pull-down timetables that show

Cut down on laundry

One way to help minimize your luggage is clever laundry management. Rather than fill your bags with a week's worth of under-garments and tote them around, consider visiting inexpensive shops to buy new under-garments as required while disposing of old laundry before it requires washing. Use your smart phone to locate clothing retail shops such as Primark or New Yorker stores that sell inexpensive undergarments. You'll also save on your airline's check baggage limit. If you fly with European budget airlines, luggage charges may exceed the price of your ticket. Rather than spend €50 to €100 on luggage fees, consider simply investing in under-garments and other disposables as you go. You'll also save time by avoiding European laundries, which often have slow wash cycles. Spend your time seeing the sights rather than washing your undies.

---

a train's complete schedule from beginning to end, listing intermediate stations. This is useful when you wish to obtain a more specific understanding of where trains go and which may be most useful to you. (See **bahn.com/en** or type *rail timetable Germany* into your browser and select "Deutsche Bahn timetable.")

Once on the site, select the pull-down menu for "Timetable & booking." (Note: while you can use this site for finding fares and booking tickets on German trains, it gener-ally doesn't supply fare information outside of Germany). Enter prospective departure and arrival points. The site will then offer a variety of stations. Be sure to select the correct station as large cities often have mul-tiple railway stations or terminals, and some stations have remarkably similar names but may be many miles apart. Once you have your end points and potential travel dates entered, the site should provide a list of trains. Not all journeys are equal, so compare the differences for the trains displayed. There are two boxes that allow you to narrow the list of trains: "Prefer fast connections" and "Local transport only." If you have either one of these ticked, the online schedule will only display the trains that fulfill these categories, and thus may not give you a complete picture of the level of service provided.

To activate your search, click on the red "Search" icon at the lower right of the "Timetable & booking" panel. A list of sched-uled trains should come up on your screen. From left to right, this will show you the departure and arrival stations one on top of the other. Next look under "Time" to find the arrival and departure times at those stations. Under "Duration" is a number representing the length of the journey in hours and minutes (1:57 indicates a 1 hour, 57 minute journey). The header for "Chg" will list the number of times you will need to change trains, with 0 inferring a direct train. Under the heading "Products," you will find a list of the types of trains by their common initials (Regional Express = RE, etc.). This seemly innocuous listing is very important since it may affect the speed and cost of the individual train and the type of ticket you will need to travel.

CONSIDER SERVICES

Pay close attention to the differences in travel times, train changes, and to the type of trains offered. Many European countries offer various types of service and those specific for each country are outlined in the individual chapters in this book. Germany has some of the greatest variety of services, ranging from relatively slow Regional Bahn services to the high-speed ICE (intercity express). In many countries, faster express trains require special tickets, fare supple-ments, and/or advance reservations.

Don't hesitate to consider different types of trains, but it is important to know in advance what level of service is provided. Just because a train connects two cities doesn't mean it's your best choice. Not all trains are equivalent. A regional train (even on a long run) may not provide anything more than rudimentary seating, let alone a dining car or other high-end features. Local and regional trains are useful for reaching smaller towns and exploring places that may not be served

Czech Republic is well served by its national railway network, which includes electrified main lines and meandering single-track branches that host a nice variety of trains to travel on.

by an express, but they can be painfully slow for long-distance travel. There may be trains that depart later and arrive earlier. Likewise, a fast high-speed train may cost more and get you there faster but follow a modern alignment that misses all the scenery. If you are planning a scenic journey through the Swiss Alps, don't spend the extra money on an express train from Zurich to Milan, since you'll pay more to miss the best scenery!

Consider what it may mean to change trains. If you are traveling alone and traveling light, changing trains shouldn't pose too much of a problem. On the more organized railways, such as those in Austria, Belgium, Germany, and Switzerland, detailed platform information may be provided in advance, and often changes are afforded in cross-platform transfers. However, changes can be fairly tight, and if necessary at relatively large stations with a half dozen platforms or more, they may require you to locate the correct platform and proceed posthaste. So if you are traveling with lots of luggage or have your family in tow, changing can prove challenging (especially when your arriving train is behind schedule).

Many railway passenger networks work on hub-and-spoke systems and routinely expect passengers to change at local hubs. In these instances, it may not be possible to get direct trains for the full length of your journey, especially if your destination is on a secondary route or branch line. When changing trains, pay special attention to the destination of the train you are boarding. Just because you are directed to platform 3 doesn't necessarily mean that first train that stops there is going where you are. Many Continental railways provide excellent on-platform destination displays as well as destination information on the trains themselves. It always helps to know the direction you are traveling and the end destination of the train you are planning to board.

For example: You have arrived at the Köln Hbf (Cologne main station) from Brussels on the Thalys high-speed train and are planning to continue to Mainz on the DB ICE. DB operates a variety of trains between these cities, so it is important to locate your train by number and by final destination. One way to find this information is with the Deutsche Bahn timetable site. Prior to traveling, go to

Great Britain boasts some of Europe's finest heritage railways. A postwar "Black Five" 4-6-0 steam locomotive exits the tunnel at Grosmont on North Yorkshire Moors Railway.

DB's "Timetable & booking" page and select the train that you plan to travel on. When you click the "Show details" box situated below the departure and arrival cities (at the left of the timetable), this should display a detailed listing for your train with the train number. In the example for the Köln Hbf-Mainz service, this train is ICE 27. In addition, it will show departure and arrival platforms, plus the final destination of your train, which is Wien Hbf (Vienna, Austria's main station). This information should be repeated on your ticket (if you've bought a train-specific ticket). The important point is that while you may have no intention of traveling to Vienna you know to look for Wien Hbf when changing trains.

By using the "Show details" pull-down menu, you can learn more about train schedules. Did you know that you can travel directly from Köln to Vienna on a high-speed train? So maybe you'd rather visit Vienna anyway. Another helpful insight is to know what to expect from the type of equipment on the platform. For example, a German ICE service uses a distinctive looking train—a sleek, streamlined consist painted off-white with bright red striped reflective windows

and the letters ICE boldly printed on the side. If while waiting on platform 7 at the Köln Hbf, a light red, electric multiple unit arrives that doesn't feature Wien Hbf in the destination board, this is unlikely to be your ICE train. If you are unsure as to a train's destination, it is best and show your ticket to a member of the train staff before the train departs.

TRAVEL SMART AND TRAVEL LIGHT

You'll notice that many European trains don't carry baggage cars, and there's a reason for that. By and large, European rail travelers tend to pack light. A moderately sized wheelie bag and a shoulder case are all most travelers will bring with them even when going on a relatively long journey. A smart visitor will try to emulate this style of travel. Avoid carrying anything that you really don't need. European stores are just as well stocked as those in North America, and you can usually buy whatever you need rather than overpacking. Keep the size and weight of your bags to a minimum while leaving space for things you might buy along the way.

High-speed and other intercity trains typically have space for luggage at the

European railways have undergone many changes in the last 50 years. A classic Trans Europ Express (TEE) departs Hamburg, Germany, in 1960. In the 1980s and 1990s, TEE's international network was supplanted by modern high-speed and InterCity services. *Richard Jay Solomon*

ends of carriages, while many trains have overhead luggage racks, but the compact nature of many modern trains do not facilitate movement of large volumes of luggage. Unlike in North America, where Amtrak and VIA Rail passengers are typically greeted by railroad employees, in Europe you may not meet a member of the train staff until after you are on your train. On most European railways, passengers using smaller stations are expected to get on and off trains without assistance.

Regional and local trains tend to have less space for luggage than long-distance InterCity and high-speed services. And if you are traveling at peak periods on commuter trains, the local travelers may neither be impressed nor sympathetic when you occupy valuable seats or aisles with your oversized bags.

In the UK and Ireland, high-level platforms are the rule, and these should be flush with train doors. Elsewhere in Europe, platform heights vary. Modern Continental trains tend to have low floors to facilitate access by mobility impaired travelers and feature low-floor sections by doors with space for wheelchairs and baby carriages. However to access the rest of the train, you may need to climb interior steps. Older trains, especially those in eastern Europe, require you to climb vestibule steps to reach the seats in the carriage.

Be prepared before your stop. At large stations and terminals, trains may have extended stops, but don't expect a train to hang around any longer than necessary. In German, Austrian, and other central European stations, train diagrams are posted on the platform to indicate the intended number and arrangement of carriages for each scheduled train. If your ticket has seating assignments, this will help you locate the correct place to board in advance of your train's arrival. This allows you to avoid fighting your way through the aisles and corridors once you are onboard and rolling.

When you are onboard, listen carefully to the announcements and anticipate your station. Some European railways issue announcements in multiple languages including English, but these may not be repeated,

Weekend and Sunday schedules

The more progressive central European railways operate the same schedule seven days a week. However, many railways continue to operate separate schedules on weekends, often curtailing or rearranging operating times to save money. Sunday schedules can be especially sparse, and some lines won't have any Sunday service at all. When checking train timetables, be sure you that are reading the times for the correct day, otherwise you may wait a long time for the next scheduled service.

so it's important to get the message the first time. By using DB's "Timetable & booking" page, you should be able to ascertain your intended arrival time (and the station prior to yours) so that you can be prepared to get off. Stops at small stations can be very short, so you should be ready before the train reaches the platform. By waiting too long, you may find that you face oncoming passengers and have difficulty reaching the door in time before the train is underway again.

On most trains, all doors facing platforms should be capable of opening (unless they are broken or marked out of service), but it is often the responsibility of passengers to actually open the door. Modern trains feature a small button that changes color or illuminates when the train driver has unlocked the doors. You press the illuminated button and the doors will open. Older trains may use cranks or a handle to open doors. Older trains in the UK required you to lower a window and open the door from the outside, but you are unlikely to find this arrangement today, except on preserved British railways.

Consider the days and times when you plan to travel. Trains are most comfortable and enjoyable when they aren't too crowded. You'll have more room to spread out and an easier time getting on and off. But traveling on tightly packed or oversold trains can be unpleasant even when you have reserved seats. Suburban trains are often packed at rush hour (one reason why some rail passes preclude travel in early mornings). Don't expect a seat if you are traveling into London, Paris, or other large cities before 9 a.m. on weekdays. Trains are often crowded on Friday and Sunday evenings. InterCity trains can be very busy during summer, at Christmas, and other popular public holidays. Consult a calendar to see when local holidays fall, keeping in mind that every country has popular travel times and these may not coincide with holidays in America or Britain. Check to see if there are events or festivals that may result in abnormally busy trains.

When possible, during busy travel times, you should reserve seats and if you must travel during busy periods, consider traveling first class (or its equivalent), even when you would normally travel second class. Some railways adjust their ticket prices to reflect peak travel. Even if you are traveling on a pass or prebooked tickets, a glance at the railway's website and fare inquiry pages will be worth the effort because this can give you an idea which trains may be the most crowded. Higher prices may hint at busy trains. (Not only will a busy train be less comfortable but also more expensive.) Likewise, when a railway's website is offering promotional fares on off-peak services, this may be a hint that the trains are lightly used. If your time is not at a premium, consider traveling off-peak since you may save money and have a more pleasant trip.

EURAIL AND INTERRAIL PASSES
Eurail offers non-European citizens or residents a variety of flexible flat-rate open passes which facilitate railway travel. The benefits of a Eurail pass include the ability to avoid buying tickets and the associated hassle of waiting in lines while trying to communicate with ticket agents or ticket sellers who are not fluent with your language. These passes are especially useful if you have an open itinerary and want the ability to change your plan quickly without financial penalty. Flat-rate travel allows you the freedom to explore and jump on and off trains at will. In addition they can be especially useful for cross-border travel where buying tickets is more complicated and more expensive.

Although much of the European mainline network is electrified, you can still find diesel trains on branch lines and secondary routes such as Austria's Zillertalbahn.

However, a Eurail pass may not always be the most cost-effective option. It pays to compare the cost of a Eurail pass with locally procured tickets, advance purchase options, Internet offers, and other ticketing choices.

You may get the best value from a Eurail pass if you intend to make a series of long journeys involving various participating train operating companies or countries. By contrast, if you are focusing your travels within a relatively small area, or are only planning a few short trips, the Eurail pass is probably a waste of money. Furthermore, in some countries, the value and flexibility of a Eurail pass has been diminished because railways require compulsory reservations or supplements for high-speed/intercity train travel. This is particularly true in France and Spain. In many eastern European countries, train travel is relatively inexpensive, and a pass may not offer great value compared with local tickets. Passes are not accepted on all trains, so before boarding make sure it is valid for travel. Always check which railways and trains within a country accept your ticket. Several famous mountain railways in Switzerland do not accept Eurail passes or

only offer a discount when you present your pass to buy a ticket in advance of traveling.

Eurail passes cover travel in 28 countries. First and second class travel is available and there are different rates for Youth, Adult, and Family passes. There are multiple country passes and a variety of single country passes. It's best to explore the Eurail website for the most up-to-date prices, passes, and special offers (**eurail.com/en/eurail-passes**).

If you are a European citizen or resident, you can take advantage of InterRail passes, which are similar to Eurail's and available for 30 different countries. (See **interrail.eu**.)

Various third-party agencies sell European railway tickets and passes and may simplify the process of procuring travel documents, but these don't necessarily offer the cheapest fares. (To buy passes, single or multiple journey tickets, and seat reservations see **raileurope.com**.)

Throughout this book, for each country, I highlight tickets and passes that may be most useful for travelers. Prices and the types of tickets change, so it's wise to consult an individual railway's website for the most up-to-date information.

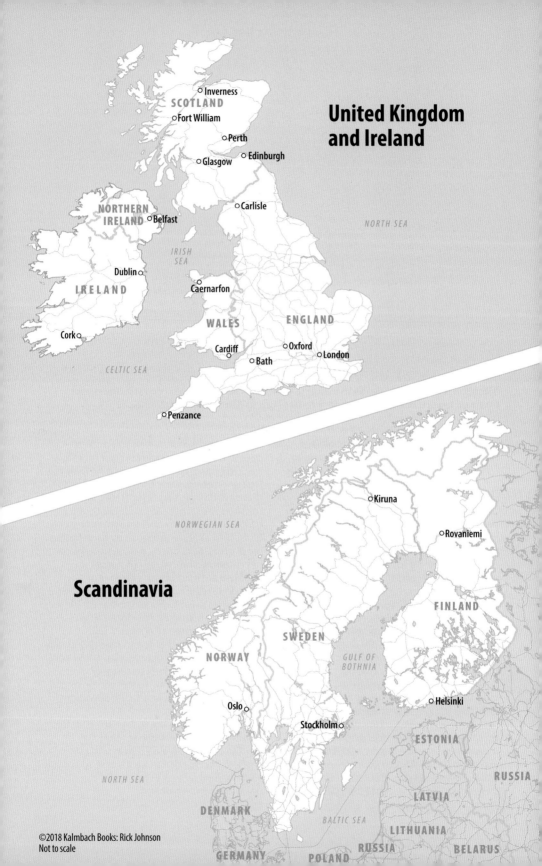

United Kingdom and Ireland

SCOTLAND
Inverness
Fort William
Perth
Glasgow
Edinburgh
Carlisle

NORTH SEA

NORTHERN IRELAND
Belfast

IRISH SEA

Dublin

IRELAND

Caernarfon

Cork

WALES

ENGLAND

Cardiff
Bath
Oxford
London

CELTIC SEA

Penzance

Scandinavia

NORWEGIAN SEA

Kiruna

Rovaniemi

FINLAND

SWEDEN

NORWAY

GULF OF BOTHNIA

Oslo

Stockholm

Helsinki

ESTONIA

NORTH SEA

RUSSIA

LATVIA

DENMARK

BALTIC SEA

LITHUANIA

RUSSIA

BELARUS

GERMANY

POLAND

Western Europe

Great Britain

378 154

Located south of London in Sussex, the Blue Bell Railway was a pioneer British preserved railway and a fine example of the many wonderful operating heritage lines in Great Britain today.

The United Kingdom includes the island of Great Britain (England, Scotland, and Wales) plus Northern Ireland, which consists of the six counties of Ulster in the northeastern part of the island of Ireland. Great Britain is served by private train-operating companies working Britain's national network that is owned, operated, and maintained by a public company called Network Rail. In addition, Great Britain has dozens of heritage railways that are largely operated independently of the national network.

The steam railway originated in Great Britain during the early 19th century as a product of the industrial revolution, so traveling by train in Britain will bring you to the very roots of railroading.

The public railway wasn't the invention of one person but represented the coalescing of ideas and technologies, driven by the desire to move goods and people faster and more efficiently. Significantly, the steam railway blended the industrial tramway with the steam engine, and extended elaborate route networks inspired by the prior development and success of inland waterway transport canals.

A London Overground train approaches Wandsworth Road against a backdrop of the famous Battersea Park Power Station, noted for its appearance on the cover of Pink Floyd's album *Animals***, and presently under adaptive redevelopment.**

The steam engine evolved from stationary pumping engines during the 18th century and advanced by the scientific investigations of Scottish instrument maker James Watt. In 1803–1804, Cornishman Richard Trevithick built and tested a full-sized, double-acting stationary steam locomotive built by the Pen-y-Darran Iron Works in Wales. Although this ran at just 4 mph (6.4 km/h), it successfully demonstrated that steam power could be used to haul trains.

In the 1820s, the future pattern for commercial intercity steam railways was established through the work of George Stephenson and his son, Robert. Britain's first common carrier (public) railway was the 12-mile Stockton & Darlington, authorized by an Act of Parliament in 1821 and opened in 1825. On September 27 of that year, George Stephenson demonstrated his locomotive *Locomotion* by hauling a 34-car train over the line. The Stephensons went on to built the Liverpool & Manchester Railway, which, when it opened in 1829, was among the most extensive industrial enterprises in the world. This line held a competition called the Rainhill Trials to encourage steam locomotive design. The winning engine was Robert Stephenson's *Rocket*, which achieved the stunning speed of 29 mph—it employed a revolutionary design that successfully combined a multi-tubular boiler, forced draft, and direct linkage between pistons and driving wheels.

The success of the L&M Railway and *Rocket* inaugurated a "railway fever" that swept across Britain in the 1830s leading to dozens of railway schemes. And soon Britain wasn't just connecting its own cities with railways but was exporting the railway and its technology to nations around the world.

By the late 19th century, Great Britain benefited from one of the world's most intensively developed and busiest railway systems. Although the network map stopped growing before World War I, Britain's railways remained extraordinarily busy. Adverse financial matters stemming in part from the effects of the war resulted in the forced grouping of lines into four large regional systems in 1923. Of these groupings, the London & Northeastern Railway (LNER), London, Midland & Scottish Railway (LMS), and Southern Railway were new creations, while the Great Western Railway (GWR) was expanded from the company established in the mid-19th century by Victorian railway pioneer Isambard K. Brunel.

The interwar period was something of a second golden age for British railways that saw the development of fast intercity express trains, electrification of some lines, and refinement of steam locomotives to new levels of performance and

An HST en route to Penzance crosses Isambard K. Brunel's famous Royal Albert Bridge over the Tamar valley at Saltash, Cornwall.

perfection. The onset of World War II brought additional changes, and despite enormously heavy rail traffic, signaled the end of railway supremacy in Britain.

British Railways came out of the Second World War with enormous traffic volumes while suffering from deferred maintenance and declining finances. As a result, the private companies were nationalized in 1948 to form British Railways. Yet the system continued to suffer from underinvestment. Although there were efforts to modernize in the 1950s, these fell short, and by the end of the decade, the growth of highway transport had resulted in rapid loss of railway traffic, especially on rural lines. A new Conservative government was elected in 1959 with a pro-highway philosophy, which brought about widespread changes to the national public transport network. Dr. Richard Beeching was hired from private industry to analyze and reshape the rail network by trimming away lightly used and unprofitable portions. As a result, during the 1960s, British Railways underwent one of the most dramatic changes of any national railway system in Europe. Thousands of route miles were cut from the map and hundreds of stations were closed. This coincided with the end of the steam era, as diesels and electric operations took over.

Beeching's overly zealous trimming had serious long-term implications for British transport. Now more than 50 years later, Beeching's shortsighted approach to rationalization continues to plague Britain's rail network, which is still one of the most intensively utilized systems in Europe, with many routes operating at peak capacity.

Additional changes occurred in the 1990s, when it was decided to return the railways to private operation. However, instead of following a traditional model in which companies owned and operated trains and track, a compromise arrangement was devised with government-allocated operating franchises put up for bid, and Railtrack was created to own and operate the infrastructure—tracks, signaling, tunnels, and most stations. Today, while there are dozens of companies operating the trains on the rail network, a variety of problems with Railtrack led the government to recapture most of the infrastructure in 2002 into the new state-controlled entity called Network Rail.

British national network today

There's lots of good news when traveling by rail in Great Britain. Since it is among the busiest railway system in Europe, its national network features many lines and very frequent service on most routes, which, combined with a variety of operators and numerous parallel lines, allows for a great many journey possibilities. (For a general route map, see **nationalrail.co.uk/css/network_rail_national_map.pdf.** For a detailed map showing a breakdown of different train operators, see **barry-doe.co.uk/railmap24.pdf**.) Most trains do not require advance reservations, but on the downside, because the railways are so heavily used, British rail travel tends to be expensive, especially if you don't take the time to investigate fare options in advance of traveling. While you can buy walk-up tickets for most journeys, this is often the most expensive way to travel. In Britain, it really pays to plan ahead. (For tips on travel and advice on tickets, check out the Man in Seat 61 at **seat61.com**.)

BASIC TICKETS

For schedules, journey planning, and tickets, see **nationalrail.co.uk** or go directly to the websites of the train companies you hope to travel on, since in some instances, individual train companies may offer reduced fares on their sites.

When planning a simple journey, for example traveling one way from London to an outlying city, a single ticket may be the most effective option. Remember that

Old train in a new dress: a 1970s-era HST working Virgin Trains' East Coast services rests under the train shed at London Kings Cross.

tickets get more expensive the closer to your trip, and that not all services on a given route are priced the same. For most routes, there are three basic types of single journey tickets. (Incidentally, a one-way journey requires a single ticket, while a round-trip journey will need a return ticket.) A **Round Robin** is a specialized type of ticket, which is explained on page 24.

The most flexible and most expensive fare is the **Anytime** ticket, less expensive are **Off-peak** tickets, while the least flexible and cheapest tickets are **Advance** tickets. All three types may be available in both first and standard (second) class, with lower fares for children and seniors.

If you are willing to lock your travel plans to a trip at a specific time on a specific train, consider buying an Advance ticket. If these are available for your route, they can provide you with substantial savings and may allow you to travel at just a fraction of the walk-up Anytime ticket price. However, Advance tickets are inflexible, and usually do not allow for a break in your journey (except where necessary to make a connection), and may be fare-specific between the two end points on your trip. Another potential advantage: a first class Advance ticket may allow you to travel in first class accommodation for approximately the same price as the Anytime standard class fare (depending on the time of day and expected demand for the train).

PASSES AND SPECIAL TICKETS

If you are hoping to explore the national railway network, desire to make circle trips, or have multiple journeys in mind, you should investigate the various **Ranger** and **Rover** tickets that are available. These offer you better value and greater flexibility than single tickets. At any time, there are dozens of different offers, many of which are focused on a specific region or line. (See **nationalrail.co.uk/times_fares/rangers_and_rovers**.)

A Rover ticket is essentially a travel pass that entitles you to unlimited travel (possibly with some restrictions) within defined geographical limits for a specified period of time, usually several days. A Ranger ticket is more restrictive, often only valid on one route (or a defined route cluster), and typically offers unlimited travel during a single day. Similar to Ranger tickets, Round Robin tickets allow unlimited travel in a circle on a defined route over the course of one day. Some tickets are exclusive to one operator's trains, while others allow ticket holders to travel on various operators within the ticket's defined area.

The National Rail website (**nationalrail.co.uk**) highlights the prices, regions, and restrictions particular to each type of ticket. Using an interactive menu, this site highlights which companies accept the ticket, lists the length of time it is valid, spells out specific restrictions, and features a useful (printable) schematic map that demonstrates the areas of validity.

The most flexible—but one of the most costly types of tickets—are **All Line Rovers**. Although the name is nominally misleading since there are a variety of lines that don't accept this pass, an All Line Rover can allow you the freedom to travel across the national railway network: exploring from Penzance to Holyhead, from Thurso to Dover, while getting on and off trains at your leisure without worrying about the necessity to purchase tickets, make reservations, or overstep the limits

Valid tickets

British train operators tend to be very rules conscious, and as a passenger, it is up to you to ensure that you have the correct ticket. In general, you must have a ticket prior to boarding a train and don't expect that railway staff will make an exception if you present an invalid ticket. If you are uncertain if your ticket is valid, it is better to ask a qualified member of railway staff prior to boarding, rather than face an unsympathetic ticket checker more eager to issue fines than aid you on your trip.

Virgin Trains operates high-speed tilting Pendolino trains on its intercity services working the West Coast Main Line.

of the pass (with some exceptions). As of this writing, All Line Rovers are available in both first and standard class and for periods of 7 or 14 days. Passes must be validated prior to their first use.

The restrictions to the All Line Rover may sound like something from a *Monty Python* sketch, and if recited to music might actually be amusing. Some intercity and long-distance operators (such as CrossCountry, East Midland Trains, and Virgin Trains) preclude the holders of All Line Rovers from traveling to or from key mainline stations (including some large London terminals and airport stations) on weekdays before 10 a.m. This restriction doesn't apply on weekends or designated public holidays—commonly known in Britain as bank holidays.

All Line Rovers are not accepted by Eurostar (international trains to Belgium and France), Heathrow Express, and various London-area rail-transit operators such as the London Underground, Docklands Light Railway, and Croydon-area trams (although it is accepted by London area suburban railways including the Overground network). As a result, the All Line Rover isn't an especially useful pass for London visitors. In addition, All Line Rovers are not accepted on most heritage

St. Pancras is a contrast between new and old; one of the latest Siemens-built Eurostar high-speed trains rests under the pioneer balloon-style shed designed by W. H. Barlow and R. M. Ordish in the 1860s and constructed by the Butterley Company of Derbyshire.

railway operators and private excursion trains. However, the Ffestiniog & Welsh Highland Railways in North Wales will accept the pass.

For travelers focused on a specific area who do not need to travel across the UK, localized Rover tickets are more cost effective. Travelers with regional Rovers need to pay close attention to both the areas and times valid for travel.

Consider the Explore Wales Flexipass, which is an open Rover-style ticket allowing unlimited travel in the greater Wales area, roughly defined by lines in the southwest running from Gloucester to Fishguard via Newport, north from Newport to Shrewsbury, Wrexham, Crewe, and Chester, and lines to the Welsh interior including the North Wales line to Holyhead, lines west of Shrewsbury, and related branch lines (as highlighted in the designated Explore Wales Flexipass map). The ticket is valid for 4 days travel within a specified 8-day period. Travelers are limited on weekdays to travel after 9:30 a.m. but not restricted on weekends and public holidays. The service area is focused on lines served by Arriva Trains Wales, but other train operators in the defined service area also accept the pass, including Great Western Railway, London Midland, and Virgin Trains.

Similar regional Rovers tickets include Freedom of the Northwest, a 4-in-8-day ticket covering a wide area in northwestern England from Leeds west to Chester, Liverpool, Blackpool, the famed Settle & Carlisle, and the coastal route via Barron-on-Furness to Carlisle and connecting lines, as defined by the Freedom of Northwest map; East Midlands Rover for 3 out of 7 days, covering a myriad of lines in the designated area; and Freedom of Devon & Cornwall Rover, available for 3 out of 7 days, and 8 out of 15 days, and valid on lines indicated by the respective map area.

An example of a regional Ranger ticket is the Cherwell Valley Day Ranger. Only available on weekends and public holidays, this is focused on Great Western Railway trains around Oxford and allows ticket holders unlimited rail travel for one day between Reading and Banbury, and on the branch from Oxford to Bicester and all intermediate stations.

London stations and environs

London boasts more passenger terminals than any other city in the world, and despite consolidation that began in the 1960s, most of London's 14 historic railway terminals have survived. These tie modern British operations to their Victorian roots. London's Victorian gems are magnificent examples of 19th century classical and Gothic architecture and remain among the most impressive railway stations in Europe. Several of London's largest stations need little introduction: Victoria, Paddington, and Waterloo have been made famous in literature, film and song, as well as by railway enthusiasts and historical interest.

ST. PANCRAS INTERNATIONAL

St. Pancras International is neither the busiest nor the oldest London terminal, but it's the greatest architecturally and a must-see for both railway and architecture enthusiasts. Constructed by Midland Railway between 1865 and 1876, it is situated just north of central London along Euston Road, adjacent to Kings Cross terminal.

St. Pancras features the pioneer balloon shed arch, designed by William Henry Barlow and Rowland Mason Ordish—Midland's top engineers. In steam days, the vast open space beneath sheltered passengers while permitting locomotive smoke to escape. Modern visitors should inspect the arches at the main platform level (elevated above the ground level) for the original Butterley Company of Derbyshire builder's plates.

The front of the station, incorporating a hotel, is an elegant architectural contrast to the iron shed beyond. The hotel's frontal façade looks like an enormous and exceptionally ornate brick castle executed in the high Victorian Gothic style, extending 565 feet (172 meters) along Euston Road, punctuated by an immense clock tower. Although converted to offices in the mid-1930s, the hotel has been since renovated and reconverted to its original purpose, now operated by Marriott as the St. Pancras Renaissance Hotel.

In addition to serving intercity trains on the historic Midland Route to Leicester, Darby, Sheffield, and Nottingham (now operated by East Midlands Trains), St. Pancras is also London's premier international terminal since its extensive renovation in the mid-2000s. Here you may board a modern high-speed Eurostar train, and soon after departing the great shed, you'll find yourself being gracefully whisked along on new tracks at 186 mph. Eurostar offers numerous daily departures to Paris and Brussels via the famed undersea Channel Tunnel (opened in 1994) between Folkstone and Calais.

On a lower level (below ground) are a separate set of platforms for Govia Thameslink Railway's electric suburban services connecting Bedford in the north to the south via London Bridge to Brighton, providing one of the few regular services that pass through London. The ground level (below the main tracks) has been developed as a large shopping mall with a variety of shops and restaurants, including a sushi bar. (See **stpancras.com/station**.)

KINGS CROSS

Kings Cross was the terminal for the Great Northern Railway, and from the 1923 grouping until 1947, it served the London & North Eastern Railway, operators of the East Coast Main Line route to Scotland via Peterborough, Doncaster, and York.

Designed by Lewis Cubitt, the station features a more sedate style than other Victorian era terminals, which makes its frontage seem more modern than it is. It takes its name from a large monument to King George IV installed at the nearby crossroads in 1830 but removed before the station was built. At the time of its opening in 1852, Kings Cross was credited for the largest single-span roof in the world.

LNER's famed *Flying Scotsman* was among the long-distance trains to serve Kings Cross. For three decades, the standard locomotives on fast express services on the East Coast Route were the elegant Gresley Pacifics (locomotives made famous by

London Kings Cross is adjacent to St. Pancras and faces Euston Road north of central London. This is the terminus for trains using the East Coast route via Peterborough, Donaster, and to York, Newcastle, Leeds, and Scotland.

Mallard, which set a world speed record for steam in July 1938 by hitting 126 mph). Today, the station is best known for its role in J. K. Rowling's Harry Potter novels, where students for Hogwarts board from magical platform 9¾. Children and tourists are delighted to be photographed at a simulated junior wizards platform located west of the 11 active platforms.

ATTRACTIONS

St Pancras and Kings Cross are near a variety of London attractions. Visit the British Museum, which hosts a vast, priceless collection of international antiquities and a fascination array of sculptures, carvings, and art that can entertain for an hour or two—or an entire day (**britishmuseum.org**). Just hop on the Underground at King's Cross/St. Pancras and travel one stop south on the Victoria Line to Russell Square and then follow signs to the museum (located just a few minutes walk across the square). Admission is free, although a donation is recommended. Best to leave your luggage at the hotel or at paid luggage storage at your arrival station. From the museum, you can easily continue farther into central London.

EUSTON

London's earliest railway terminal, Euston was the Spa Road station of the very short London & Greenwich Railway, and thereafter became the city's first mainline terminus, originally serving the London & Birmingham Railway (a line engineered by Robert Stephenson). Eventually, Euston evolved into one of the capital's most important stations, serving the West Coast route with trains to Birmingham, Manchester, Liverpool, Scotland, and the North Wales Coast with boat connections to Ireland.

For more than a century, Euston's portal gateway was an immense classical Doric arch designed by Phillip Hardwick. This served little practical function but marked the importance of the railway station. Despite a groundswell of public protest, the iconic arch was demolished in November 1961 as the first stage of the station's total redevelopment, conducted in conjunction with West Coast route electrification. The new station facilitated direct connections to the London Underground and provided retail space. Queen Elizabeth II dedicated it on October 14, 1968. Modern, but often decried as London's ugliest station, Euston will again require massive rebuilding as part of the HS2 West Coast high-speed rail project. It is expected that this will transform the property into a thoroughly modern terminus.

From Euston, take the Underground toward central London, but be aware there are two Northern Line routes. More useful for tourists aiming for prime attractions is the westerly route via Charing Cross that runs to stations at Tottenham Court Road, famous for its electronics shops, and Leicester Square, noted for its cinemas, theaters, and nearby restaurants. Northern Line's easterly route takes a more circuitous path, running via Bank and stopping at London Bridge.

MARYLEBONE

Comparatively small, Marylebone Station is architecturally glamorous on the outside and functionally austere inside. It opened in 1899, the last of the major London terminals completed. As built, it served both as terminus and company headquarters for the Great Central Railway—the last major railway to open in England. It has just four platforms. During the Beeching era, most of GCR's route beyond the London suburbs was abandoned, yet Marylebone survived, and today, it serves trains to Aylesbury, Banbury, Birmingham, and Oxford via Bicester Village.

Marylebone is reached by London Underground's Bakerloo Line. Use this route to travel southeast toward Elephant & Castle. Just three stops bring you to Oxford

London Marylebone was the last of the London terminals and historically served as the headquarters and terminus for the Great Central Railway. Today, it is largely a terminal for suburban services.

Circus, a popular shopping street, and one more stop lands you at the famous Piccadilly Circus, location of various posh and high-end shops.

PADDINGTON

Paddington, one of the most impressive London stations, was built by Victorian master engineer Isambard K. Brunel for his broad gauge Great Western Railway. It opened in 1854 to replace GWR's original but cramped station located a short distance to the west. Paddington's great shed was originally a three-span wrought iron roof (one of the first train sheds inspired by Sir Joseph Paxton's Crystal Palace of 1851).

Broad gauge services concluded in 1892 with a major re-gauging of the GWR network, and the station was expanded on several occasions to accommodate burgeoning passenger traffic. The old shed was augmented in 1914 by a fourth span constructed from steel and glass yet retaining the spirit of the original roof. Eight tracks are located below the 1854 roof and two are under the 1914 span, with additional tracks in less glamorous surroundings below London Road.

London Paddington Station is an urban classic. Despite the many changes to British railways and London, the old train sheds designed by Isambard K. Brunnel in the mid-19th century are still in use today.

During the 1990s, the station was rehabilitated and the concourse, known as the Lawn (as a reference to its role as a station master's gardens before the terminal occupied the area), was expanded, modernized, and opened to retail development. In 2004, Paddington Station was designated a UNESCO World Heritage Site. Fronting the station is the old Great Western Hotel, one of the earliest large railway hotels in England. It was refurbished in 2001 and is now operated as the Hilton Paddington Hotel.

Paddington is one of the farthest main terminals from central London, but it is well served by the London Underground. The Bakerloo Line is the closest Underground line to the main terminal and perhaps the most useful for reaching central London shopping districts and other attractions. Passengers may reach the Metropolitan, Hammersmith & City, and Circle Lines via long underground passages.

Ongoing construction of the London Crossrail network promises to transform Paddington once again. This network will link the old Great Western routes via the new Elizabeth Line Tube under central London with services to Abbey Wood and

First Great Western HSTs idle beneath Brunel's Victorian train shed at London Paddington. This is the terminus for trains using the GWR route to Bristol, Devon, and Cornwall.

Shenfield in London's eastern suburbs. The new Paddington Crossrail Station will be located to the south of Brunel's 1854 station and is scheduled to be completely operational by the end of 2019.

VICTORIA

Of the terminals serving routes running south from London, the most impressive is Victoria, which was originally two stations built to serve the fashionable West End district. Today, it is a busy suburban terminal, which also hosts Gatwick Express airport trains. Despite numerous changes to the terminal buildings over the years, its classic train shed (designed by Sir John Fowler) survives to the present day. Visitors to London may wish to consider staying at the Grosvenor Hotel, located at the northwest corner of the station complex with direct access to the concourse. Platforms are numbered 1 to 17. Third-rail electric operations began in 1925, and today, most trains serving Victoria, as well as the rest of the old Southern Railway, operate with third-rail electric multiple units, considered the most extensive third-rail network in the world.

ATTRACTIONS

Victoria passengers are afforded easy access to and from the Undergound with direction connections within the station to Victoria and Circle/District Lines. Travel east on a Circle/District Line—it's one stop to St. James Park, and two take you to Westminster, where you can see the Houses of Parliament and the famous clock tower housing Big Ben, which chimes every quarter of an hour (unfortunately silent for the next few years as it's being refurbished).

Travel west on the Circle/District Line two stops to South Kensington to visit the V&A Museum and the Science Museum. The latter is a great place for children of all ages (and features a variety of railway exhibits including Robert Stephenson's *Rocket*).

WATERLOO

Waterloo Station, which gets a prominent mention in the Kinks' 1967 hit song "Waterloo Sunset," is located near the famous bridge that takes its name from the Belgian town where Napoleon was defeated. Although this is Britain's busiest terminal station, featuring 21 platforms, Waterloo offers little to detain the tourist. The building largely dates from the 1920s, and it shares none of the Victorian charms befitting other large London terminals. However, it's a useful starting point for trains to Basingstoke, Guildford, Poole, Portsmouth Harbour, Southampton, and Weymouth.

Nearby is the Imperial War Museum, a worthy attraction just an 11-minute walk to the south. If you are interested in watching the parade of trains from Waterloo, take a train one stop to Vauxhall or continue on toward gigantic Clapham Junction, where more trains pass by than any other station in the UK.

LONDON BRIDGE

Famous in name, the modern London Bridge Station, while exceptionally busy, isn't especially attractive. It is near a variety of interesting attractions. Europe's tallest building, known as The Shard, towers 1,004 feet (306 meters) over the tracks and is adjacent to the station. The observation deck is highly regarded but admission isn't cheap. Consider an advance purchase for £26, which comes with a fair weather guarantee. If clouds obscure your view, you can return anytime within three months for another visit (**theviewfromtheshard.com**).

From the station, it's a 13-minute walk east along the Thames to the famous Tower Bridge. Cross this magnificent span and visit the famed Tower of London, a

Part of the extensive London Victoria Station complex is the Grosvenor Arms, an elegant hotel with an interior entrance that leads directly to station platforms.

medieval castle that variously served as a royal palace, prison, and torture chamber.

OTHER STATIONS

Charing Cross is a suburban terminal located near Trafalgar Square that, despite its architecturally impressive Victorian frontage, is purely functional within. Cannon Street and Blackfriars are functional suburban stations located relatively near to central London attractions. Fenchurch Street offers a classic building and is among London's smallest stub terminals. It serves trains to Shoeburyness. London Liverpool Street was once decried as London's bleakest big terminal, a condition undoubtedly resulting from its status in the 1920s as world's most intensive steam-hauled station. Years of soot removed during its refurbishment in the 1980s cleaned its Victorian shed and brightened the concourse. In addition to Stansted Airport trains, Liverpool Street also serves trains for Brentwood, Cambridge, Clacton-on-Sea, Colchester, Ipswich, and Norwich. Adjacent Broad Street Station was one of the few large London terminals closed as result of route consolidation.

London transport

London has one of the most extensive and heavily used public transport systems in Europe. Key is the London Underground, which operates the famous Tube. (For a journey planner and up-to-the-minute information, see **tfl.gov.uk/modes/tube**.) Technically the *Tube* referred to deep lines bored through London clay and thus has smaller cars, but today the *Tube* is a term synonymous with the whole Underground network, including the older lines with larger cars. (For history, vintage maps and perspective, see **underground-history.co.uk**, or **insider-london.co.uk/tours/london-underground-and-tube-tour for** tube tours.) In central London, the majority of the Underground network is below ground; however, out in the suburbs, it tends to run above ground and, on some routes, shares lines and tracks with the national network. (For a Tube map, go to **tubemaplondon.org**.)

London is also famous for its buses, many of which are classic red double-deckers. Among the newest double-deck buses are the unusually styled "Boris Buses" (colloquially named for the London mayor Boris Johnson who procured them).

Single tickets on London transport are expensive. If you have a day or more to spend in London, consider buying a **Travel Card** or an **Oyster Card**, which allow much greater flexibility and unlimited travel (with certain restrictions).

Travel cards are sold as 1- to 7-day passes and valid on most forms of London transport. They can be bought as paper tickets or loaded onto an Oyster Card. In general, they offer much better value than single tickets and give you the freedom of being able to switch from one mode to another without hassle. These are zone-based and can be bought in Off-peak and Anytime varieties (**visitorshop.tfl.gov.uk/help/travelcard**.)

The Oyster Card is a smart card that can be loaded with tickets and/or pay-as-you-go travel credit. It eases fare paying between modes, while offering discounted fares, and is valid on most forms of London transport including the Underground, Docklands Light Railway, Croydon area trams, London buses, London Overground, and most Network Rail suburban services operating within the allotted urban area. Oyster Cards require a £5 deposit (**tfl.gov.uk/fares-and-payments/oyster** or **oyster.tfl.gov.uk**). There is a special version called the Visitor Oyster Card (**tfl.gov.uk/travel-information/visiting-london/visitor-oyster-card**).

The **London Pass** is an option for visitors planning to see a variety of sites and museums that includes the option of an Oyster Card as well as featuring a hop-on/hop-off bus tour (**londonpass.com**).

A Tube train accelerates out of the Caledonian Road Station on the London Underground.

LONDON TRANSPORT MUSEUM

Located at Covent Garden, this interactive museum tells the story of London transport and displays a great variety of historic vehicles including vintage trains, trams, and buses. It may amaze some visitors to learn that the original London underground lines were operated with steam locomotives. The museum is ideal for visitors of all ages. (See **ltmuseum.co.uk**.)

National rail journeys

The extensive nature and complexity of the British railway network makes for almost endless possibilities for railway journeys, limited only by the amount of time and capacity for travel of an individual. Owing to the wide range of tickets, including Rover, Ranger, and other passes, it is easy enough to combine journeys and break journeys to explore locations en route or change your travel plans mid-journey as you see fit.

The most common journeys in Britain are on fast trains along busy main lines, yet some of the most interesting train rides are on secondary lines off the well-beaten path, where spectacular scenery mandates difficult engineering. Take the time to explore branch lines as well as main routes.

SETTLE-CARLISLE RAILWAY

Take a train through wild moors, where treeless hills catch ever-changing light shaped by flowing mist and clouds that sweep like a paintbrush across the landscape. You can roll across towering stone viaducts, through long tunnels, and past quaint stone buildings that have stood since the 19th century. One of the greatest mainline train rides in Britain is the famed Settle-Carlisle Railway.

Despite being remote and flanked with parallel electrified main lines, this rustic route has survived waves of cuts because it is so spectacular. Attempts to cull it owing to its apparent redundancy in the 1960s and 1980s failed because of a public backlash against anti-rail policies, and this ultimately helped preserve the route as a through main line. Closed stations along the line were restored and reopened, and the line has become popular with hill walkers as well as visiting tourists and avid train riders.

The Settle-Carlisle was constructed in the 1870s, relatively late for a British main line, but it was pushed forward by the Midland Railway's desire to reach Scotland independent of its competitors. When the railway opened in 1876, it was primarily intended to carry express trains, and despite the rugged scenery, it was engineered with the most efficient grades, requiring 14 tunnels, 325 small bridges, and 21 multiple-span viaducts.

Today, the raw character of the line is among its principal attractions. There's a noticeable lack of population along the central Settle-Carlisle Route, noted for its remote windswept landscape of rolling barren hills, raised bogs, grass, and moss. To the delight of visitors, Settle-Carlisle's country stations still highlight signal towers that retain their old-school, upper quadrant mechanical semaphore signals.

Between Settle and Garsdale, the line runs northward through the scenic Yorkshire Dales National Park following the Ribble valley via Stainforth and Helwith

The Dockland Light Railway (DLR) is a relatively modern component of the London transport network that opened in the mid-1980s and now serves East London and South London. A DLR train is seen departing the impressive Canary Wharf Station.

The HST (high speed train) is a 125 mph train that saved British intercity rail service in the 1970s. HSTs have operated in various liveries, and many still work today. An HST sails across the stone viaduct at Liskeard on the old GWR route.

Oxford makes for an excellent day trip from London. It is home to Oxford University, which is the oldest English-speaking university in the world and one of its leading learning institutions. Many of its constituent colleges are housed in medieval buildings built of yellow-tinted Headington limestone. Visit the neoclassical Radcliffe Camera building, the university's main science library, and stroll across the Christ Church meadows.

Among the highlights of the GWR route via Swindon to Bristol is Bath, so named because it was the site of Roman baths. Sit on the right and you'll get splendid overviews of this stunning British town as the line sweeps into the Avon valley, revealing its characteristic buildings made from golden stone. The main station is aptly named Bath Spa, and it is only a short distance from the town center. Visit the Bath Abbey and the Roman Baths Museum, where you can catch a glimpse of ancient history unearthed for the world to study. West of Bath, the line passes Twerton Long Tunnel, famous for its elaborately decorated castle-like portals.

Continuing toward Devon, at Saltash west of Plymouth the railway crosses Brunel's unique Royal Albert Bridge completed in 1859 to span the Tamar valley.

Oxford University is a decentralized learning center comprised of 38 independent colleges. Many have been active for centuries and are located across the town.

This magnificent bridge demonstrates Brunel's engineering genius and, after nearly 160 years, remains in daily traffic.

There are several interesting branch lines off the main GWR. At Liskeard, you can change to a shuttle train that navigates the line to Looe, which requires hook-and-eye routing via Coombe in sight of a tall multiple-arch viaduct on the main line. This big bridge is characteristic of viaducts on the western end of the GWR route. The branch works southward through St. Keyne and Sandplace to the popular village of Looe, situated on a natural harbor off the English Channel.

At Bodmin Parkway, there's a junction with the Bodmin & Wenford Railway, a preserved line normally operated with steam. This line aims to recreate the atmosphere and operation of a rural GWR branch line prior to the nationalization of British Railways in 1948. It is the only steam railway operating in Cornwall (**bodminrailway.co.uk**).

From Truro, another branch extends southward 12.4 miles (20km) to Falmouth Docks, while St. Erth is the junction with the 7km branch northward to St. Ives—a splendid popular seaside town with a warm micro-climate.

Although you are unlikely to find any pirates in Penzance, this is as far west as

Ruins of abandoned tin mines are silhouetted in a silvery sunset over the Celtic Sea on the Cornwall coast.

the railway goes. This pleasant Cornwall town is a jumping off point for further exploration. Head out to Lands End or explore the north Cornwall coast, where you can see evidence of the once-important tin mining industry. Then plan to watch the sun set into the wide expanse of the North Atlantic.

Great Western Railway is presently the name of the franchise operating long-distance trains on the historic GWR route. (This is owned by the FirstGroup, and although both companies have Great Western Railway in their name, there is no historical lineage between them—FirstGroup is simply paying tribute to this route's history.) In addition to day trains from London, the Night Rivera sleeper runs to Penzance. It departs Paddington at 11:45 p.m. and arrives at Penzance before 9 a.m. (For schedules and tickets, see **gwr.com/tickets**.)

OVERNIGHT TO SCOTLAND

Among the wonderful passenger train anomalies in Great Britain are the nightly sleeping car trains operating from Euston Station to the Scottish Highlands. These work up the high-speed West Coast Main Line. One service runs to Glasgow and another runs to Edinburgh Waverly, where the train divides into three sections and

Located less than 15 minutes from Oxford by train, the Didcot Railway Centre offers a steam-era railway experience based on its collection of Great Western Railway locomotives.

Didcot Railway Centre

The Didcot Parkway Station is adjacent to the Didcot Railway Centre, a small museum focused around former GWR locomotive sheds. This living museum features a short section of running track. It is home to the Great Western Railway Society and houses more than a dozen former GWR steam locomotives. It's generally open to the public on weekdays from June to September and weekends year-round. See the museum website for details and operating days when locomotives are under steam (**didcotrailwaycentre.org.uk**).

runs to Aberdeen, Fort William, and Inverness. Passengers have a choice of accommodations on board the train.

The Fort William leg takes a spectacular journey running along the Clyde Estuary in the wee hours and then ascends the Scottish Highlands, running via the Bridge of Orchy and over Rannoch Moor. This is a stark, windswept, rolling landscape that catches cosmic light when the early morning sun burns through layers of billowing mist. The railway line twists and turns until it crests at Corrour Summit, where there's a lightly used station some 1,338 feet (408 meters) above sea level. It's downhill from here, as the line descends toward Loch Trieg and stations at Tulloch, Roybridge, and Spean Bridge before reaching its terminus at Fort William.

You can continue your journey west by day via the stunning West Highland Line that continues to the remote coastal port of Mallaig. En route, the railway spans Glenfinnan Viaduct, a 21-arch concrete bridge constructed in 1901. Nearby is the Glenfinnan Monument, which honors those who fought in the Jacobite Risings in 1745. Mallaig is a quiet place where most visitors waste little time before catching the ferry to the Isle of Skye.

The Inverness leg runs via Stirling and Perth to Pitlochry through the Killiecrankie Tunnel to Blair Atholl, over Drumochter summit, 1,484 feet (452 meter) ASL, to Dalwhinnie, Aviemore, and finally to Inverness—the town on Loch Ness undoubtedly best known for its most elusive resident. (However, here you are more likely to be met at the station by a clown in a monster suit.) Rail connections continue to Kyle of Lochalsh and to the far north of Scotland at Wick and Thurso. The latter point is the northernmost reaches of railway service in Great Britain and the jumping-off point for ferries to the Orkney Islands. Although there are no railways on the Orkneys, these wild, windswept islands beckon your visit, and it's worth a few days to explore this unusual and distant landscape.

The Aberdeen leg of the sleeper runs northward over the famed Firth of Forth and Tay Bridges to Dundee, and finally to its namesake city.

Britain's heritage railways

Step back in time; find a rural country station where a coal stove fills the atmosphere with a warm inviting aroma, potted flowers decorate the platforms, and a helpful station master wearing a classic uniform offers to aid you in your travels. Soon a semaphore snaps to attention, and a distant shrill whistle announces the arrival of an incoming train: a locomotive comes chuffing to a stop and the station comes alive. Buy a ticket, hop on board, and enjoy railway travel the way it was meant to be.

One unanticipated positive consequence of Beeching-era railway rationalization was that it spurred a wide-scale railroad preservation movement. The end of steam operations in 1968, combined with rural line closures, both freed equipment and lines for preservation while stimulating nostalgia for the old network operations.

Today, there are dozens of wonderfully preserved railways across the UK that are well worth exploring and are often more enjoyable than traveling on the national network.

On the final leg of its overnight journey from London to Fort William, the Caledonian Sleeper crests Corrour summit on Rannock Moor in a heavy fog.

BLUEBELL RAILWAY

One of Britain's most charming historic lines is the preserved Bluebell Railway in West Sussex, located southwest of London. It's the pioneer example of a standard gauge preserved railway line. This is an easy day trip from London. You can travel directly to East Grinstead on a third-rail electric train from Victoria Station (departing from platforms 16 to 19). These run every half hour on weekdays and make the journey in 55 minutes. Alternatively, you can depart from St. Pancras Thameslink platform or Blackfriars Station and change at East Croydon for East Grinstead services, or if you desire the experience of a harried London commuter, try going from Waterloo Station and change at the ever-busy Clapham Junction.

While the modern train to East Grinstead offers a pleasant foray down a rural branch on the periphery of the London area suburban network, this is just a taste of what's to come! Upon arriving at East Grinstead, exit the mainline station and walk to the nearby Bluebell platform and buy your tickets. There are several options: rather than scrimp and get a single ticket, get the All Line return, which is slightly more expensive but a much better value. This will enable

Preserved South Eastern & Chatham Railway locomotive number 65, a 0-6-0 type built in 1896, works the Bluebell Railway grade northward from Horsted Keynes.

Bluebell Railway, a preservation pioneer

Bluebell Railway is the pioneer example of a British standard gauge historic railway, and it set preservation precedents that have been emulated across the UK. Today, it's a national treasure and one of Britain's most famous and most popular preserved steam railways.

The line was built in the 19th century as Lewes & East Grinstead Railway and was later a component of the London, Brighton & South Coast Railway. During 1923, it was melded into the Southern Railway; nationalization in 1948 saw it briefly operated as part of British Railway's southern region.

Declining traffic after World War II doomed the line as part of the national network, and since the Bluebell route via East Grinstead ran parallel to the primary London-Brighton Line via Haywards Heath, it was viewed as inferior and redundant and subsequently cut. Revenue passenger service was discontinued in 1955, prompting early preservation efforts a few years later. Bluebell's first steam excursions operated in 1960. Early operations were on the south end of the line between Sheffield Park and Horsted Keynes.

Tracks were gradually rebuilt northward, and in 2013 Bluebell Railway reestablished a connection with Network Rail at East Grinstead. Not only did this facilitate a convenient connection for passengers traveling by train from greater London, making the line more accessible to the general public, but it allowed possible through all-rail movements to and from the railway.

you to get on and off trains and more thoroughly explore the railway and its wonderfully restored stations. Discounted tickets for children and families are available.

Bluebell's schedule varies seasonally and by the day of the week, so it helps to

Scotland's famous Firth of Forth Bridge spans 1.5 miles (2.5km) across its namesake estuary near Edinburgh. Completed in 1890, this is one of Great Britain's landmark railway structures, and it still carries trains today.

check in advance online to see when trains are operating. Tickets are also available for advance purchase (**bluebell-railway.com**).

Traveling south from East Grinstead on the Bluebell is a trip back in time as the railway's identified periods appear to get older as the train chuffs along. Not long after leaving East Grinstead, you'll cross the multiple-arch Imberhorne Viaduct. The nominal climb forces the locomotive to bark as it works upgrade.

Kingscote features a station on the east side of the tracks. Although a quiet layover point, the railway discourages visitors by automobile from beginning their journey here. South from Kingscote, the line reaches the bottom of a sag and then starts to climb toward the former West Hoathly Station before dipping into the 2,193-foot-long (668 meter) West Hoathly Tunnel.

Bluebell's station at Horsted Keynes may invoke a case of déjà vu since it has often been the set for films and television programs including the popular *Downton Abbey* series. This is a classic country junction station designed by Thomas Myres and built in 1882. Myres was a prolific architect for the old London, Brighton & South Coast Railway. The station has an island platform accessed by a below-track pedestrian subway—an unusual feature on a preserved line—and yet the station environment embodies the atmosphere of a British railway from the late Edwardian era.

Locomotive *Blackmore Vale*, a postwar Southern Railway West Country class 4-6-2 Pacific type, working on the Bluebell Railway, dramatically exits Horsted Keynes in the pouring rain.

Interestingly, the old Southern Region branch to Hayward's Heath had been electrified with third-rail, and so for a few years, British Railways suburban trains shared Horsted Keynes Station with Bluebell's steam trains. Today, the short branch is truncated (a portion it used to store preserved equipment pending restoration), but there are long-term efforts that may eventually see the branch rebuilt and reopened.

Sheffield Park Station is named for Lord Sheffield, a 19th century railway director. This is the southernmost station on the Bluebell line and one of the best places to reach the line by road. This station hosts the railway's engine sheds, a small railway museum, and the railway's pub called Bessemer Arms where you can get lunch and a pint of ale.

SEVERN VALLEY RAILWAY

Take a scenic steam train to the cradle of Britain's industrial revolution on one of Britain's most popular heritage railways. The scenic Severn Valley Railway (SVR) meanders for nearly 17 miles (27km) along the famous river that lends its name to the line, placing it among Britain's longest standard gauge preserved railways.

On a lush morning in the Severn valley, locomotive *Bradley Manor* works toward Arley as a black lamb looks on. The SVR re-creates a secondary railway line with all the sentimental trappings of a bygone era.

The ascendancy of the highway industry was a dark time for Britain's railways, resulting in many shortsighted decisions that included severing the Severn Valley route in 1963. So, today's wonderfully preserved SVR was among the unintended consequences of Dr. Richard Beeching's system pruning. Beeching was especially unsympathetic to lightly used branch lines and secondary routes. The charm of rural railways didn't fulfill his arbitrary financial standards. The groundswell of nostalgia in the wake of British Railway rationalization led to the Severn Valley Railway Society being formed in 1965. Operations began in 1970, initially in the form of excursions on the north end of the line, but by the mid-1980s, the Severn Valley had been restored the full distance from Bridgnorth to Kidderminster, where it connects with the mainline network.

Today, SVR is among Britain's finest preserved railways and far more than a mere steam train ride. It encompasses the whole atmosphere of a classic British country railway, including nicely adorned passenger stations, fully functioning Victorian signal towers with mechanical semaphore signaling, coal stoves, old engine sheds, period railway infrastructure, plus well-mannered and properly uniformed railway

Taking the train to SVR

SVR's Kidderminster Station allows for easy interchange with mainline trains. If you are traveling from London, you'll need an early start to make the most of your visit.

One of the best options is to travel via Marylebone Station and change trains at Birmingham Moor Street, which takes 2 hours, 49 minutes. It's slightly longer, 3 hours, to go via Paddington Station and change at Worcester Shrub Hill.

Traveling from Birmingham Moor Street, trains take about 45 minutes, while from Birmingham Snow Hill, the journey is just under 40 minutes.

people who welcome visitors. This is a pleasant time warp that contrasts with the world the highway made. Enjoy a visit back in time when Britain's railways reigned supreme.

Purchase a Freedom of the Line open ticket. (If you buy online in advance, you may get a discount.) You can travel the whole line in as little as 3 hours, but you may wish to stop and visit the small stations along the line, take in the atmosphere of this special place or explore portions of the valley on foot. At Kidderminster, there's a quaint railway museum filled with railway memorabilia.

SVR's seasonal schedule varies from four daily trains to upwards of seven round trips during peak times and special events. During the winter, SVR offers only limited service and trains don't operate everyday.

Board at Kidderminster for your ride down the Severn valley. After departing the station, the line traverses a tunnel before making its first stop at the old junction station at Bewdley. This is a fine old railway station with working signal towers at each end. Immediately after leaving the station, the line crosses the Wribbenhall Viaduct—a stone bridge of eight arches—and then wanders for nearly 4 miles toward Arley. A short distance before the station, you'll cross the cast-iron Victoria Bridge over the Severn.

Arley completely embodies the spirit of a classic British country station. This is a great place to get off and wander around. There is a passing siding here, and your train may meet another coming the other way. Hiking trails run up and down the valley from Arley. If you're hungry, head down the road and stop in at the local pub called the Harbour Inn for a pint of bitter and some local fare. Across the Severn is the Arley Arboretum & Gardens, where you'll find several tea rooms.

Highley is further up the line, where in addition to an award-winning station, SVR maintains an engine house where you may see restored steam locomo-

A Severn Valley Railway train from Bridgnorth to Kidderminster makes for a timeless scene as it crosses the Wribbenhall Viaduct as it approaches the station at Bewdley.

tives. Hampton Loade is another quaint little station and also the location of an active signal tower complete with a friendly signalman. SVR's line terminates at Bridgnorth.

There's variety in SVR operations owing to the wealth of serviceable steam locomotives on the line, and more than five dozen restored passenger cars from various periods. This gives passengers the opportunity to sample different trains. In addition, it's not unusual to find visiting engines on the line. (For tickets, timetables, information, and photos, see **svr.co.uk**.)

GREAT CENTRAL RAILWAY

Most preserved railways are single-track lines, typically branch lines embracing the nostalgia for bygone days when short ambling trains connected towns and villages. By contrast, Great Central Railway (GCR) bills itself as "the United Kingdom's only mainline heritage railway." Significantly, GCR has rebuilt and operates a portion of the historic Great Central double-track main line. Today, GCR offers a rare opportunity to experience steam trains passing at speed.

Great Britain's historic Great Central Railway has a mythic quality because the company name was lost during the 1923 grouping, while four decades later much of the route was closed and lifted, essentially erasing its route from the national network.

Historic Great Central Railway

Britain's last major network was the Great Central Railway, renamed and expanded from the Midlands-based Manchester, Sheffield & Lincolnshire Railway. In the early 20th century, GCR emerged as a competitor to traditional railway companies including the parallel Midland Railway.

For most of its independence, GCR existed on precarious financial footing and survived under the creative management of Sir Sam Fay and chairman Sir Alexander Henderson. Its London operations were focused on its Marylebone terminal. To better compete for traffic, in 1903, it introduced fast express trains between London and Midlands cities. Great Central lost its independence in 1923, when it was melded into the newly created London & North Eastern Railway.

In the 1960s, Beeching viewed the old GCR route as redundant and culled most of its lines from the national network. Portions in the London area survived, and short segments around Loughborough have been rebuilt as the preserved Great Central Railway.

GCR's 1899-built Loughborough station is its base of operations and the location of locomotive sheds. The grounds have been restored to approximate its 1950s appearance from the British Railways era. GCR's station is a 15–20-minute walk from Loughborough's mainline railway station, but a bus also connects the two railway hubs.

Great Central Railway's double-track mainline-style operation distinguishes it among Great Britain's heritage railways. A spring excursion works toward Loughborough.

GCR offers a variety of tickets. The railway's Day Rover provides unlimited travel and makes for the best value. Family, Child, and Senior tickets are also available. A mix of diesel and steam excursions operate on weekends year-round, with weekday trains at various times.

There are several stations along the line running south towards the railway's terminus at Leicester North. Visit the Quorn & Woodhouse Station, where the central island platform is typical of many stations on the old Great Central system. Scenic highlights include waterside running along the Swithland Reservoir. (For information, timetables, and tickets, see **gcrailway.co.uk**.)

Although the old Great Central Railway route is no longer intact, you can still travel by train from London to ride the Great Central heritage railway. Through express trains operate from St. Pancras International twice an hour to Loughborough. It's best to select a limited-stop service (departing London ahead of the stopping service) which makes the journey in 1 hour, 13 minutes using diesel express trains. Passengers from Midland destinations may find it practical to travel to Loughborough by changing trains at Leicester since express trains run from Leicester to Loughborough in under 10 minutes.

engine type as the world-famous *Mallard* noted for its steam speed record. Old *Sir Nigel Gresley* won't be racing over the Moors at anywhere near high speed, but it does retain its flamboyant streamlined shrouds.

The North Yorkshire Moors Railway is at the periphery of the UK national network, a long way from London to Whitby by train. Visitors to the NYMR may wish to budget at least two days for a round trip. A 5-hour journey beginning at Kings Cross at 7 a.m. will get you to Whitby by noon, but you'll need to change twice, first at Darlington and then at Middlesbrough. From York, the railway journey requires 2 hours, 45 minutes and also requires a change at Middlesbrough. From Edinburgh, it's 4 hours, 30 minutes with changes at Darlington and Middlesbrough. Traveling from Holyhead can take more than 8 hours and up to four changes. Despite the distance, the remoteness is part of the region's charm, and it's well worth the effort to make the trip. Once you get to the NYMR, you won't want to leave!

FFESTINIOG RAILWAY

Most of Britain's national network had adopted Stephenson's standard gauge—4 feet 8½ inches between inside rails—which established the precedent embraced by many countries across Europe and North America. Among the exceptions to this standard were the commodity-specific Welsh lines built with narrow gauge tracks.

Running from Blaenau Ffestiniog to Porthmadog, the slate-hauling Ffestiniog Railway was a pioneer narrow gauge railway, proposed very early in the railway age. Its construction commenced in 1836 with a track gauge of just 23½ inches. This was not an arbitrary choice, but rather an expansion of an established standard used by the slate companies' tram lines within their quarries, where tight curvature was a functional necessity. In its early configuration, Ffestiniog was gravity operated—train loads of slate were rolled in a carefully controlled manner from quarries to the docks, and empties were returned upgrade by horse.

In the 1860s, Ffestiniog adopted locomotive haulage and introduced scheduled passenger services. Interestingly, Ffestiniog was the pioneer application for the unusual double-ended Fairlie-type locomotive, which enabled greater hauling power on its lightly built tracks. Although adopted elsewhere (even the Rio Grande in the United States owned one), these curious engines emerged as a Ffestiniog trademark and remain in action on the line today.

Standard gauge construction brought tourists to the Welsh mountains but siphoned away lucrative freight traffic from narrow gauge lines. In the 1920s, the

NYMR history

The Whitby & Pickering Railway was among the oldest railway lines in Yorkshire, engineered in the mid-1830s by none other than Britain's famed railway pioneer George Stephenson. The route between Whitby to Pickering was completed in 1836. Its formative operations required trains to ascend the steeply graded Beckhole Incline, which climbed sharply from Grosmont using a primitive system of cable haulage.

Since this line was much too steep for locomotives, growing traffic demanded a better route during mid-19th century, so the old inclined line was abandoned in favor of an all-new route via Goathland with a easier gradient. Today, the old Beckhole Incline is a rail trail; portions of the old grade can be seen from the train as you climb up the mountain from Grosmont to Goathland.

In the 20th century the route was part of the London & North Eastern Railway. Dr. Beeching's reports had devastating effects on the railways around Whitby, but nostalgia for the old railway resulted in the formation of The North Yorkshire Moors Railway (NYMR) in the mid-1960s.

connecting 25-mile Welsh Highland Railway opened from Porthmadog over the scenic Aberglaslyn Pass to Caernarfon, primarily serving as a passenger line. Although popular with passengers, diminishing freight traffic resulted in Ffestiniog's closure during World War II.

Yet the Ffestiniog survived because of its endearing charm. During the early 1950s, preservation of the nearby Talyllyn Railway led to a movement to reopen the Ffestiniog. Ultimately the operation and ownership was conveyed to a charitable trust. Through the dedication of railway preservationists, most of the railway was rebuilt. Today, Rheilffordd Ffestiniog Railway (note the spelling change) is among Britain's most significant preserved railways, running 13.5 miles between its historic terminals.

Connections with national network services are available at Blaenau Ffestiniog, where Ffestiniog shares a station with standard gauge trains running from Llandudno Junction. Additional connections are available at Minffordd Station.

Several intermediate stations are worth visiting. The station names are classic Welsh tongue twisters, but the scenery is fabulous. Dduallt is the location of a complete helix constructed in the preservation era as part of a line relocation around a reservoir. Tan-y-Bwlch is a pleasant layover point with a passing siding and a small platform café. Reconstruction of the Welsh Highland Railway now allows for an expanded narrow gauge journey all the way to Caernarfon. Consider buying a Wales Wander ticket that offers discounts on 10 of Welsh tourist lines, including the nearby Talyllyn. (For more information, see **festrail.co.uk** or **ffestiniograilway.org.uk**.)

The pioneering Dublin and Kingstown ran 6 miles (10km) from Westland Row in Dublin to Kingstown (now Dún Laoghaire). As built, this used the British standard gauge (4 feet 8½ inches), however this track width wasn't ultimately adopted as the Irish standard because other early Irish lines used a variety of track widths leading to compatibility problems. To sort this out, eventually a broad track gauge (5 feet 3 inches) was established as the Irish standard and this remains to the present day. As a result, Irish railways are unusual among European lines featuring both a non-standard track width as well as an unusual loading gauge, making its rolling stock physically incompatible with the rest of Europe. Since Ireland is an island, this might not appear to be a problem, yet it has resulted in higher costs for some new trains.

Ireland's historically predominantly poor agricultural population didn't develop a train-riding culture to the same degree as Britain or the more developed Continental nations. Thus the golden age of railways was less pronounced in Ireland than elsewhere in Europe. Yet by the end of the 19th century, railways connected most major Irish towns, with networks focused on the primary population centers in Belfast, Cork, Dublin, Limerick, and Waterford. Route development continued after 1875 with construction of narrow gauge peripheral railways linking outlying points with broad gauge hubs. The most famous narrow gauge lines were Tralee & Dingle, West Clare, Londonderry & Lough Swilly, and the bizarre Listowel & Ballybunion that was built using the Lartigue monorail system.

Republic of Ireland

In the 1920s, Ireland's 26 southern counties (today the Republic of Ireland) gained independence from the United Kingdom, which coincided with the subsequent partition of the six northern counties (now Northern Ireland) that have remained part of the UK. This preceded a long period of economic stagnation that froze railway development and contributed to the long slow decline of railway route mileage. Waves of line cuts from the 1920s through to the 1970s pared back the network to primary core routes largely focused on Dublin, although a few radial routes have survived. The narrow gauge routes are all but a memory, except for a few segments rebuilt as preserved lines.

Following World War II (known in neutral Ireland as "the Emergency") Irish railways were nationalized and combined with other public transport. Today, Irish Rail is a quasi-autonomous component of the semi-state transport company known in Irish as Córas Iompair Éireann (CIÉ), which is the primary railway operator in the Republic of Ireland.

During the Celtic Tiger boom years, Irish Rail invested in quad-tracking a portion of its Dublin-Cork main line in suburban Dublin. A set of Irish Rail intercity railcars (ICRs) pass Stacumny Bridge as Belmond's Grand Hibernian (in distance) races toward Dublin.

Over the last 15 years, Irish Rail has invested in infrastructure and equipment providing comfortable convenient intercity services, including a regular interval timetable on several primary routes radiating out from Dublin to the larger towns and cities. Dublin and Cork also enjoy suburban rail services integrated with intercity routes. The Dublin Area Rapid Transit (DART) services are electrified.

Irish Rail's standard type of train consists of modern intercity railcars, self-propelled diesel trains built in Korea by ROTEM. These operate in configurations of three, four, and five cars at speeds up to 100 mph in mainline service. In addition, General Motors (American-designed, Canadian-built) locomotives work push-pull intercity trains assigned to Dublin-Cork and Dublin-Belfast (Enterprise) services. Although boxy in appearance, these locomotives will sound familiar to American ears.

IRISH RAIL TICKETS

Irish Rail requires that all passengers have valid tickets prior to boarding trains (except on some rural branches where it may not be possible to purchase a ticket in advance). Most large stations have staffed ticket windows and/or automated ticket machines. In many instances tickets purchased at stations or from machines on the day of travel have the highest fare.

A better way to buy Irish Rail tickets is via the company website, **irishrail.ie**. Online advance ticket purchases often provide better fares, which may be at a fraction of the walk-up fare. Irish Rail at times offers promotional fares, so it pays to investigate ticketing options before traveling, especially on the Dublin-Cork and Dublin-Tralee routes where trains are in the highest demand. On Fridays, Sunday evenings, and during public holidays, rail tickets can be expensive and trains crowded. Likewise, trains tend to be well patronized when sporting events are scheduled in Dublin (often on summer weekends).

Purchasing tickets online also allows you to select and reserve seats in advance (reservation information is displayed above your seat on a digital display). When purchasing tickets online, you have the option of collecting paper tickets from ticket machines.

Irish Rail has a mobile app available via iTunes that is useful for planning journeys and obtaining up-to-the minute schedule information: however, as of this writing, it didn't allow users to purchase tickets.

In addition to regularly scheduled Irish Rail trains, the Railway Preservation Society of Ireland, Rail Tours Ireland, and Belmond operate excursions using steam locomotive-hauled heritage equipment.

Dublin

Many visitors to Dublin get their only glimpse of Irish railways when a train crosses the river Liffey on the maligned Loopline Bridge in the city center. Unlike many continental cities that are crisscrossed by modern railway lines, most of Dublin's railway infrastructure dates to 19th century planning, and so while Dublin benefits from railway services, its stations tend to be on the periphery of the city center and not useful for visiting primary tourist areas. Despite this, Dublin's suburban network offers some excellent short trips, including one of the most scenic commuter rail journeys in Europe.

Dublin's primary railway terminals remain as active vestiges of the Victorian era, landmark examples of 19th century railway architecture. Dublin's stations, along with other primary terminals across Ireland, were renamed in 1966, the 50th anniversary of the Easter Rising, for the 16 leaders executed in 1916.

In 2016, Irish Rail repainted the class leader of its 071 class in its as-delivered livery for the 40th anniversary of this versatile General Motors diesel-electric in Ireland. Locomotive 071 is seen under the train shed at Limerick's Colbert Station.

PEARSE STATION AND ITS ENVIRONS

Dublin's Pearse Station, originally called Westland Row (named for the street that runs in front of the elevated station building), is claimed as the world's oldest city terminal in continuous use. It was the terminus for the Dublin & Kingstown Railway), the line engineered by the Wicklow-born William Dargan, heralded as the father of Irish railways and a protégé of Britain's acclaimed engineer Thomas Telford. Today, very little remains of the original structure, and the station is no longer a stub-end terminal. It is now dominated by a balloon-arch train shed dating from 1884, and the 1891 connection with the Loop Line at its west end that spans Westland Row on an ornate iron bridge.

Pearse is an important station on Dublin's DART electrified suburban service, also served by a variety of outer suburban routes as well as southeastern intercity trains destined for Rosslare Europort Station. Nearby is Dublin's illustrious Merrion Square (walk south on Westland Row, jog left on Lincoln Place to reach Merrion Street Lower and continue south), once home to a variety of Irish celebrities including the flamboyant writer Oscar Wilde, who is recalled by a reclining bronze statue in the

Early suburban railway

Ireland claims the world's first suburban railway. Unlike most early railway schemes built as industrial lines or for intercity transport, Ireland's pioneer Dublin & Kingstown was conceived as connecting Dublin with its seaside suburbs and began operations carrying suburban passengers and mail (forwarded from Packet ships running between the Welsh port at Holyhead and Kingstown).

An 1840s-era extension of the route to Dalkey was built and initially operated as an atmospheric railway, whereby trains were propelled in the uphill direction using vacuum cylinders and returned downhill by gravity. Radical in its day, vacuum propulsion offered quiet smoke-free operation; while functional, it was soon found to be unreliable, so it was replaced with conventional steam locomotive-hauled trains after only a few years.

fenced park in the center of the square. The park also features a selection of vintage gas lamps, characteristic of the Victorian era, and a reminder that before the advent of gas lighting, Dublin would have been a scarily dark place after sundown.

Opposite the west end of the square are two prominent Dublin museums. The National Gallery of Ireland exhibits prominent examples of Irish and international art, including paintings by John "Jack" Butler Yeats (brother to the world-famous Irish poet) and watercolor sketches by 19th century English painter J. M. W. Turner (displayed every February). Primary entrance to the gallery is off Clare Street to the west of Merrion Square. (See **nationalgallery.ie**.)

The National Museum of Ireland-Natural History is a curious treasure. Known colloquially as the "Dead Museum" for its displays of stuff animals, animal skeletons, preserved insects, and fish and sea animals, the museum is fascinating for its Victorian-era appearance. This is what many museums used to look like before the advent of interpretive exhibits and interactive displays.

Take the corner of Merrion Square and follow it around to the Georgian House Museum at 29 Lower Fitzwilliam Street. Gaze down Fitzwilliam Street for the impressive view of Georgian terrace houses known as Dublin's Georgian Mile. Alternatively, from the corner at the Natural History Museum, continue southward along Merrion Street Upper and walk by the gate to Irish Government buildings, including the Department of the Taoiseach (Irish Prime Minister).

At Baggot Street Lower, you will be at the heart of one of Dublin's more affluent areas. Cross Baggot Street and turn left and head for Toners Pub to visit an authentic Victorian pub serving excellent pints of stout. Turn right and you'll reach St. Stephen's Green—one of Dublin's finest city center parks with flower gardens

An Irish Rail ICR passes Islandbridge Junction as it departs Dublin Heuston Station. The obelisk at the left is the Wellington Testimonial located in the southeast corner of Dublin's Phoenix Park.

and duck ponds. The west side of the green faces Stephen's Green Shopping Centre—a multistory mall and the top of Grafton Street—Dublin's premier pedestrianized southside shopping district. St. Stephen's Green is a busy stop on the LUAS Green Line tram route (See LUAS on page 74).

HEUSTON STATION AND VICINITY

Dublin's Heuston Station is another rare active example of a very early railway terminal. Not only does its main buildings still exhibit the essence of 1840s-era architecture, albeit partially modernized inside, but the station still serves as Irish Rail's primary intercity terminal for points south and west of Dublin. If you compare an early watercolor drawing of Heuston with its appearance today, you will only find nominal changes.

As built, Heuston was the main passenger terminal for Ireland's Great Southern & Western Railway. Opened in 1848, the station features a neoclassical motif designed to be consistent with Dublin's other civic structures. The station's three-story head house consists of a lower story dressed in stone blocks, its higher level a Corinthian colonnade that rises to meet an ornately decorated cornice, and the main structure flanked by two short decorative towers that offers a pleasing symmetry for the frontal façade. The upper floors house office space, while the ground floor hosts the passenger station and accompanying shops and restaurants.

Beyond the station building is Heuston's classic cast-iron shed covering roughly 2.5 acres and spanning tracks 2 to 5. The shed is credited to Great Southern & Western Railway chief engineer Sir John Macneill. It was completely renovated in the mid-2000s with new skylights installed. Passengers may now enter directly through the front of the building from the LUAS tram and bus stops, although traditionally passengers were encouraged to enter at the southern entrance that leads directly to the booking hall (main ticket desk). If you come in this way, take a look at the vintage clerestory ceiling with ornate plaster molding. Compared with major city terminals on the continent, Heuston Station is only a modest facility. In 2002, additional platforms were added (tracks 6, 7, 8) to the north and west of the older platforms. At the north side of the station is the Galway Hooker, a bar and restaurant that features arrival and departure boards so passengers can mind their trains while having a meal and a drink.

Heuston serves Irish Rail's Portlaoise/Kildare outer suburban trains and all regularly scheduled intercity trains to Cork (departing at the top of the hour from 7 a.m. to 9 p.m., with most trains offering connections to Limerick city via Limerick Junction and to Tralee and points in County Kerry via Mallow). In addition, Irish Rail also operates a few direct trains to Limerick and Tralee. Irish Rail has two hourly departures to Galway and Waterford with at least eight trains daily to both cities, and three trains a day to Westport, County Mayo (via Athlone and Roscommon with connections to Ballina via Manulla Junction). If you are traveling to a popular destination, there may be long lines to board trains.

Heuston is a long walk from Dublin's city center but has several useful public transport connections. The LUAS Red Line stops in front of the station and trams run eastward toward the city center, Busáras (central bus station), and Connolly Station, or to the Dublin Docklands (destination "The Point," which refers to the old Point Depot). Buses stopping in front of the station include route 90 to the city centre (operates at peak times), route 145 that runs toward Bray via the City Centre, and route 747 to Dublin Airport (journey time is about an hour, and the fare is €6, which is higher than ordinary Dublin city buses). Additional bus stops are located on the St. John's Road West near Heuston's south entrance, serving routes 25a, 25b, 25d

Ireland's only electrified lines are those used by Dublin Area Rapid Transit. Shortly before Christmas, an outward DART, on its way to Bray, approaches Dublin's Pearse Station (formerly known as Westland Row). Visitors should be aware that Irish Rail shuts all service on December 25 and 26.

and 25x running toward Merrion Square via the city centre, and 51d and 51x running toward University College Dublin (UCD) at Belfield. Cross the Liffey on the cast-iron Seán Heuston Bridge (that carries the LUAS tram tracks), and there's another bus stop on the far side of the road that serves routes 25, 26, 66, 66a, 67, and 69 running east toward the city center and Merrion Square.

NEARBY SIGHTS

Attractions within a 15-minute walk of Heuston Station include Phoenix Park (considered the largest park within a European city limits), which features the towering obelisk known as the Wellington Testimonial (commemorating the Duke of Wellington, British general and military commander), and the Dublin Zoo, among the world's oldest zoos.

The National Museum of Ireland-Decorative Arts & History is about a 5–10-minute walk east, or one stop on LUAS toward the city center. Set in a former British army barracks, it features an exhibit on the Easter Rising in addition to a host of collected items include vases, porcelain, and curiously ornate antique household items. Admission is free.

Guinness Storehouse

On many days, the aroma of roasting malt will greet visitors as they get on and off trains because the famous Guinness Brewery is located across from Heuston. To visit the Guinness Storehouse, follow the LUAS tracks up Steeven's Lane and turn left on James's Street. Signs will point you toward the storehouse entrance, which is located in an alleyway. Then follow Ecclin Street to the Old Harbour Bar, left on Grand Canal Place (that once encircled a now-defunct canal harbor) to Bellevue.

Undoubtedly, you'll see a parade of fellow visitors making the same pilgrimage since the Guinness Storehouse is one of Dublin's primary attractions. Notice the narrow gauge tracks in the cobblestone streets. Guinness once had its own internal railway that was needed to move components of the beer-making process within the brewery complex as well as laden and empty kegs to and from the canal and railhead at Heuston. Guinness kegs were last shipped by canal boat about 1960 and cross-country by Irish Rail freights in 2006.

Heuston Station

Designed in 1845 by English architect Sancton Wood, Heuston was originally known as Kingsbridge (after the nearby 1828 cast-iron span over the river Liffey commemorating King George IV's royal visit to Dublin in 1821). Both the bridge and the station were renamed for Seán Heuston, the Irish patriot martyred for his role in the 1916 Easter Rising. A plaque commemorating him is located on the wall inside the station near platform 2.

Walk west on St. John's Road West and turn left (south) on Military Road and follow the signs to the Irish Museum of Modern Art (IMMA), located on the grounds of the 17th century Royal Hospital at Kilmainham. The museum features both permanent and traveling art exhibitions (**imma.ie**). Adjacent to IMMA (down the stairs to the right) are some beautifully manicured gardens, located virtually within sight of Heuston station's railway yard yet secluded by rows of trees and hedges.

Continue through the old hospital grounds toward Kilmainham Village. Before you reach the great stone gate, look to your right and you'll see Bully Acre, one of Ireland's oldest and strangest burial grounds.

Kilmainham Gaol (Jail) is an old-school prison building with great national significance and a popular tourist attraction. It was here in 1916 that British authorities executed Irish patriots

A crescent moon rises over Dublin's Heuston Station. Located on the south banks of the river Liffey, and originally known as Kingsbridge, this Dublin terminal hosts intercity trains to Cork, Galway, Limerick, Tralee, Waterford, and Westport.

responsible for the Easter Rising, the event now considered to be the founding of the modern Irish nation. After your gaol tour, visit The Patriots Inn across the street.

CONNOLLY STATION AND CITY CENTER ATTRACTIONS

Irish Rail's Connolly Station is a busy suburban and intercity station situated east of Dublin's city center where Talbot Street intersects Amiens Street. (It was officially Amiens Street Station until being renamed in 1966 for trade unionist and Easter Rising organizer James Connolly). The principal station building is an Italianate-style Victorian structure dating to the 1840s. Tracks 1 to 4 are stub-end terminal tracks covered by a vintage train shed, while tracks 5 to 7 are through electrified tracks used by DART, suburban, and some intercity services. Connolly is the terminus for the Dublin-Belfast Enterprise services, as well as Sligo Line and Wexford/Rosslare intercity trains. Connolly is served by a short stub-end branch of the LUAS Red Line: however, it is only a 2–3-minute walk to the Busáras (main Dublin intercity bus terminal) LUAS stop, which offers more frequent service. Connolly is served by a variety of city buses, while route 747 airport buses stop outside Bus Aras. Inside the station

In the blue glow of evening, a LUAS Citadis tram glides down Dublin's Harcourt Street heading for St. Stephens Green. Modern trams contrast with Dublin's Georgian-style terrace houses.

is Madigan's restaurant, as well as a newsagent, ATM machines, ticket counters, and ticket machines.

Among attractions near Connolly Station is Dublin's famed 18th century Custom House designed by James Gandon, a classical British architect responsible for several of Dublin's most prominent Georgian-era structures. This building faces the river Liffey in the shadow of the lattice Loopline Bridge. Walk east along the north quays to see tragic statues commemorating victims of Ireland's 1840s-famine and genocide—an event that precipitated mass emigration from Ireland to America and around the world. The *Jeanie Johnston* is a re-created "famine ship" moored nearby, and tours are available daily (**jeaniejohnston.ie**).

To reach Dublin's busy O'Connell Street shopping district, walk due west on Talbot Street toward the towering stainless steel Spire of Dublin—a monument

Dublin's Connolly Station features this classic Italianate-style Victorian head house dating to the 1840s. In addition to DART services, Connolly hosts a variety of outer suburban trains, plus intercity trains to Rosslare, Sligo, and Belfast.

completed in 2003 (designed to replace Nelson's Pillar that had been blown up by terrorists in 1966). Near the spire is Dublin's General Post Office, an iconic structure that was the center of the 1916 Easter Rising. This is an active post office but also features the An Post postal museum (**anpost.ie/anpost/history+and+heritage/ museum**). Alternatively, you can take the LUAS two stops (tram direction Tallaght/ Saggart) to Abbey Street and walk to O'Connell Street from there. The famed O'Connell Bridge over the river Liffey is located at the south end of the street. This bridge is wider than it is long.

DUBLIN PUBLIC TRANSPORT AND LEAP CARD

In addition to DART and outer suburban passenger trains, Dublin is served by a modern urban tram system (LUAS) and city buses operated by Dublin Bus. LUAS is based on the French model and uses sleek Alstom Citadis articulated low-floor trams on two primary routes. Its east-west Red Line runs from the Point Depot in the Docklands via Busáras and Abbey Street in the city center to Heuston Station and beyond to the western suburbs. One Red Line branch goes to Tallaght and the other goes to Saggart. (A short branch from Busáras to Connolly Station serves as a turn-back facility for some city center services.)

The LUAS Green Line is a north-south route connecting the southern suburb terminals at Brides Glen and Sandyford with St. Stephen's Green, via the Cross City line to the north city center and beyond to an Irish Rail-connection with the Sligo/ Maynooth line at Broombridge Station that opened in late 2017.

LUAS tickets may be purchased from automated vending machines on tram platforms. When paying with coins, be patient and drop the coins into the machine one at a time. LUAS uses an honor system with fare checkers periodically boarding trams to inspect tickets. (See details at **luas.ie**.) Dublin Bus operates dozens of routes across the city and fares may be purchased from the drivers.

If you are planning multiple journeys on Dublin-area public transport, Dublin's Leap Card is easier and cheaper than paying for individual fares. This is a contactless, rechargeable plastic card that can be purchased from local newsagents, related shops and other vendors, and Irish Rail ticket machines. To use the card, charge it with a fixed amount and then tap it on specially allocated fare sensors when boarding public transport. It is valid on LUAS, Dublin Bus, some Bus Éireann local services, and Irish Rail suburban services (including DART and Cork suburban lines). When boarding Dublin Bus, you state your destination to the bus driver and hold the card

Irish Rail assigns its push-pull Mark 4 trains to many Dublin-Cork services. On St. Patrick's Day 2017, a Cork-bound Mark 4 races through lush scenery between Mallow and Kent Station, Cork.

to the sensor—you do not need to tag off on buses. However for LUAS and Irish Rail suburban journeys, you will need to tag on and tag off on platform-based sensors. Cards can be filled online (**about.leapcard.ie/dublin**).

DUBLIN TO CORK

You'll begin your railway journey to Cork at Irish Rail's Heuston Station. Cork service is one of Irish Rail's premier trains and most use the push-pull CAF-built Mark 4 trains that offer both first and standard class accommodation and carry a café/dining car operated by Rail Gourmet. (First class includes an in-seat dining option.) Shortly after departing Heuston, you'll pass Islandbridge Junction, and you may glimpse the Wellington Testimonial—and you are just a short distance from your author's Dublin apartment. Another railway line, which runs from Dublin's Connolly Station and North Wall freight yards joins here.

After about 10 miles of west Dublin suburbs where the railway's modern four-track operation is evidence of Celtic Tiger boom years—when Ireland invested in

Cork area suburban service: a Kent Station to Cobh diesel railcar is seen on the causeway to Harper's Island after passing Cobh Junction, Glounthaune, where the line to Midleton (seen in the distance) diverges.

new infrastructure and housing—you'll reach rural countryside. For long stretches, top speed is 100 mph—the fastest railway operation in Ireland. Near Kildare, you'll cross the Curragh—public grasslands where sheep graze. Beyond Kildare, Cherryville Junction is where the Waterford Line diverges, and a few miles later at Portartlington is the junction to Athlone, Galway, and County Mayo.

The scenery improves as you roll farther south and west. County Tipperary features lush green fields with distant low mountain ranges visible on both sides of the line. Near Limerick Junction (the connection for shuttle trains to Limerick City and a secondary route to Waterford) look to the south (left-hand side) to spy the misty silhouette of Galtee Mountains. The scenery is at its best in County Cork.

At Mallow, all trains pause for connections to County Kerry, where local trains serve all stops to Killarney and Tralee. Enjoy the last leg of the run, where you'll see lush bucolic scenery with fields full of sheep and cattle and low rolling hillsides. When you plunge into the inky darkness of the Cork Tunnel, you are only minutes away from arrival at Cork's Kent Station.

Cork is a wonderful small city with its city center just a 10-minute walk from the station. Walk west via Glanmire Road and follow the signs to the city center. Much

An Irish Rail intercity railcar working a Dublin-Portlaoise suburban service approaches its final stop. The old Great Southern & Western Railway station at Portlaoise (formerly called Maryborough) is among Ireland's oldest passenger stations.

Dublin to Cork

Irish Rail's Dublin-Cork main line was originally the Great Southern & Western Railway (GS&WR) that reached Cork in 1849. (The route in Cork City was materially improved in 1855 when the long tunnel was finished.) Several GS&WR country stations including Portarlington, Portlaoise (formerly Maryborough), and Thurles were the designs of architect Sancton Wood, who also did Dublin's Heuston Station and portions of GS&WR Inchicore Works—the primary shops located a few miles west of Heuston. Cork's Kent Station (historically Glanmire Road) dates to around 1890, and features an unusual train shed on an exceptionally tight curve as result of its location between the tunnel and the Cork waterfront. This classic Victorian facility is presently undergoing restoration and improvement to make it more accessible to the Cork city center.

of central Cork is built on an island in the river Lee, and here you'll find plenty of quaint pubs and restaurants, shops, and local curiosities. Cork was once a rail hub with lines radiating out to rural points in every direction, and there's still evidence of some of its old railway stations near the south quays at Albert Quay.

Irish Rail provides two suburban rail services running east from Kent Station: trains to Midleton (famous for its whiskey distilleries), and to the scenically sublime port of Cobh (pronounced *cove*, and formerly known as Queenstown). The lines split at Glounthaune. The Cobh Route is the most interesting as it island hops its way on causeways and short viaducts to its namesake. There's a secluded stop at Fota for the Island Wildlife Park and adjacent resort. Cobh is famous as the final port of call for the ill-fated *Titantic*. Visit the Cobh Heritage Centre, a museum adjacent to the Cobh railway station. High on the hill is majestic St. Colman's Cathedral.

DART, HOWTH, AND THE DUBLIN & SOUTH EASTERN ROUTE

Take a spin on the world's oldest suburban railway, which is also the most scenically stunning line in the Republic. Taking a cue from California's Bay Area Rapid Transit, when Irish Rail electrified and re-equipped its busy Dublin north-south suburban services in the early 1980s, it renamed the service Dublin Area Rapid Transit (universally known as the DART). Service from Malahide on the northern line, and trains from the Howth Branch, run via Dublin's Connolly Station through the city center on the elevated Loop Line and out the old Dublin & Kingstown Route via Pearse Station to Bray and Greystones.

DART south from Connolly provides some of the finest views of any commuter line in Europe, running along the shore of Dublin Bay for a few miles between Booterstown and Dún Laoghaire, before coming inland and navigating a tight curved tunnel south of Dalkey, emerging on a shelf above the Irish Sea where the scintillating waters make for a spectacular view from the left side of the train as it glides down toward the beach at Killiney. Some DART services terminate at Bray, a classic Victorian-era seaside getaway now an outer Dublin suburb. Roughly every second train continues around Brayhead to Greystones, and here you'll get some of the picturesque seaside views.

In addition to DART electric services, Irish Rail operates three intercity round trips daily from Connolly Station to Rosslare that continue south from Greystones along the southeastern route. For visitors, these trains offer several advantages: they run express south of Dublin (only stopping at major stations such as Dún Laoghaire and Bray), the seating is more comfortable, and there's typically a snack cart for most of the run.

South of Greystones are miles of beachfront running to Wicklow. Then the line turns inland up over Glenealy Bank to Rathdrum, where it begins its sharp descent through a short tunnel before passes the scenically sublime Vale of Avoca.

Rosslare trains make stops at the villages of Arklow, Gorey, and Enniscorthy. Scenery south of Enniscorthy includes passage through a few more short tunnels, and view of the ruins of an old castle at Ferrycarrig, before reaching the old Viking

DART trains pass near Killiney Beach against a misty backdrop of the Wicklow Mountains. Dublin's DART running south along the Irish Sea is one of Europe's most scenic suburban routes and unquestionably the oldest.

town of Wexford—a popular holiday destination. Beyond Wexford Station, the line runs along Wexford Quay, unusual in a country where the railway is almost always fenced, or located on high embankments or deep cuttings. Rosslare Strand is a junction with the now disused scenic line via Wellington Bridge to Waterford. Trains continue a short distance along the eroding waterfront to Rosslare Europoort, where there are ferry services to Wales.

MIDLAND ROUTE TO SLIGO

You can get a sense of the old ways of transport when you travel on Irish Rail's Sligo Line tracing the path of the old Midland Great Western Railway (MGWR), which built west along the Royal Canal toward Mullingar. Although effectively abandoned by the mid-20th century, the canal has since been restored and refilled with water. Today, you can see an occasional pleasure boat working its way through the old locks.

The railway was among Irish Rail's operating antiques until 2005 when the old system of individually manned mechanical signal towers concluded and the line

The Emerald Isle Express operated by Railtours Ireland First Class is seen on the "Irish Rivera"—the scenically situated and very pricey area along the Irish Sea between Dalkey and Killiney on the historic Dublin & South Eastern route to Wexford.

was converted to remotely control modern color light signaling operated from a centralized office in Dublin. Some of old cabins can be seen at various points along the line. The largest cabin is at Mullingar, once an important junction with Midland's line to Galway.

Irish Rail's Mullingar Station is a Midland Railway gem. The stone building is located in the wye between Sligo and Galway platforms. Although today the Galway side is largely derelict, it still hosts occasional RPSI steam excursions and permanent way maintenance trains, yet nothing uses these tracks beyond the yards immediately west of the station. It is among Ireland's ghost railways—this once busy main route running toward Athlone via Moate is now a bicycle/hiking path. Irish Rail's Galway and Westport trains run via the old Great Southern & Western Line from Portarlington via Clara to Athlone, where they rejoin the old MGWR route.

West of Mullingar, the line is pastoral. Just a few minutes after Mullingar, you'll be running along the northeastern shore of Laugh Owel, where a windy day will result in some remarkably choppy waters. You pass stations at Edgeworthstown, Longford, Dromod, Carrick-on-Shannon, Boyle, Ballymote, and Collooney before you reach

Although Dublin's Broadstone terminal hasn't served a passenger train since the 1930s, the new LUAS cross-city tram line (opened in December 2017) now transits a purpose-made cutting in front of the station's classic façade.

Midland Great Western Railway

Historically, Ireland's Midland Great Western Railway (MGWR) served Dublin at its elegant but inconvenient Broadstone terminal, executed in a neo-Egyptian style and situated on the city's north side near the King's Inn, about a half mile from Dublin's General Post Office. This site was originally a Royal Canal basin, which required canal boats to cross the adjacent road on an over bridge (long removed).

In the 1920s, the recently formed independent Irish Government encouraged the amalgamation of railway companies echoing similar changes in Britain. As a result, the Dublin & South Eastern, Great Southern & Western

Railway, and MGWR were melded in a new company called Great Southern Railways in 1925. Retrenchment followed and among the changes was the realignment of passenger services from Dublin's Broadstone to Westland Row in 1937.

The old Broadstone station survived as a steam depot until the end of the steam era in early 1960s; some freight traffic lingered but rails were lifted in the 1970s. Now the MGWR line has been re-laid to Broombridge for LUAS Cross City services, while the old station building remains as the headquarters and main depot for Bus Éireann.

Sligo. As you approach this famous seaside town, you'll catch an impressive view of Benbulben, which looms like an iridescent mesa. This impressive land scale caught the attention of poet W. B. Yeats, whose grave lies at Drumcliff in sight of Belbulben, 4.3 miles (7km) from Sligo.

RAILTOURS IRELAND FIRST CLASS

Railtours Ireland First Class is an Irish based rail-tour operator that operates a suite of 42 different tours running from 1 to 11 days in length. Most tours use reserved cars on scheduled trains combined with a fleet of luxury coaches (buses) that allow visitors to explore Ireland carefree without the need to drive. Among the most famous attractions and iconic sites are along the Wild Atlantic Way—destinations include Cork, Blarney Castle, Ring of Kerry, Cliffs of Moher, and Giant's Causeway. The company also operates the 5-star Emerald Isle Express—a weeklong tour of Ireland using a private beautifully presented heritage train (limited to 50 guests). Overnight accommodations are in a luxury castle, as well as country and city hotels. (See **railtoursireland.com**.)

BELMOND GRAND HIBERNIAN

Belmond, famous for its luxury rail excursions including the Venice-Simplon Orient Express, operates weekly deluxe sleeping car excursions around Ireland from April to October. Belmond has a specially equipped 10-car train of Mark 3 carriages, each converted into plush rolling transport festooned with traditional elegance while benefitting from modern conveniences. The highly regarded Mark 3 design was developed in the 1970s for British Rail's HST and imported to Ireland in the 1980s. The carriages now employed by Belmond had been Irish Rail's premier intercity passenger equipment until made surplus by newer CAF-built Mark 4 and ROTEM-built intercity railcars.

In preparation for its new exclusive sleeping car excursion, Belmond completely transformed its Mark 3s into Ireland's first modern luxury train (and the first to carry sleeping cars on Irish rails in living memory). Each of the sleeping cars contains just four bedrooms. Among the highlights of the train is the observation car with large side and rear-facing windows designed to allow passengers to take in the lush Irish scenery. A full bar onboard the train offers a selection of Irish whiskey and stout, while storytellers and musicians provide live entertainment. On most legs of its run, the excursion train is led by an

Belmond's specially outfitted 10-car Grand Hibernian is the longest regularly scheduled train in Ireland. It is seen passing Islandbridge Junction in Dublin on its way to Waterford.

Irish Rail class 201 General Motors diesel-electric locomotive specially painted navy blue to match Belmond's carriages. Select Irish Rail operating crews are in charge of running the train, while Belmond supplies professional staff to accommodate its passengers.

Belmond's Grand Hibernian operates weekly trips allowing passengers the choice of booking two-night, four-night, and week-long railway holidays. All trips start in Dublin and work down country over Irish Rail and NI Railway lines to premier destinations. The two-night excursions are billed as The Taste of Ireland and work to Belfast and Waterford; the 4-night trip is called Legends & Loughs running to Cork and Killarney, and to Galway with a side trip to the beautiful Connemara National Park. The Grand Tour of Ireland combines the two excursions along with an walking tour of Dublin. Prices vary depending on the specific itinerary and availability, but a typical week-long trip costs in the vicinity of €9,000 per person. (For a review of the train plus prices and itineraries, see **belmond.com**.)

Northern Ireland

The six counties of Northern Ireland are some of the most picturesque on the whole island and well worth a visit. Northern Ireland is among the smallest countries in Europe operating its own intensive passenger railway. Although a part of UK, its trains are run by Northern Ireland Railways (NIR)—a component of Translink, which has four primary routes with regular interval timetable services. Northern Ireland and the Republic are linked via Belfast-Dublin Enterprise services which is among Ireland's most scenic intercity trains. In addition, Northern Ireland enjoys regular mainline heritage excursions operated by the RPSI, and host two important railway/transport museums and Ireland's only fully functional broad gauge heritage railway. (Northern Irish railways, like those in the Republic use broad gauge tracks that are 5 foot 3 inches between the rail instead of the common standard gauge of 4 feet 8½ inches used in Great Britain and most of continental Europe.)

TAKE A RIDE ON THE ENTERPRISE

Dublin-Belfast cross-border service is one of Ireland's only daily named trains, marketed as the Enterprise. This runs express from Dublin's Connolly Station to Belfast Central Station, only making intermediate stops at Drogheda, Dundalk, Newry, and Portadown. The Enterprise name stems from steam days, when Great Northern Railway operated the train using its sharp looking sky-blue 4-4-0 express steam locomotives.

Today, the train uses push-pull carriages built by French manufacturer De Dietrich, similar in design to carriages used on the high-speed TGV trains. American-designed General Motors diesel locomotives are coupled at the Belfast end of the consists. Standard class interiors feature subdued tones with three-tone wine-colored seats, gray side and ceiling paneling, and navy blue carpeting. Seating is in two-by-two configurations with some seats grouped in facing sets of four on both sides of a central table and others in pairs with airline-style folddown trains. First class is more spacious with two-tone slate-colored seating and burgundy headrests, in one-by-two arrangements with and without central tables. First class passengers may order meals from their seats, including a full Irish breakfast on morning trains. In addition, all Enterprise services carry a café car that sells snacks and drinks, and features a pushcart with drinks and snacks making its way up and down the train.

The Dublin-Belfast Enterprise is jointly operated by Irish Rail and NIR using specially procured and decorated French-built De Dietrich push-pull trains powered by American-designed General Motors 201 class diesel-electric locomotives.

Departing Dublin, the Enterprise uses the same tracks as DART and outer suburban services and tends to plod along at suburban speeds; once beyond the DART electrification at Malahide, the train noticeably picks up speed and is allowed up to 90 mph on the old Great Northern main line. Among the scenic highlights are the low causeways across coastal estuaries at Malahide and Rogerstown, views of the Irish Sea between Balbriggan and Laytown, the high crossing of the river Boyne immediately north of Drogheda Station, and the lush and rugged hills that occupy the border zone between Dundalk and Newry.

North of the Newry station stop, the line crosses a curved multiple-arch stone viaduct and then begins its ascent of Poyntzpass, an especially bucolic area that typifies Northern Ireland's pastoral landscape. All along the way, you can relish the lush Irish greenery that characterizes the Great Northern route where fields of sheep or cattle quietly graze under mixed lighting—one minute the sun is shinning brightly, the next it's pouring rain, and soon the sun is out again so watch for a rainbow in the ever-changing tapestry of the Irish sky.

Enterprise services make eight round trips Monday to Saturday and five on Sundays. The trains are jointly operated by Irish Rail and Northern Ireland Railways and may be booked through the Irish Rail website **irishrail.ie**, which also allows you to select and prebook seats in both standard and first class. As with most Irish Rail services, you are required to purchase a ticket prior to boarding the train. Passengers to Belfast can present their train ticket for buses at Belfast central station for passage into the city center, while Dublin-bound passengers can use their ticket for travel on DART to Tara Street and Pearse Stations.

Plans are underway to relocate the Enterprise's Belfast terminus from the present Central Station (which isn't especially convenient for most travelers visiting Belfast's city center) to NIR's suburban rail hub at Great Victoria Street Station. As of 2017, passengers must transfer at Central Station for local trains to Great Victoria Street and other NIR stations in greater Belfast. You will need to purchase an NIR ticket for travel to destinations across the NIR/Translink transport network. Ticket desks are located beyond the barriers at Central Station.

BELFAST

Decades ago, Northern Ireland's capital and largest city was known for its dark days of the Troubles, when civil strife and acts of terrorism made headlines and frightened away most visitors. In the 20 years since the Good Friday Agreement of 1998 calmed Northern Ireland's sectarian violence, Belfast has been transformed, and now has much to offer visitors including pleasant riverfront walks, classy shopping centers, and excellent pubs and restaurants.

If you arrive at Great Victoria Street Station, turn left on the station's namesake walk to reach Howard Street and then turn right, and you'll soon reach Donegall Square, location of Belfast's impressive gated neoclassical city hall. On sunny days, visitors and residents can be seen relaxing on the grass around the building. Tours are available weekdays. Donegall Square is near shopping areas, restaurants, and pubs. Head south on Bedford Street to Harlem Café, an eclectically decorated place where you can get a lovely full Irish or full English

Titanic

If you want to learn more about the ill-fated luxury ship, visit the recently redeveloped Titanic Quarter where Titanic Belfast (on Queens Road) is the leading attraction. This interactive interpretive museum cleverly tells the story of the *Titanic*, which was built at the Belfast docks in 1912. (For more information, see **titanicbelfast.com**.)

The staple train cars of Northern Ireland Railways are its CAF-built diesel railcars, as typified by this train seen crossing the river Lagan in Belfast.

breakfast along with a Bloody Mary. For lunch or dinner, try Granny Annies Kitchen, a bar and restaurant on Chichester Street east of Donegall Square (and opposite the posh Victoria Square Shopping Plaza). Locals recommend the salt and chili chicken.

Belfast's Lagan-side waterfront has been redeveloped. Riverfront parks and walkways make for a pleasant way to explore the city. Visit the leaning Albert Memorial Clock and then check out the Big Fish, a 32-foot-long interpretation of a Salmon covered in blue and white ceramic tiles depicting Belfast history. Walk across the Lagan on a pedestrian bridge that offers nice views of the river and the iconic yellow Harland and Wolff shipbuilding cranes famous for their role in the construction of the *Titanic*. This bridge is also a good place to photograph NIR's trains, and since trains run every few minutes on this route, you shouldn't have to wait long before a set of yellow-fronted silver and blue railcars come gliding across the bridge on their way to or from Central Station.

Belfast's Cathedral Quarter is located on the north side of the city centered on Saint Anne's Cathedral. Visit the Dirty Onion pub and Yardbird restaurant which

A Northern Ireland Railways train heading to Belfast runs along the river Foyle and is about to pass below the Derry/Londonderry Peace Bridge, a footbridge opened in 2011.

West of Coleraine there is some of the most scenically impressive running in Northern Ireland. The railway crosses the Bann Estuary and then follows the west shore of the navigable body toward Castlerock. This is a beautiful pastoral landscape with lush greenery, punctuated in-season by yellow gorse—a flowering shrub that makes for fine grazing. Castlerock is a compact seaside village, with a relaxed little pub called the Temple Bar located in the old station building adjacent to NIR's platforms. It's a short walk north on Sea Road to the promenade and Castlerock beach.

After departing Castlerock, the line plunges into a long tunnel below a seaside bluff, emerging briefly with views of the sea on the right only to be engulfed again by darkness. Upon exiting this second tunnel, passengers are treated to some of the finest scenes afforded from a train anywhere in Ireland. Rugged bluffs on the left lead up to the National Trust-Downhill Demesne and Hezlett House with the Mussenden Temple that overlooks the sea, while on the right are stunning views across the sea. As the line continues, you'll see cozy cottages nestled against sharp cliffs with cascading waterfalls on the south side of the train. The line was recently rebuilt, affording some fast running with speeds up to 90 mph. Gradually the

Downpatrick and County Down Railway operate a vintage 1950s A class diesel-electric among other Irish heritage equipment. St. Patrick's Church on the hill to the left marks the burial place of its namesake saint, the patron saint of Ireland.
Colm O'Callaghan

Downpatrick & County Down Railway

by Honer Travers

Positioned in the heart of County Down, the Downpatrick & County Down Railway (D&CDR) is Ireland's only 5 foot 3 inch gauge preserved steam railway. Here, you can experience an exquisite view of pastoral County Down from preserved carriages while being hauled by a heritage locomotive on historic Belfast & County Down Railway lines

The D&CDR hosts an original Belfast & County Down Railway structure referred to colloquially by the museum personnel as the loop platform, which is one of the original platforms used by passengers traveling to and from Belfast to change trains for the seacoast resort branch trains to Ardglass and Newcastle. Significantly, the platform is still protected by an original B&CDR canopy.

The area is rich in history and there's more than just railways to explore. Among the attractions are the historic Inch Abbey (part of famed St. Patrick's Trail) and the crossing at the river Quoile to the alleged gravesite of Viking King Magnus.

The museum showcases various antique railway items, including preserved steam engines and beautifully overhauled carriages. In addition to the variety of rolling stock, some beautiful historic structures and artifacts are featured.

If traveling from Dublin, the best way to reach this railway is to take the Enterprise to Newry and use bus connections to Downpatrick town. If traveling from Belfast, regular bus services (routes 15/215) leave the main Europa Bus Station. The D&CDR station is located in the main carpark directly behind the bus station at Downpatrick.

The D&CDR caters to the interests of various audiences and age groups by hosting annual theme events, including the St Patrick's Day Steam, Easter Eggspress, and the occasional vintage Diesel Gala and Christmas themed Lapland Express that everyone in the family may enjoy. D&CDR's annual open dates can be found on their website at **downrail.co.uk**.

scenery opens up across a broad coastal plain with mesa-like hills to the south. There's a remote station at Bellarena, beyond the line closes in on the Foyle Estuary where cosmic weather effects often result in golden light with shafts of sun penetrating coastal mists. The railway hugs the Foyle on its approach to Derry, with the majority of the old town visible on the west side of the estuary. You are near the end of the line when passing below the modern Peace Bridge pedestrian crossing.

Although NIR's modern railway station is a small, functional, and unimpressive building, nearby are the old Belfast & Northern Counties railway station buildings. You can either take an FY17 bus into Derry city center or walk back to the Peace Bridge and cross the Foyle by foot, which offers some nice views of Derry as well as the railway line.

Derry has a compact city center imbued in history, famous for its strife, and yet makes an excellent destination for a day trip, or to spend a few days exploring. Take a walk around its intact city walls where you can inspect cannons that were cast in the 16th and 17th centuries. Visit the Guildhall, which features some amazing stained glass and dramatic interior spaces. The more adventurous may consider wandering into the Bogside area on the north side, where large murals depict Derry's dark days of troubles, best remembered by Bloody Sunday, when in 1972, British paratroopers fired upon and killed more than a dozen Catholic civilians—an event made famous by the song "Sunday Bloody Sunday" by Irish rock band U2.

RAILWAY PRESERVATION SOCIETY IRELAND

The Railway Preservation Society Ireland is an operator of historic passenger trains in both the Republic of Ireland and Northern Ireland. It maintains a small fleet of authentic Irish steam and diesel locomotives and traditional passenger carriages for periodically scheduled mainline excursions. In addition, it occasionally borrows diesel locomotives from Irish Rail and NIR.

Popular mainline trips include its Portrush Flyer (Belfast to Portrush), steam and jazz themed excursions from Belfast, Belfast-Dublin Steam Enterprise, plus Dublin-based trips on the Dublin & South Eastern Route to Wicklow, Gorey & Rosslare, on the Midland Route to Maynooth and Mullingar, and the annual Radio Train day trip to Kilkenny. In May, RPSI hosts an annual steam tour that makes a 2- or 3-day exploration of Irish railway lines (routes and destinations vary annually). In December, steam-hauled Santa specials operate for the benefit of young enthusiasts. These run multiple trips over successive weekends from Belfast and Dublin, and typically sell out months in advance.

Among the RPSI's most popular trains are its annual steam-hauled Santa specials operated out of both Belfast and Dublin on December weekends. Trains often sell out months in advance.

Irish Rail and NIR locomotive crews are specially trained to work vintage steam locomotives and help carry on traditional knowledge that has been passed down through generations. Members volunteer for maintenance work, equipment repair and restoration, logistics planning, and as car hosts and guides. (For scheduled trips and tickets, see **steamtrainsireland.com/events**.)

RSPI operates the Whitehead Railway Museum at its locomotive and carriage sheds in Whitehead, County Antrim. This displays the society's active and static equipment, including historically significant passenger carriages such as the Irish State Coach, along with exhibits on Irish railways. The museum has limited hours and is only open from Tuesday to Saturday from 10 a.m. to 4 p.m., and visits should coincide with one of three daily tours of the premises that are normally offered at 11 a.m., 1 p.m., and 2:30 p.m. The museum is a short walk from NIR's Whitehead Station that is served by regularly scheduled trains running approximately every 30 minutes to and from Belfast Great Victoria Street via Belfast Central Station. (For museum information, see **steamtrainsireland.com/museum-tickets**.)

Germany

The scenic Mosel River route follows its namesake river valley from Koblenz to beyond Bullay. A DB Regional Express passes the Pfarrkirche St. Johannes Catholic church at Hatzenport.

Germany has one of the most interesting and varied railway networks in Europe. The vast number of routes combined with very dense traffic and a large variety of freight and passenger operators make for a fascinating study in railway dynamics. In other words, it's a wonderful place to ride, watch, and photograph trains. Almost every town of any size has regular passenger service. Most main routes are electrified and built with at least double-track. The German railway system is truly a network, and you can set off in almost any direction and return via a different route. Deutsche Bahn (DB) is the national railway and operates lines across the country. Since Germany borders on Denmark, Poland, Czech Republic, Austria, France, Luxembourg, Belgium, and the Netherlands, it is a central European crossroads.

European railway liberalization has resulted in the national railways of the adjacent countries routinely operating trains on German rails. In addition, there are

A DB class 152 electric banks into a curve exiting the Bettunnel on the Rhine left-bank line south of St. Goar in the Rhine gorge.

numerous open-access and other third-party operators with the effect of providing tremendous variety in the types of trains on the move.

DB operates a range of passenger services, including local S-Bahn suburban locals, Regionalbahn all-stops locals (RB), Regional Express trains serving limited stops (RE), InterCity domestic express trains (IC), EuroCity international express trains (EC), and InterCity Express high-speed trains (ICE). In addition to DB services, there are a myriad of other operators, some operating local or regional services formerly run by DB and others competing with DB for internal or international intercity traffic.

The wide variety of routes could take months, if not years, to adequately explore. Descriptions of German railways could easily fill a book 10 times this size. The versatility of rail travel in Germany makes it a very useful and comfortable way to travel and see the country. Excellent airport connections make it easy to begin your rail exploration of Europe here.

The DB site features one of the best organized and the most extensive journey planners for all European railways, so even if you aren't traveling on Germany railways, check out **reiseauskunft.bahn.de** to plan your trip. The site has an English option in the upper right-hand corner. However, if you are traveling on DB, you can use the site to plan your trip and purchase tickets as well. DB Navigator is an interactive mobile app for Apple iPhone, Android, and Windows that can be downloaded free at **bahn.com/en/view/booking-information/booking/db-navigator-app.shtml**.

Bavarian Alpine railways

Austria and Switzerland aren't the only countries in Europe with stunning Alpine railways. A trip to the top of Germany involves one of the great European mountain lines. The narrow gauge Bayerische Zugspitzbahn (Bavarian Zugspitz Railway) serves as the connection between DB's standard gauge network at Garmisch and various winter resorts and ski areas in the Zugspitz area. This continues to near the top of its namesake mountain, which at 9,718 feet (2,962 meters) above sea level is the highest in Germany. From here, you can experience an Alpine panorama that will leave you breathless (and even if it doesn't, the thinner air at the higher altitude probably will!).

This mountain ascent has several defined stages, beginning with your arrival at Garmisch, where you change to the Zugspitzbahn, and continue through a high Alpine valley toward the looming namesake rock that towers high above you while

German's Bayerische Zugspitzbahn is every bit as thrilling as its Alpine counterparts in Switzerland. At Grainau, passengers change to a rack train to ascend the steep line to the summit.

passing intermediate stations for local resorts. Some of these are request stops (make your request in advance or the train might sail right on through without stopping).

Kreuzeck is a transfer point for the Kreuzechbahn and Alpspitzbahn, two aerial tramways that connect with their namesake ski area resorts. The Alpspitzbahn also serves Osterfelderkopf, where there's an aerial tramway to Hochalm.

Your train continues to a small station at Hammersbach and beyond to Grainau, where Zugspitzbahn's steep-grade rack line begins. You'll change to the waiting electric rack-railway train (similar to those in Switzerland with a central rack located between the running rails to lift the train upgrade). The gradient to Eibsee Station reaches 14 percent, well beyond the limits of steel wheel-steel rail adhesion. You'll see Eibsee on your right. This is the transfer point for another aerial tramway that offers an alternative means of reaching the Zugspitz. (For a circle trip, you may consider traveling up the mountain by train and returning by aerial tramway. But if you have a fear of heights, the thought of hanging hundreds of feet over a rocky snow-covered landscape as you drop rapidly by a wire cable may not be the most comfortable form of transport.)

From the summit of the Zugspitz, you can return to lower elevations via an aerial tramway, which drops steeply over rocky terrain.

From Eibsee, the rack train ascends a ramp-like 25 percent grade, resulting in the cog clattering loudly below the floor as it engages the rack. Clinging above the tree line, the line enters the Riffelriss Tunnel, which brings the train to an underground terminal station. Follow signs to the Gletscherbahn aerial tramway for the final stage of your journey. At the top, you'll enjoy a 360-degree panorama, and in clear weather, you may be able to glimpse Munich in the distance to the north, identifiable by the brown haze above the city. The peaks of the Austrian Alps are to the south.

TICKETS AND SCHEDULES

At Garmisch, Bayerische Zugspitzbahn's station is adjacent to DB's station. It is not part of the DB network, and you'll need to buy a separate ticket for the Zugspitzbahn journey. Mile for mile, it's an expensive line but worth every euro for its scenic value and gravity-defying thrills. It's not a fast trip—the 12 miles (19km) take more than hour. You won't be alone, as this is a well-traveled, popular line. It features hourly service over the length of the route from Garmisch to Partenkirchen, and half-hourly service between the intermediate station at Grainau and the Zugspitzplatz summit.

A DB electric multiple unit at Lahn, Austria, traverses the line running southwest from Garmisch-Partenkirchen and straddles the German-Austrian border to offer magnificent Alpine views. Trains run every two hours.

Looking for adventure

On mountain journeys, an indirect trip offers greater adventure and more opportunities to explore and take in views of snow-capped peaks.

Consider taking the connecting branch line from Garmisch-Partenkirchen that straddles the German-Austrian border serving Ehrwald (southwest of Zugspitz). It provides stunning mountain panoramas and an opportunity for an alternate route to Munich. Plan your connections carefully since you will need to change trains at Reutte in Tirol and Kempten.

These Bavarian towns have many attractions including their exceptional brewing tradition. Stop over for a beer in Kempten, which has a pleasant town center and ample accommodation.

Then you can travel by train north and northwest via Memmingen to Ulm and Stuttgart, or northeast via Kaufbeuren (home to Aktienbrauerei, brewers of excellent pilsner, lager, Oktoberfest, and helles styles of beer) and Buchloe toward Munich.

A charming branch south to Füssen diverges near Kaufbeuren, while a dead-end line to Obertsdorf runs south from Immenstadt, just 16 minutes west of Kempten on the line to Lindau.

Consider purchasing the **Zugspitze** ticket (day pass) for your visit, which despite its relatively high initial price gives you greater flexibility than the more expensive single (one-way) ticket. The Zugspitze ticket allows unlimited travel on the Zugspitzbahn and Gletscherbahn aerial tramways. The **Two-Peak** ticket is more expensive but allows for a greater travel area. Child (ages 6–15) and Youth (16–18) tickets offer discounted fares. There are also discount options for families traveling together. Prices vary depending on the season, and the greatest demand is during ski season (**zugspitze.de**).

Traveling to the Zugspitz is an easy day trip from various destinations across Bavaria and western Austria, with connections allowing for a circle trip rather than simply returning back the way you came. DB's national mainline network operates a hourly through service from the Munich Hbf (main railway station) to Garmisch. Regionalbahn (RB local trains) typically depart from platforms 27 to 29 at 32 minutes past the hour, and running time is 1 hour, 22 minutes. The single (one-way) fare is about €20. Check the destination board carefully since some trains may terminate at Mittenwald or Reutte in Tirol, which are located beyond Garmisch. Other trains provide a through service to Innsbruck (in cooperation with ÖBB). Garmisch to Innsbruck trains depart every two hours at 2 minutes past the hour, and take 1 hour, 22 minutes. In addition, there are scheduled runs requiring a change of trains to the Innsbruck S-Bahn at Seefeld-in-Tirol.

Rhine journeys

If you like to watch trains, come to the Rhine valley. DB lines from Köln (Cologne) running southward toward Frankfurt and Basel, Switzerland, are among Europe's busiest main lines. They feature an impressive schedule of hourly local, regional express, and intercity passenger services, while serving as one of the Continent's busiest north-south freight corridors.

The scenic Mittlerhein (Middle Rhine) is one of the greatest German mainline railway trips. Here, splendid scenery, historic castles, and quaint villages are combined with heavily traveled double-track lines on both sides of the river, providing an exceptional volume and variety of trains in a beautiful setting.

European Union initiatives aimed at liberalizing Continental railways plus the strategic importance of the Rhine valley lines has attracted a large number of open-access freight operators on this route producing an endless parade of trains.

Historically, freight was concentrated on the right-bank tracks south of Köln, but since the 110-mile (117km) Köln-Frankfurt high-speed line opened (which runs inland east of the Rhine), track capacity on the once largely passenger left bank has left plenty of room for freight. So for the delight of train watchers, now freights ply both sides of the river (with route flexibility depending on traffic conditions).

The Rhine is a corridor of commerce. A northward DB InterCity train led by a class 101 electric overtakes a slow-moving barge on the river near Boppard.

TRAVELING ON THE RHINE

Many travelers do little more than board an InterCity train at Köln, Dusseldorf, or beyond and enjoy the pleasant rolling panorama of the Mittlerhein traveling south-ward on the left bank. You will get a sense of the history and natural beauty of the river, which becomes especially scenic south of Koblenz toward Bingen.

This section is an UNESCO World Heritage Site. The Rhine gorge is known for exceptional rich scenery. For many miles, the tracks are close to the river as trains wind their way south past castles perched upon cliff sides and rustic river villages with clusters of antique and multistory buildings, punctuated by a church steeple, the vestige of an old fortress, or some other relic of centuries past.

The ships navigating the river hint of a slower pace with which to enjoy this wonderful place. In summer, rain may streak down your window one minute, and you'll round a bend, pass a tunnel, and suddenly the sun is out again. If you want a truly cosmic experience, take a very early train in autumn and watch as the sun gradually gets higher, burns off the river fog, and illuminates the wonders of the Rhine gorge.

A cruise ship pauses at St. Goarshausen on the right bank of the Rhine north of narrows by the famous Lorelei Rock.

The Rhine River

With headwaters in the Swiss Alps, the Rhine flows through Germany to ultimately reach the North Sea at Rotterdam in the Netherlands. Julius Caesar viewed the river as the border between the Roman Empire and Celtic lands. It served as Napoleon's eastern frontier.

Today, the Rhine is one of Europe's most important rivers, serving as a primary conduit for freight and passenger ships. The parade of ships adds to the sense of commerce in motion.

Along the Mittlerhein, the many medieval castles and fortresses in the narrow river gorge hint at the historical strategic importance of this waterway during prior ages of independent fiefdoms.

Consider taking a week or more to explore the Rhine at your own pace. This a great way to enjoy your German holiday if you are not pressed for time and have tired of touring an endless array of museums, art collections, and cathedrals while navigating the bustling urbanity of large European city centers. This is a rich area where each twist in the river offers new sights. A week-long Rhine interlude may be easily accomplished by train and may combine train-watching with a cultural and adventurous exploration. The mix of Mittlerheinbahn local trains, DB regional

A DB Regional Express running north toward Koblenz passes medieval towers and walls at Oberwesel on the Rhine's left bank.

expresses, and DB Intercity/EuroCity and ICE express runs on the left bank, augmented by an hourly stopping service on the right bank. Local ferries, river ships, and cruises open the way for an endless variety of travel itineraries.

Germany's multimodal air-rail interfaces are some of finest in the world. Rather than make your way to the country from some faraway destination all by rail, consider flying directly to Köln or Frankfurt and beginning your rail journey there. Focus on the Rhine and avoid the temptation to book an ICE train between the two cities. While fast, the new high-speed route misses virtually all of the scenery and comes at a premium price.

Köln (Cologne)

Situated in the shadow of the famous twin-spired Cologne Cathedral, the Köln Hauptbahnhof (main station) is a very busy place and an impressive gateway to the city. It is also a wonderful site to watch trains. Designed by J. E. Jacobstahl, Köln Hbf is a pioneer example of classic European station design: the tracks are elevated above the street while station facilities are located below track level. Immediately east of the station is a six-track railway bridge with an unceasing parade of passenger trains. Pedestrian walkways allow you to cross the bridge on foot. Thousands of love-locks have been attached to bridge railings and fences in recent years by amorous young Germans and visitors, and they make an interesting study in European romance. Walk to the east end for an impressive view looking back, with Köln's monumental cathedral looming over the station and bridge.

The bridge, station, and cathedral were badly damaged during World War II by the hundreds of air raids that devastated the historic city. Köln has regained its vibrancy, but the ancient cathedral is still being repaired. The cathedral is one of the city's principal attractions. For many years, this was the world's tallest structure and was visible from many miles around.

Nearby are some excellent beer halls and restaurants. Sample the Kölsch, a distinctive style of beer brewed locally. It is served in moderate quantities in characteristically narrow glasses. (In many beer halls, when you finish your glass of

---

Construction of Cologne Cathedral began in 1322 and continued into the 19th century. Allied bombs rained down upon the famous church during WWII, and its reconstruction is still ongoing.

The views from KölnTriangle includes this elevated perspective of the massive six-track railway bridge over the Rhine with the Dom looming beyond.

Köln panorama

For a superlative elevated view of greater Köln, cross the railway bridge and follow the footpath along the tracks toward the KölnTriangle Panorama, a 360-degree, glass-lined viewing platform on top of a 29-story skyscraper.

Railway enthusiasts will be impressed by the view to the east of the nearby Köln-Messe/Deutz Station (located at an important junction and served by many RB, RE, IC, and ICE services, which offer an alternative means of reaching the panorama) and adjacent railway yards.

However, most visitors come to look 180 degrees in the other direction across the Rhine and the sprawling city completely dominated by the cathedral's presence.

Admission is €3, with discounts for groups of five or more. Hours from May to September are 11 a.m. to 11 p.m. on weekdays and 10 a.m. to 11 p.m. on weekends and holidays. From October to April, it is open noon to 8 p.m. weekdays and 10 a.m. to 8 p.m. weekends and holidays.

beer, it will automatically be refilled until you place your glass face-down to signal the server that your thirst has been quenched.)

Bonn

Bonn is best remembered as the birthplace of German classical composer Ludwig van Beethoven, and the city relishes its most famous resident. A Beethoven festival has taken place annually since 1845. Beethovenhalle (Beethoven Hall), home to the

A Mittlerheinbahn Siemens Desiro ML electric railcar is seen from Oberwesel's medieval city walls on a clear autumn afternoon.

Mittlerheinbahn

Since 2008, German regional passenger rail operator Mittlerheinbahn (Trans-Regio rail operator) has operated Köln-Koblenz-Mainz left-bank local services. Its trains are modern Siemens Desiro ML three-section, bidirectional, semi-streamlined electric railcars. These lightweight high-powered trains allow rapid acceleration with a top speed of 100 mph (160 km/h).

Passenger cars are designed with two doors per section, low floors, and capacious interior passageways to facilitate rapid loading and unloading while being easily accessible for mobility impaired passengers. Trains operate at least hourly, with greater frequencies at peak times. (See **mittelrheinbahn.de**.)

Tickets are available from automated vending machines on station platforms and on the trains themselves. Mittlerheinbahn also accepts the flexible Rhineland-Palatinate day ticket (See **bahn.com/en/view/offers/regional/regional-day-tickets.shtml**.)

Beethoven orchestra, is presently being refurbished (and closed) in preparation for the celebration in 2020 of the 250th anniversary of the composer's birth. The hall is scheduled to reopen in fall 2018. (See **beethovenhalle.de/en**.) The Beethoven-Haus (Beethoven House) has a museum displaying artifacts and maintains an archive of the composer's work.

Following World War II, Bonn was established as the capital of the German Federal Republic (West Germany). German reunification in the 1990s saw the capital move back to Berlin.

A southward Rhein-Main-Verkehrsverbahn train of Stadler Flirts passes Rhine vineyards south of Lorch on a beautiful September morning.

Right-bank Flirts

Rhine right-bank local passenger services are provided by Rhein-Main-Verkehrsverbahn (RMV) using modern Stadler Flirts (stream-lined, electric multiple unit railcars) operated by VIAS Gmbh as Stadt expresses. They make local stops between Koblenz Hbf (on the left bank) and greater Frankfurt. Hourly trains run from Neuwied via Koblenz down the right bank to Weisbaden and Frankfurt. At peak times, additional half-hourly services run between Koblenz and Kaub.

RMV's modern Flirts glide along the supremely scenic Rhine valley and collect passengers between the seemingly endless procession of freight trains on the same tracks. The brightly painted cars stand out nicely against lush backdrops and can make for interesting photographic subjects or props in the scenic Rhine gorge.

RMV's mobile app for schedule information, maps, and tickets are available at Google Play and Apple iTunes (search for RMV Rhein-Main-Verkehrsverbund). Among the great features of RMV's app are its schematic maps of Frankfurt area rail services that help untangle this complicated German network in an easy to read format. (For general web searches, use **rmv.de**.)

Bonn's tram system is operated by SWB Bus and Bahn. The network's core transits the city center via a short subway. Trams run via three overlapping routes: lines 61 and 65 run northward from Dottendorf via the Hauptbahnhof (main railway station) and Stadhaus, with line 61 taking a left turn toward Auerberg, while route 62 continues to the Beethoven-Haus, crosses the Rhine to serve the right-bank railway station at Bonn-Beuel, and continues southward to Ramersdorf and Obercastle.

A Bonn tram destined for the main railway station (Bonn Hbf) glides down Wilhelmstrasse at the intersection of Oxfordstrasse.

Tram line 65 traces portions of lines served by 61 and 62 but allows for through journeys from Auerberg to Ramersdorf. In addition to city trams, two interurban routes connect Bonn with Köln's tram subway.

Tram and bus tickets may be purchased from automated vending machines at designated stops. The variety of different tickets are priced to reflect the length of your intended journey. Bonn, like many German transit systems, relies on the honor system with random spot inspections. To avoid a fine, be sure you have the correct ticket and validate it. (The Bonn tourism website has information on transport and attractions: **bonn.de**.)

Koblenz and the Rhine gorge

As mentioned, the lush twisting Rhine gorge between Koblenz and Bingen offers passengers the most interesting views. The scenery and wonderful historic architecture combine with quaint villages to provide both a pleasant rolling panorama and a rewarding destination.

Koblenz, where the Mosel flows into the Rhine, is a moderately sized river city with ancient origins. The Romans called it Confluentes, (Confluence). Tourists will delight in the Altstadt (old city) with its medieval architecture and Mittelrhein Museum. If you're hungry (or thirst for local beer or wine) make your way posthaste to the Florinsmarkt to soak in the charm and sate your appetite.

Looming above the city on the right bank is the impressive Festung Ehrenbreitstein, a massive stone fortress. Access is afforded on foot, by taxi, or via a Rhine-spanning aerial tramway. Visit in the morning or late afternoon for stunning views of the city and of trains working up the right bank.

One of the interesting aspects of the Mittelrhein is its dearth of bridges. Instead, small ferries shuttle cars and pedestrians back and forth. Koblenz features some of the region's only railway bridges, which allow convenient left-bank and right-bank interface.

The Koblenz Hauptbahnhof (main station) is a busy modal hub that serves both Rhine lines as well as the picturesque Mosel valley route (see page 123) making it a popular place to change trains. Its proximity to the most scenic area of the Rhine and Mosel valleys, combining excellent railway service with ample cultural and culinary attractions, makes it an ideal base for regional exploration. Consider renting a bicycle for peddling around the area. (For an organized bike tour in English, see **rent-a-guide.com**.)

Down the river, Boppard is another town dating to Roman times. Once praised for its baths, this quaint village is situated on the left bank at a bend in the river, which makes for an impressive setting (but a challenge for river navigation). Its rows of hotels and restaurants along the Rheinallee promenade facing the river served visitors arriving by boat (and some continue to do so) before the railway was built.

Curiously, despite Boppard's excellent railway and river service, many vacationers arrive by highway. Nonetheless, there is a variety of fine hotels a short walk from the railway station, and the old town with its classic Marketplatz and rustic medieval buildings make for an ideal spot to enjoy the river for a few days. Near the railway station are ruins of a medieval stone castle tower. At sunset, a golden glow envelopes the town as river boats ease up, and the river's hue changes and water swirls to reflect the colors of the sky and surrounding hills. A small ferry shuttles back and forth across the river to link Boppard with Filsen on the right bank.

The short Drachenfelsbahn is a rack railway built to bring tourists to its namesake's scenic overlook on the Rhine's right bank.

Drachenfelsbahn

A few miles south of Bonn on the right bank of the Rhine, a volcanic crag named Drachenfels (Dragon Rock) rises 1,053 feet (321 meters) above the river's flowing waters. This is an icon of the Siebengebirge (Seven Hills).

To reach the top, travel on the Drachenfelsbahn, a suitably named 1-mile-long rack railway built for tourist travel. Today the line is electrified, but when it opened in 1883, it was originally operated with steam locomotives. These were specially designed for steep slow-speed cog service for uphill working with grades as steep as 20 percent (1 foot ascent for every 20 traveled), and one of these relics is on display.

Round-trip fares are €10 for adults, €8 for children, with reduced fares for one-way travel and groups. Hours of operation vary seasonally. During most of the year, trains run every half hour, but the line is shut from the middle of November through New Year's. (See **drachenfelsbahn-koenigswinter.de**.)

A southward DB InterCity train splits the medieval towers at Oberwesel, as viewed from a tower on the city walls. Access to this vantage point is free and only a short walk from Oberwesel Station.

Mosel valley

One of the most pleasant German journeys is traveling up the Mosel valley from Koblenz to Trier and Luxembourg. This transits a famous wine-producing region characterized by steeply pitched terraced vineyards in a winding river valley. Colorful villages are nestled between hillsides with needle-like church steeples and lofty castles marking the valley.

The Mosel begins in France (Moselle), where small streams in the Vosges Mountains join to become a mighty flowing river, which like the Rhine is a navigable body. Scheduled river cruises ply the waters, as do freight barges, so you may wish to make a circle trip and travel one way by ship and the other by train. The experience on the water is sufficiently different in that the Mosel takes on a whole new character when viewed from a ship. Yet passage is slow since the river winds around and ships need to pass through several locks, which not only aid commercial shipping but help protect the valley from flooding. You may wish to make an extended adventure and

A southward freight on the right-bank line passes Kaub and the Pfalzgrafenstein Castle located in the middle of the Rhine.

combine a Mosel trip with a tour of Mittelrhein. If you are short on time, begin at Köln and travel by train to Koblenz, where you may change for the ride by rail westward along the Mosel.

Soon after departing the Koblenz Hauptbhanhof, the line swings southward through suburbs and then crosses the Mosel on a double-track deck bridge at Moselweiss. It passes the station at Koblenz-Gulsand, and a little more than a mile later joins the river's left bank, largely staying in sight of the river for the next 30 miles. The river coils back and forth like an enormous snake, passing quaint villages every few miles.

Lof is small but pleasant, and Hatzenport is idyllically situated with two churches, one perched on a hill high above the tracks and the other nearly lineside, while vineyards blanket the valley high and low.

A few miles later, you come upon Moselkern, a resort town with a remarkably nice old station building on the riverside of the tracks. Built on a hill divided by the tracks, Moselkern is quiet with some nice small hotels and restaurants. This is a good place to visit if you have no agenda so bring a good novel to pass the time. Nearby

A Regional Express train from Luxembourg City via Trier to Koblenz crosses the Hangviadukt (hanging bridge) in the Mosel valley near Bullay. These trains run with a mix of German and Luxembourg railway equipment.

member state and Germany. Alternatively, you can stay within Germany and take the line up the Saar valley towards Saarbrucken.

Trier

Trier is Mosel's most important regional railway hub and an interesting historic city. This is another ancient city with a compact center with plenty to see and do and is best explored on foot. It's often claimed as Germany's oldest city—it was already well established when the Romans arrived. But Roman influence developed it into a strategic northern conurbation, and it is dotted with Roman ruins, most prominently the Porta Nigra, a city gate with a vestige of city walls. This is northwest of the Trier main railway station at Porta Nigra Platz. Exiting the station's west side, it is a 5–10 minute walk following Bahnhofstrasse to either Theodor-Heuss-Allee or Christophstrasse. You'll see the old gate on your left.

South from Porta Nigra is the pedestrianized Simeonstrasse. This is the core to the city's vibrant central shopping district, which in the evening is filled with resi-

The German city of Trier has ancient origins. The downtown features a pedestrian shopping area along Simeonstrasse with shops and restaurants.

dents, students, and tourists out for a stroll. Visit the Hauptmarkt and the cathedral. You'll see the ruins of Roman imperial palace baths (Kaiserthermen), which is a UNESCO World Heritage Site. Karl Marx was born in Trier, and his home is preserved at Brückenstrasse 10. (For Trier tourist information, see **trier-info.de/english**.)

TRIER TO GIROLSTEIN AND KÖLN

Travel off the beaten path and take a spin on the nonelectrified line that runs northward from Trier to Girolstein and ultimately reaches Köln. This is the old Eifelbahn that takes its name from the Eifel Mountains that it passes through. North of Trier, the line passes bucolic woodlands, open meadows, and narrow valleys as it meanders along the Kyll River (A Mosel tributary), passing quaint villages at Kordel and Philippsheim. At Kyllburg, the line leaves the river and passes directly below the town through a short tunnel that features impressive castle-like tunnel portals. The north portal is near the station.

Girolstein was important for the Eifelbahn in the days of steam, when yards, shops, and a roundhouse were kept busy servicing engines. This was also a junction with

BERLIN STATIONS AND TRANSPORT

Historically, Berlin was a major railway hub with lines extending to cities all across Germany. Among the projects implemented following reunification was construction of a unified Berlin Hauptbahnhof, the city's central station, conveniently situated north of the Spree River near the main business district and convenient to main tourist attractions. This impressive modern station is one of the finest in Germany and offers a unified multimodal node that connects local, regional, and intercity transport. It opened in 2006, replacing the old Lehrter Bahnhof, and features mainline rail services on two levels that cross perpendicular to each other under a capacious train shed, with direct elevator connections between all platforms on both levels.

DB offers direct ICE and IC services from here to most major German cities, plus international trains to adjacent European capitals including Amsterdam, Bratislava, Budapest, Prague, Vienna, and Warsaw, as well as dozens of other cities outside Germany. Several regional S-Bahn lines converge here. Airport services (RE7 and RB14) operate on approximately 30-minute intervals with a trip time of about 30–35 minutes. Berlin has a variety of smaller and suburban stations that also serve regional and long-distance services.

Berlin enjoys excellent urban public transport consisting of S-Bahn, U-Bahn, tram, and bus routes. However, deciphering the tangle of complex routes can be challenging. (For an overview of Berlin transport, see **berlin.de/en/public-transportation**.)

Berlin's S-Bahn is a subsidiary of DB but operates as part of the Transport Association Berlin-Brandenberg VBB that allows for unified ticketing between transport modes. In addition to S-Bahn's east-west spine and its north-south routes is the famous Ringbahn that completely encircles the city on a 23-mile (37km) loop. Berlin's 91-mile (146km) U-Bahn consists of 10 routes and features some of the world's most interesting underground stations. The 20-route tram network is largely focused on the former East Berlin (with some modern connections to the west).

There is a variety of public transport ticketing options. An inexpensive short-distance ticket called a **Kurzstrecke** allows for a three-stop ride on S-Bahn and U-Bahn trains (allowing for a change) or six stops on a single tram or bus (no change permitted). Slightly more flexible is the one-way ticket sold as **Eizelfahrschenin** which permits a 2-hour, one-way trip across the city, but you must progress away from your starting point.

A gilded statue of the Goddess of Victory sits atop Berlin's 19th century Victory column located at the center of a traffic circle in the Tiergarten.

Open since 2006, the Berlin Hauptbahnhof is a busy station with tracks on two levels neatly blended with a huge shopping mall.

For the best value visitors should consider buying one of several varieties of day tickets that include a 1-day pass, 7-day pass, and a group ticket that allows up to five people to travel on one ticket (with certain restrictions).

You can purchase tickets using automated vending machines on station platforms or from machines inside trams or buses. All paper tickets must be validated using red or yellow validation boxes located on S-Bahn and U-Bahn platforms and inside trams and buses.

A free mobile app called Fahrinfo Plus is available for Apple and Android smart phones. In addition to trip planning, it allows you to download and display tickets on your smart phone. (For tickets, information and maps, see Berlin Verkehrsbetriebe BVG's webpage **bvg.de/en**.)

BERLIN ATTRACTIONS

Berlin, Germany's capital, is rich with history and culture. Badly damaged during World War II and then divided during the Cold War, Berlin has rebuilt itself into a modern city with a diverse collection of historical and modern attractions. (For

Berlin's U-Bahn features some of the world's most impressive underground stations.

details on Berlin's numerous and myriad attractions see the official Berlin website **berlin.de/en/attractions-and-sights.**)

The fiery destruction of the German Reichstag in February 1933 symbolized Nazi domination of German politics. The 1890s building was left in ruins for decades and then gradually restored. Following reunification, the building was rebuilt for its intended purpose, including a spectacular glass dome deigned by Sir Norman Foster. Since April 1999, it has been the official assembly for the German Bundestag (German Federal Parliament). It is located on the Platz der Republik facing the Tiergarten, immediately north of the iconic late 18th century Brandenburg Gate, and within sight of the Berlin Hauptbahnhof located to the north across the Spree River. The views from the dome are outstanding and especially impressive at sunset. Admission is free, and the dome is open daily from 8 a.m. until midnight (although the last admission is at 10 p.m.).

The Brandenburg Gate is one of the city's most recognizable symbols. Built in neoclassical style to emulate the Athenian Acropolis, the gate was located in East Berlin and the scene of political strife during the DDR years. It was restored to its former glory after reunification.

Sir Norman Foster's glass dome is the most iconic feature of the rebuilt German Reichstag in Berlin.

Located at Berlin's near-geographic center, the Tiergarten is the city's largest park and is near a variety of other attractions. Historically, this was a hunting reserve but crafted into a city park in the 1830s. It's a popular place for Berliners and visitors to walk and take in the air.

Checkpoint Charlie was the most famous crossing point between East and West Berlin, and thus symbolic of the divided city. It was here that non-German visitors would line up to cross into the DDR, and the gatehouse was flanked by ominous barricades, barbed wire, and tense soldiers. Today, little remains of the Berlin Wall; however, you can visit the museum called Haus am Checkpoint Charlie to see a reconstructed guard tower and try to imagine the international tensions at this place between 1960 and its fall in 1989. Located at Friedrichstrasse 43-35, you can take the U-Bahn to Kochstrasse to get there.

The Deutsches Technikmuseum is devoted to a variety of German technologies featuring a wide range of displays with something for everyone to enjoy (**sdtb.de/museum-of-technology**). Permanent exhibits include displays on film and photographic equipment, historic beer brewing, textiles, and manufacturing,

Built in 1791, Berlin's neoclassical Brandenburg Gate was a symbol of both Berlin's postwar division and then, since 1989, Germany's reunification. It is just a short walk from both the Reichstag and Berlin Hauptbahnhof.

with several sections focused on transportation including municipal Berlin transport, navigation, and aerospace. Railway enthusiasts will be delighted with one of the museum's specialties which includes an extensive collection of German railway rolling stock that is exhibited in the former works of the Berlin-Anhalt Railway. The museum is on Trebbiner Strasse 9, a short walk from the Gleisdreieck U-Bahn station.

Dresden

Dresden was a beautiful German cultural capital that sadly remains most famous for the tragedy of its sudden destruction during World War II. The German populace believed that Dresden wasn't a strategic target and so was seen as a safe haven for refugees from other cities trying to escape the horrors of war. However, it became a symbolic target, and on the evening of February 13–14, 1945, Allied bombers honed in on the sleeping city. Air raid sirens screamed as thousands of bombs fell, creating a vast firestorm that rapidly consumed the city and killing tens of

Since this view in 2002, many of Dresden's iconic buildings have been cleaned of the charring from the terrible 1945 firestorm that had destroyed much of the city.

thousands of people. Its destruction was so sudden and so complete, and seemingly so unnecessary, that Dresden emerged as symbol of the wasteful destruction of war. Novelist Kurt Vonnegut, a POW who survived the bombing, wrote of his experience in his famous novel *Slaughterhouse-Five*.

Dresden, like so many European cities faced rebuilding after the war. Although its destruction remains evident more than 70 years later, like the phoenix of legend, it has been reborn and is again a vibrant city. The city offers visitors a blend of modern and historic architecture, although much of it has required substantial postwar restoration and re-creation.

Alstadt (old town) is on the left bank and Neustadt (new town) is on the right bank of the Elbe. An irony of the firestorm is that Alstadt seems modern, while Neustadt faired better in the bombing and today retains a greater concentration of older buildings.

Among Dresden's gems is the early 18th century Zwinger Palace built between the old city walls. A classic example of baroque architecture, it was noted for its fire-scarred walls and charred statues of cherubs that became tragic symbols of postwar

Following German reunification, East and West German railways were recombined; however, it took more than a decade to repaint all the equipment. In 2001, a class 143 electric seen at Dresden Neustadt still wore the old East German paint scheme, albeit with DB lettering.

Germany. Today, much of the palace has been cleaned and restored, and it houses several museums. (See **der-dresdner-zwinger.de/en/home**.)

Dresden's other delights include its Royal Palace, Stable Yard, historic fortress, and the Grand Garden famous for the Dresden Park Railway, which offers seasonal train steam train rides on its miniature equipment (**grosser-garten-dresden.de**).

The city has two fine railway stations: its Hauptbahnhof (main station) is situated near the center of Altstadt, and Neustadt Station is on the other side of the Elbe. These are similar in design and feature expansive iron and glass train sheds (the Hbf has tracks on two parallel levels). There is frequent service between them.

Dresden has excellent public transportation with 29 bus routes and a 12-line tram network, which is unusual because freight trams also ply the city streets (**dresden.de/en** and **vvo-online.de**).

In addition to its Transport Museum (located at Augustusstrasse 1 and closed Mondays), Dresden also has an historic tram fleet, a vintage cable-hauled funicular known as the Standseilbahn, plus a marvelous hanging railway called the Dresden Schwebebahn (**dvb.de/en-gb/excursions/hillside-railways/schwebebahn**).

129

DRESDEN TO PRAGUE

Take a pastoral Elbe journey between two of central Europe's most intriguing cities. Dresden's urban area is relatively compact, so not long after departing the city center, the railway passes rural scenery and wooded hills and soon follows the Elbe, where it hugs the river valley's sinuous course through the scenically sublime Nationalpark Sächsische Schweiz (Saxon Switzerland National Park). This rugged valley is famous for its magnificent sandstone rock outcropping and excellent hiking trails. Stations at Pirna, Königstein, Bad Schandau, and Schöna serve different areas of the park. (For details, see **nationalpark-saechsische-schweiz.de**.)

Königstein is a pleasant town nestled in a bend in the Elbe. Medieval buildings and newer structures topped with red terra-cotta roofs are tightly spaced between the river and the hills to the west. Situated high above the town is the 15th century fortress Festung Königstein, its stone battlements visible many miles away. There isn't an Elbe bridge here, so a small ferry provides access to the east bank of the river and trails of Sächsische Schweiz. Take a walk up to the public park near the church for a view that overlooks the village and the river valley.

The Elbe is a conduit of commerce. From here, you can witness a procession of tour boats, as freight and passenger trains roll by every few minutes. The tourist office is on Bahnhof Strasse not far from the ferry dock; from the station, walk west back toward Dresden. Enjoy a stroll along the Elbe in the fading light of a summer's evening. Various attractions are situated upriver from the main village along Schandauer Strasse east of the station, including the Elbefriezeitland Konigstein amusement park.

Bad Schandau is a quaint village along the river to the south. This historic spa town is quite a distance from the railway station, as the town is on the right bank and the station is on the left. To reach the town, you can either walk across the Elbe bridge or take the 252 local bus. Change to the 253 bus to reach the Sächsische Schweiz park or take the historic tram that works its way along the roadside and into the park. Alternatively, there a Regionalbahn branch train that runs hourly and uses a line that crosses the river to Rathmannsdorf and then wanders through the park via Sebnitz to Rumburk, Czech Republic.

After Bad Schandau, the river enters a deeper, narrower part of the gorge where the railway is tight to the western shore. Schöna is the last station in Germany. Walk down to the ferry that brings you across the river to Hrensko in the Czech Republic and explore the side gorge of the Kemenice River, which features hotels and roadside attractions including a casino. The line continues southward to Děčín and Prague.

Located in the scenic Elbe River valley, Schöna is the border station between Germany and the Czech Republic and the end of the Dresden area's regional rail service. A ferry brings passengers across the river to Hrensko in the Czech Republic.

Departing Dresden, you have a choice of through EuroCity services to Prague and other Czech cities or taking S-Bahn local trains. Trains call at both of Dresden's primary stations. Dresden's S1 S-Bahn serves the German portion of the journey, working on half-hour intervals throughout the day and terminating at Schöna on the German-Czech border. These trains use comfortable bi-level cars with numerous stops along the line that allow you to make layovers and explore the towns along the way. This is a pleasant day trip from Dresden, or you could also take several days. If you are traveling with two to five people, consider a day ticket to get the best value and freedom of travel on the line after 9 a.m. (See **bahn.com/en/view/offers/regional/regional-day-tickets.shtml**.)

Zittauer Schmalspurbahn

Located in a far corner of German Saxony and surrounded on three sides by the frontiers with Czech Bohemia and Poland, the colorful narrow gauge Zittauer Schmalspurbahn (Zittau narrow gauge railway) makes for a delightful interlude and a relaxing ride. Its two-pronged route operates south-ward into the mountains from Zittau—a quaint German town characterized by tightly spaced buildings with terra-cotta roofs punctuated by narrow church spires. The 2-foot 5½-inch (750mm) gauge railway opened in 1890 to connect Zittau with health resorts in the mountains. This line handled both freight and passengers until the 1980s when freight traffic ended. In 1994, the Saxon-Upper Lusatian Railway Company (known by its initials in German as SOEG) was formed and two years later assumed full operation of the Zittauer Schmalspurbahn.

The railway is famous for its continued use of historic 2-10-2T steam loco-motives; however, some weekend services operate with a vintage Triebwagen diesel-powered railcar. This curious antique is a delight to travel on but has very limited seating.

The railway is busiest from the end of March to the end of October, with its most intensively scheduled service on weekends, when between 8:45 a.m. and just after 4 p.m., it operates up to nine trains from Zittau toward Bertsdorf. However, its winter operations are very limited. The line divides at Bertsdorf with one route continuing southwest toward Kurort Jonsdorf and the other southeast to Kurort Oybin. In addition to through trains from Zittau, the railway also operates direct service between Kurort Jonsdorf and Kurort Oybin, running via Bertsdorf to give visitors greater choice of travel options.

Bertsdorf is its operations hub where locomotives are serviced, maintained, and stored. The locomotive shed is a working museum open to the public as is the signal tower, where visitors can watch historical signaling apparatus in action.

The line is key to regional tourism as it connects with the Zittau Mountains Nature Reserve (opened in 2008) and the castle and monastery at Oybin. The nature reserve is an area of scenic beauty, famed for its unusual sandstone and volcanic rock formations and popular for networks of hiking and biking trails.

Connections with national rail passenger services can be made at the Zittau station. Express trains to and from Dresden take 90 minutes, and every other hour they use Siemens Desiro diesel railcars. Additional all-stops service takes longer. Hourly services to and from Görlitz (on the German-Polish frontier) take 40 minutes. There are also some through trains to Liberec, Czech Republic. (Zittauer Schmalspurbahn's website is in German, but it offers up-to-date information: **zittauer-schmalspurbahn.de/aktuell**.)

Bad Schandau, formerly located in East Germany, enjoys one of the shortest German tram lines, which runs from the town 5 miles (8km) up to the famed Lichtenhainer Waterfall.

Dresden area steam–Weisseritz Valley Railway

When visiting Dresden, you don't need to go far into the countryside to enjoy a relaxing, ambling journey behind a steam locomotive. One of the Dresden's railway gems is the 16-mile-long scenic narrow gauge railway ascending the Weisseritz valley (named for the Red Weisseritz River) to Kurort Kipsdorf from its standard gauge connection at Freital Hainsburg (a suburban station just 12 minutes from the Dresden Hbf by S-Bahn local train). The railway's summer schedule is in effect from June to September. Its scheduled steam passenger trains are hauled by the comparatively heavy class K-57 2-10-2T locomotives, and typically make two daily 90-minute round trips between Freital Hainsburg and Kurort Kipsdorf, departing Freital at 9:25 a.m. and 3:42 p.m. An additional short midday trip does the run halfway up the line to Dippoldiswalde in just 45 minutes.

This quaint picturesque line boasts being the oldest surviving narrow gauge railway in Germany. Its construction dates to 1881, and it was completed to Kipsdorf by September 1883. From the beginning, tourist traffic to the Kipsdorf resort area was key to the railway's business. However, it also developed freight traffic that served

There are numerous small stations on the line. Most popular is Moritzburg, location of the opulent fairytale Moritzburg Castle. This colorful baroque hunting palace is situated on a manicured island; it features cream-colored walls and four circular towers each capped with red terra-cotta tile. Nearby is the related Fasanenschlösschen (Little Pheasant Castle). Standard admission for Moritzburg Castle alone is €8, with a joint ticket for both sites €11. (See **schloss-moritzburg.de.**)

The line continues via Bärnsdorf and Berbisdorf to its terminus at Radeburg. Be aware that Rade**burg** is a different town than Rade**berg** (also rail-served in the Dresden area). A few years ago, services were curtailed, and the section between Moritzburg and Radeburg was under threat of being closed altogether. A compromise resulted in scaled-back service, with relatively frequent Radebeul-Moritzburg services while trains going beyond to Radeburg became less frequent. (See **traditionsbahn-radebeul.de.**)

Harz Mountain lines

If you are seeking more steam locomotives, head to Germany's Harz Mountains and you won't be disappointed. The Harz is the setting for Goethe's Faustian legends, popular with tourists owing to its scenic splendor, medieval villages, and, of course, its amazing narrow gauge railway network.

The region was near the carefully guarded border between East and West Germany, and during the Cold War, the top of Brocken Mountain served as an East German listening post. The curious combination of DDR's constrained economy and strategic importance of the Harz resulted in the narrow gauge railway surviving as a steam railway and as part of the national network many years after such lines were discontinued in the West. The 87-mile (140km) network is the most extensive narrow gauge railway system in Germany.

Today, the Harz Mountain lines are operated by a private railway called the Harzer Schmalspurbahnen GmbH (HSB). Although largely focused on tourism, HSB is more than a tourist railway, and it remains part of the regional transportation system. Steam locomotives, while important for HSB's daily operations, are only part of the story, as diesel trains are also scheduled. HSB connects with Deutsche Bahn at Nordhausen, Quedlinburg, and Wernigerode.

HSB has three operations with cross-platform connections between trains. Harzquerbahn is HSB's north-south trunk that runs from Nordhausen 38 miles

The Harzer Schmalspurbahnen is the most elaborate of the surviving East German narrow gauge networks and operates steam trains on many of its routes. A scheduled steam service departs Eisfelder Talmühle en route to Nordhausen.

(61km) to Wernigerode, a medieval town popular with tourists. At Drei Annen Hohne (1,771 feet/540 meters above sea level), passengers can change to the Brockenbahn, a steeply graded railway that follows a spiral to the old Soviet-era listening post at Brocken located 3,704 feet (1,129 meters) above sea level. This is HSB's busiest steam operation. On this route, HSB's old 2-10-2T tank engines with small driving wheels are well suited to the stiff climb, and popular with visitors who take in the thrill of the steam and smoke. The third HSB route is the Selketalbahn, which connects with the Harzquerbahn at Eisfelder Talmühle and runs to Gernrode and the mazelike medieval town of Quedlinburg, an UNESCO World Heritage Site.

Both Nordhausen and Wernigerode are 3- to 4-hour mainline journeys from Berlin; take an ICE train to Erfurt and change to a RE (Regional Express) for Nordhausen or an ICE to Halle (Saale) Hbf and change to an HEX (Transdev Sachsen-Anhalt regional train) to Wernigerode. Dresden to Wernigerode is also 4 hours, changing at Halle Hbf. Frankfurt to Nordhausen is a 3½-hour one-way journey requiring one or two changes. (For Harz Mountain information, tickets, and times, see **hsb-wr.de/en**.)

High-speed TGV services connect Paris with many cities across Europe. A Paris-Milan TGV set rests alongside a double-deck TGV Duplex at Paris Gare de Lyon.

reach Paris. During the 1870s, a state-operated company, the Etat, was created to serve areas of Brittany and north Channel ports (later melded with Réseau de l'Ouest.)

By the turn of the 20th century, Paris was among the primary European hubs for international and luxury passenger trains, as exemplified and best recalled by the Paris-Budapest-Istanbul Orient Express.

One the eve of World War I, the French network spanned some 30,000 miles making it the fourth largest national network in the world after the United States, Russia, and Germany. By the 1930s, the French railway system was suffering from the effects of highway competition, and in 1938, the railways were nationalized into the Société Nationale des Chemins de Fer Français (SNCF).

Further effects of competition resulted in rationalization and scaling back of the system after World War II but also encouraged pioneering efforts to increase operating speeds to make long-distance services more competitive with other modes (see TGV history on page 143).

SNCF's high-speed services connecting French and Swiss cities are marketed as TGV Lyria and operate with specially painted trainsets such as this one at Paris Charles de Gaulle Airport Station.

French high-speed trains

Gliding along at super high speeds, while gazing at the tapestry of the French countryside blur past, is one of the great pleasures of European long-distance train travel.

SNCF operates Europe's most extensive high-speed network, consisting of hundreds of departures daily. What began as a largely new super railway running from Paris to Lyon has been gradually extended in every direction from the French capital. Today, the French high-speed network connects most major points in France, while serving some 230 destinations in 15 countries across Europe.

The French high-speed network blends modern highly engineered high-speed lines called LGV that allow top speeds of up to 199 mph (320 km/h), while traditional rights-of-way allow SNCF's TGV trains to directly connect major cities without the need to change trains.

Among SNCF's premier TGV domestic services are those radiating from Paris to outlying cities including Avignon (2 hour, 45 minutes), Bordeaux (3 hours), Lyon (1 hour, 50 minutes), Marseille (3 hours, 20 minutes), Montpellier (3 hours, 20 minutes), Nice (5 hours, 40 minutes), and Strasbourg (1 hour, 45 minutes).

TGV international services include direct trains from Paris to Switzerland marketed as TGV Lyria: Basel (3 hours), Berne (4 hours, 30 minutes), Geneva (3 hours), Lausanne (3 hours, 30 minutes), and Zurich (4 hours). Other TGV international services include direct runs between Paris and Milan and other northern Italian cities, Paris to Brussels via Lille, Paris to German cities including Stuttgart and Frankfurt, and Paris to Spain.

Although may modern high-speed lines and TGV services are focused on Parisian terminals, key to SNCF's modern timetable are high-speed services that avoid central Paris by using specially built radial diverting lines. A secondary high-speed hub is SNCF's Lille Europe in northeastern France. It allows passengers traveling via Eurostar trains from London (running via the Channel Tunnel) and Thalys high-speed trains (connecting Paris with Antwerp, Brussels, and Liege in Belgium, Köln in Germany, and Dutch cities) to change to TGV services that run to cities south of Paris while avoiding the complexity of crossing Paris to change trains. Many through services call at the Paris Charles de Gaulle Airport Station, making this an ideal European airport to begin or end a railway tour of the Continent.

TGV services are the backbone of SNCF's intercity train services and work intensive schedules, so SNCF tends to emphasize TGV services over most traditional trains. Traveling by TGV is like flying on steel rails but with greater comfort and flexibility. On the inside, TGVs are clean but functional. Most trains carry first and second class seating with electrical outlets. There isn't much difference between the two except that first offers slightly more legroom and nominally larger seats while giving solo passengers the option of booking single seats since first class has one-by-two seating. Some first class TGV journeys may also come with a complimentary meal.

There are several varieties of TGV trains. These may be comprised of either single-level or double-deck carriages. International sets are often tailored to a specific service, such as Paris-Milan, in order to comply with the individual signaling and overhead electrical arrangements peculiar to railways outside of France. Intensive high-speed operations often result in TGV train exteriors showing the signs of heavy use presenting a tatty appearance in contrast with SNCF promotional imagery.

SNCF's high-speed trains feature a TGV bar car, in which passengers can buy snacks, light meals, and drinks. You are able to sip a glass of wine as the scenery blurs by at almost 200 mph.

TGV HISTORY

France has been a leader in European high-speed railway development since the 1950s, when SNCF began pushing the limits of conventional steel wheel on steel rail travel using highly refined conventional railway technologies. In March 1955, SNCF was the first rail operator in the world to break the 200 mph barrier in a famous test run. More relevant to everyday passengers was SNCF's introduction of regularly scheduled high-speed intercity trains in the 1960s. These routinely traveled at 125 mph in daily traffic.

SNCF's decision to help expand its passenger business by constructing new high-speed railway routes for very fast trains was specifically intended to allow the railway to effectively compete with automobiles and airlines. These purpose-built high-speed lines were called Lignes à Grande Vitesse (LGV) and offered several benefits. Not only were these engineered for exceptionally fast running, but they were aimed to shorten distances through innovative construction while relieving congestion on existing SNCF trunk lines.

SNCF's original TGV trains of the 1980s were painted in an attractive orange, brown, and white livery, which by 2001 had been phased out in favor of blue and silver. *Denis McCabe*

SNCF also worked with manufacturers to develop exceptionally powerful new electric trains designed for rapid acceleration and sustained high-speed running on new LGV lines. These became known as Trains à Grande Vitesse (TGV). (Be careful not to confuse LGV and TGV.)

SNCF's new LGV infrastructure was designed to augment the existing steel-rail network, and new TGV trains were designed to operate on both LGV and conventional lines to enable high-speed services to extend beyond the limits of the new infrastructure. So while TGV may operate at superfast speeds on the specially built LGV routes, TGV schedules benefit from the mix of super fast, high-speed operation and connections to older lines that allow high-speed trains to access most of the SNCF system.

The French government authorized construction of the first new LGV route in the early 1970s, focusing on the heavily traveled Paris-Lyon corridor. The Paris-Sud Est route not only connected Lyon but also served a variety of destinations in southeastern France and as a gateway to Switzerland. Construction began in 1976, and on September 27, 1981, the first new TGV service was inaugurated, advertised as

Although French high-speed services are now the domain of electrically powered TGV sets, until the early 2000s, SNCF operated moderately high-speed gas-turbine-powered "turbo trains" on nonelectrified routes. Amtrak imported similar French trains for US Midwest services in the early 1970s. *Denis McCabe*

the fastest regularly scheduled passenger trains in the world, temporarily eclipsing Japan's Shinkansen, which had held the title since the 1960s. Although in the early years maximum TGV speed was only 161 mph (260 km/h), SNCF's top commercial running speeds were gradually increased through improvements to high-speed infrastructure and train technology.

SNCF's TGV trains are powered through high-voltage AC overhead electric systems. Since the purpose-built, high-speed lines were aimed at connecting major cities while largely traversing lightly populated areas, there are few intermediate stops on the new routes. Some TGV services operate as expresses from terminal to terminal, much in the manner of a commercial airline flight.

SNCF's TGV/LGV network is remarkable in several ways, and it set important precedents for high-speed railways elsewhere in Europe and around the world. Since TGV services may reach city centers directly on existing routes, providing high-speed train service avoided the astronomically high construction costs and disruptions involved with building completely new high-speed railway lines

A diesel railcar working a regional TER service approaches Sete in southern France. Modern self-propelled railcars are typically assigned to many French regional trains.

transportation in this corridor than the airline could, so domestic plane services were curtailed.

Over the last 35 years, successive French governments have made enormous investments in the high-speed network to produce the current system of TGV routes radiating from Paris, while European Union integration has encouraged high-speed rail investment all across Europe.

SNCF's TGV Atlantique routes west of Paris (Montparnasse Terminal) opened in 1989 and 1990, and raised TGV's operating speed to 186 mph (300 km/h). Additional high-speed routes were extended across France and beyond including TGV Nord to the Channel Tunnel and Belgium, TGV Est routes toward Metz and Strasbourg, lines southward to Spain, radial high-speed connecting lines around Paris, and extensions of existing routes, including lines that opened in 2017 to Rennes and Bordeaux.

SNCF INTERCITY AND REGIONAL TRAINS

TGV high-speed services dominate SNCF marketing, but these are only one part of the railway's national passenger network. Regional trains marketed under the TER

French locomotive-hauled passenger trains are in decline, yet many SNCF Intercités services, such as this train arriving at Bordeaux, still use traditional locomotive-hauled consists.

heading serve more than 20 French regions and account for some 7,500 daily services around France that connect an estimated 5,000 stations and carry some 1 million passengers daily. TER trains are comparatively inexpensive, and unlike TGV and other long-distance trains, the fares are fixed and can be purchased from up to four months before to right up to the moment of travel. Most TER trains are modern self-propelled railcars and may be either electrically or diesel powered.

SNCF once operated one of the finest and most extensive schedules of traditional intercity passenger trains. Over the last 35 years, these services have gradually been overshadowed by expansion of the TGV network. Yet SNCF's Intercités network remains, and it's one of Europe's larger "ghost-rail" networks.

According to SNCF's website, in 2017, it still operated 340 Intercités services daily (including up to a dozen night trains), which served more than 360 stations and carried some 100,000 daily passengers. Despite this, trying to find schedule information or booking Intercité trains on SNCF's website is difficult. Visitors aiming to travel on traditional trains may seriously consider buying an open pass, such as Eurail or InterRail, or buy single tickets at local stations at the time of travel. The

Among the distinctive features of French locomotives is an inward slanted windshield, such as on these electrics in Intercités service at Paris Gare du Nord.

SNCF schedules

Obtaining accurate and complete TER and Intercité scheduling information using SNCF's website can be challenging, owing to the site's myopic focus on TGV services. SNCF offers a TER mobile app, but the site is only in French.

A better choice for travel planning is German Railway's DB scheduling site at **bahn.com**, which covers railway services inside and outside of Germany. When navigating the DB site, unclick the box called "Prefer fast connections," which focuses the search engine on through trains such as the TGV. Then try the same search but with the boxes ticked to compare the results.

most popular Intercité routes run from Paris Gare Saint-Lazare to Le Havre and Caen, Paris Gare du Nord to Amiens, and non-radial services in the south of France.

SNCF TICKETS

If you plan to travel by TGV, SNCF offers several types of tickets. Since TGV uses an airline model, SNCF's TGV fare prices are on a sliding scale that reflect demand and when you book your tickets. Late booking and ticket flexibility cost more money. As a result, you will often get the lowest price ticket if you make your plans well in advance and are willing to remain locked to a specific journey.

Generally, the cheapest fare comes with **TGV Prem's** tickets, which are sold up to 90 days in advance and are not flexible. Don't buy one unless you are positively

SNCF's TGV service is like flying on the ground, yet offers greater comfort and flexibility than airline travel.

certain you will travel on a specific scheduled train since Prem's tickets are neither exchangeable nor refundable. Furthermore, they are only sold in very limited numbers and for select routes.

The **TGV Leisure** ticket has a higher fare, but it is exchangeable and up to 90 percent refundable if you decide not to travel. It is also sold up to 90 days prior to travel.

TGV Pro is a high-fare fully flexible ticket. You can get a full refund up to 2 hours prior to travel, and when purchasing an E-ticket, you may cancel up to 30 minutes after departure if you miss your train.

One option is to purchase tickets (or at least check prices) online using SNCF's website. This attractive site offers an English language option (click the arrow near the world map at upper right and select EN for English), but it can be counter-intuitive and clunky. Although you may find it useful for learning about SNCF's various products, be aware that it's a journey planner, which doesn't appear to offer a full view of scheduled trains and it can be challenging to obtain detailed information unless you are traveling by TGV high-speed train.

151

Begin your Eurostar journey beneath the classic train shed at Paris Gare du Nord. The international particulars of this journey make boarding the Eurostar more complicated than most other European railway journeys. This isn't a condition of Eurostar or the trip, but of the relations between the UK and Continental countries.

Come prepared—print your boarding pass in advance and allow ample time for the boarding process, which may take up to an hour as you'll need to pass through both passport controls and a security check. This is an exercise in bureaucratic procedures: first French border control officers will inspect your documents, and if you're traveling on American passports, expect an exit stamp. Then you'll proceed to British passport control. Non-EU travelers to the UK will need to fill out a "landing card."

Passengers are normally allowed to bring two suitcases per person; however, while undergoing the luggage inspection, you are typically required to handle your own bags and lift them onto the X-ray machine's conveyor belt. Keep this in mind if you are traveling with large or heavy bags. You'll proceed to a boarding lounge to wait for your train. Eurostar trains are unusually long and if you have a seat toward the London-end of the train be prepared for a healthy walk to reach your seat. Similar boarding procedures are in place at Brussels, Lille, London, and other Eurostar stations.

Eurostar seats are comfortable, its staff is accommodating, and you'll find the overall second class Eurostar experience to be better than first class on SNCF's TGV. Once departing Paris, Eurostar transits fast, but not superfast, track through the northern Paris suburbs. You glide past high-occupancy housing that is more typical of the average Parisian residence than the luxury apartments in the center of the city. Soon you'll be up to speed, and the train will be traveling 3 miles a minute as it races toward the Channel Tunnel. Most trains stop at Lille Europe Station, northeastern France's high-speed hub. Then you'll sail across rolling agricultural lands toward Calais. You'll pass the Calais station and see the sprawling staging yards for freight and vehicle shuttle trains before your train descends the ramp into the Channel Tunnel.

If all goes to schedule, you should be through the tunnel in a little more than 20 minutes. However, this is an exceptionally busy railway route, and it's not unusual for trains to slow or stop in the tunnel to wait to cross over or wait for traffic ahead to clear. If the train stops, you may catch a hint of briny seawater and hear dripping. This is normal as the tunnel is always leaking, and pumps run continuously to keep it dry.

The distinctive silhouette of the Eiffel Tower on a frosty late December afternoon is seen from along the Seine River in Paris.

Soon you'll be back up to speed and flying across East Sussex toward London. England's high-speed Channel Tunnel link runs parallel to older lines, and you'll probably overtake slower moving trains as if they are standing still. Finally, you'll loop around the city and enter the grand balloon train shed of London's St. Pancras International, a fitting end for your journey. (For information on Euro Tunnel's Le Shuttle train ferries, see **eurotunnel.com/uk**.)

EUROSTAR TICKETS

Eurostar offers three classes of travel with widely diverging ticket prices. Check Eurostar's website for deals and prices (**eurostar.com**). It has several nationality and language options including United States, which quotes ticket prices in US dollars.

The least expensive tickets are in **standard class**, where advance purchase, low-fare, single (one-way) tickets from Paris to London can be purchased from between $65 and $272. Tickets bought less than a week before traveling are the most expensive so plan your journey as soon as you can. For this same journey, **standard premier class** tickets range from $155 to roughly $350 one way, depending on

155

RATP operates most Paris public transport, including the famous Metro. RATP's Metro line 6 operates above ground and crosses the Seine near the Eiffel Tower.

the time of purchase and projected travel demands. **Business premier** tickets cost $402 one-way regardless of the time of purchase or the time of travel. Among the advantages offered by Eurostar business premier class are shorter check-in times (up to 10 minutes prior to departure), more spacious comfortable seating, and specially prepared meals developed by Raymond Blanc.

Paris

Known as the "City of Light" or the "City of Love," Paris is unquestionably one of Europe's top destinations. What better way to arrive than by rail? For some European travelers, Paris may be the focus of their trip; for others, it is the jumping-off point for Continental adventures. Paris Charles de Gaulle Airport serves as one of Europe's biggest intermodal transport nodes, so many visitors will sample Paris-area transport even if they never see the famous Eiffel Tower.

Paris benefits from some of the most intensive rail-based public urban transport on the Continent, and most visitors will avail of its two overlapping urban rail

The Parisian RER network provides frequent-interval rapid transit that connects central Paris with the suburbs using SNCF's electrified multiple-track main lines.

networks—the Metro and the RER. Simply gazing at a map will unlikely aid visitors, as the multitude of entangled colored lines representing different routes are not easily deciphered at first glance. So it's advisable to learn a little bit about how Parisian public transport functions prior to arrival.

PARIS METRO

The Metro is to Paris as subway is to New York City and the Underground is to London. Short for *Métropolitain*, the term *metro* has evolved into an international synonym for electrified underground urban transport. Paris opened its first subway line in 1900, and today, the Paris Metro consists of 14 routes (identified numerically from w1 to 14) and 300 stations (identified with a large letter M at their entrances). This is an entirely grade separated network, and while much of the system is below ground, there are some open-air and elevated sections too (notably line 6 which crosses the Seine on a bridge with views of the Eiffel Tower).

The Metro is famous for its early stations that were built with stylized Art Nouveau architecture, especially the iconic street level entrances, many of which

While much of the Paris Metro is below ground, portions of the system, including most of line 6, operate above ground.

have been preserved. Another unusual characteristic of the Paris Metro is its use of rubber-tire propulsion on some modern lines, which reduces noise and allows for rapid acceleration and comparatively steep ascents. Trains operate on most routes daily from 5:30 a.m. until after 1 a.m. Paris Metro suffers from limited access for mobility impaired passengers. The Metro along with surface transport is operated by RATP (**ratp.fr/en**).

RATP's extensive bus network includes routes 20 to 99 that serve the city, while routes 100 to 199 are aimed at serving outlying suburban areas (although a few routes continue into Paris proper for the convenience of passengers). A network of late-night Noctilien buses operate after the Metro concludes daily operation, which provides Paris a 24-hour public transport network. In addition, electric trams (routes T1 to T11) serve peripheral areas of Paris. These are excellent examples of modern tramway systems but serve Paris suburbs rarely visited by tourists.

In central Paris, RER routes are largely underground and very heavily traveled. RER route D, pictured, provides connections between Gare du Nord and Gare de Lyon.

PARIS RER

RER is short for Réseau Express Régional, which links Paris with the île de France (the Paris Region), and both supplements and augments the Metro in central Paris. It is a joint effort between RATP and SNCF with both operators cooperating on RER routes A and B, and SNCF operating routes C, D, and E. Use of letters helps distinguish RER lines from those of the Metro (useful to remember in central Paris where the two systems complement one another).

Visitors should be aware that while most tickets and passes are accepted on both the RATP Metro and RER systems in central Paris, once beyond the city limits, the RER often requires a separate ticket, especially when traveling to a Paris airport. RER B runs northwest to two stations at Charles de Gaulle Airport (one jointly with TGV routes), while both RER routes B and C run southward to Orly Airport. (To download detailed Paris transport maps, see **parisbytrain.com/category/maps**.)

American artist Albert Herter's most famous painting depicts soldiers boarding a train for World War I. This is displayed at Gare d l'Est. Herter's son was killed in the war.

TICKETS

The most basic RATP fare, the **Ticket T+**, is valid for is single (one-way) journeys. This may be used on the Metro, buses, and trams, and allows a free transfer between buses and trams with validation. Ticket T+ fares are valid on RER lines in Paris but not to outlying suburbs. Tickets may be purchased from ticket windows in Metro stations or from ticket machines, and are available singly or in a bundle of 10 (a Carnet) at a reduced price. Reduced-fare Child tickets are intended for children ages 4 to 9 (children under 4 may travel free).

Among the more useful tickets are day cards called **Ticket Mobilis**. These can be purchased for Zones 1–2 and Zones 1–5. The Zones 1–2 fare covers transport in Paris, while Zones 1–5 is also valid on suburban transport, with restrictions on travel to airports (except on some bus routes).

This Sunday morning view in April looks down Rue de Lyon toward Gare de Lyon, the most architecturally impressive Parisian terminal.

The old Gare d'Orsay is now one of the premier Parisian art museums appropriately known as Musée d'Orsay. The tracks are long gone but it still has the aura of a railway station.

Gare d'Orsay

Gare d'Orsay was a sensation when it opened in 1900. The station was the vision of Parisian architect Victor Laloux, a well-known professor at the École des Beaux-Arts, which stressed balanced architectural design to fulfill intended functions. Laloux previously designed the railway station at Tours. (Beaux Arts architectural theory had a great influence on American railway stations in the late 19th and early 20th centuries.)

Gare d'Orsay was constructed between 1897 and 1900 and considered by many as Laloux's masterpiece. Its opening (along with Gare de Lyon built at the same time) coincided with the Paris Exposition of 1900.

Gare d'Orsay was fully electrified to obviate concerns of steam, smoke, and coal dust from locomotives that had afflicted traditional railway stations.

By merging waiting areas and the concourse into a single, large open space, Laloux transcended traditional design and brought trains directly into the station. Passengers reached platforms using staircases from the waiting area.

This radical arrangement influenced a new station at Hamburg in Germany (opened in 1906) and Denmark's Copenhagen Central Station in Denmark (opened in 1911). Both Orsay's third-rail electrification and its platform design inspired New York City's 1910 Pennsylvania Station and tunnel complex, while the all-new Grand Central Terminal of 1913 is a significant American example of Beaux Arts station architecture.

By the early 1960s, Gare d'Orsay had fallen out of favor, although its through tracks were repurposed for the new RER line C. In the early 1980s, Orsay was reopened as the Musée' du XIXe (Museum of the 19th Century), better known as the Musée' d'Orsay, a prominent museum of art.

Stark February sun illuminates Paris Gare du Nord's impressive façade that faces Place Napoléon III. This is your gateway for a railway journey to London, Brussels, Amsterdam, or Köln.

The old Paris-Lyon-Mediterranée (PLM) terminus at Gare de Lyon now serves SNCF trains, including TGVs running south to Lyon, Marseille, Avignon, southwestern Switzerland, and northwestern Italy. Lyon is the most visually impressive Parisian station. Located in the Quinze-Vingts area, its opulent façade faces Parvis (Place) Louis Armand and the Boulevard Diderot beyond. Its architect lavished embellishments inside and out, including an immense clock tower and risqué statuaries that generated criticism at the time of construction from pundits who judged railway stations as functional rather than beautiful.

Don't miss out on the jewel of the French Belle Epoch, Gare de Lyon's fame Le Train Bleu restaurant located up an opulent flight of stairs from beneath the shed. Operationally, the station is divided into three "halls" (groups of tracks and platforms). Hall 1 is in the older part of the station immediately beyond the building and beneath the expansive train shed. Hall 2, a newer addition, is set back on the left and not immediately visible from Hall 1. Hall 3 serves two lower track levels for RER lines A and D, reached by escalators and a mezzanine.

a symbol of France and attracts millions of visitors from around the world. The tower is open to visitors year-round from 9:30 a.m. to 11:45 p.m., with extended hours in the summer. You have a choice of taking an elevator all the way to the top, or saving a little money and walking up numerous stairs to the second level and then taking an elevator to the top. Walking offers magnificent views from the staircases and mezzanines. One of the best times to visit is right before sunset, when rays of golden light sweep across the city. You'll catch glimpses of the Metro crossing the Seine as well as RER line C along the riverfront. Yet if you are not in top shape or suffer from a fear of heights walking may not be the best option, so spending an extra 10 euro for the elevator may be worth it. You can reach the Eiffel Tower by taking the Metro to Bir Hakiem or RER line C to Pont de l'Alma.

The impressive Arc de Triomphe was Napoleon's magnificent monument to his armies, himself, and his unifying marches around Europe. This classic monument emulates the great Roman arches and today sits at the center of one of Europe's most dizzying traffic circles where a dozen streets converge along the Champs-Élysées. Go to the top of the arch for great Parisian views. Look south to the Eiffel Tower, or simply gaze with wonder at the maelstrom of automotive traffic swirling around down below. The arch is reachable by several Metro stations including George V to the west. The closest railway transport hub is Charles de Gaulle-Étoile served by RER line A.

PARIS MUSEUMS

You could spend weeks perusing Paris museums, saturating your senses with the world's finest collections of art, satisfying your historical curiosity, and observing the countless objects, artifacts, and architecture that can only be experienced in Paris.

The Musée du Louvre is arguably the world's greatest art museum. Most visitors want to see Leonardo DaVinci's enigmatic *Mona Lisa*, unquestionably one of the world's best-known works of art. If you arrive at noon in June, the lines to a catch a brief glimpse of this one painting will rival the long lines simply to get into the museum.

Yet pick a rainy Wednesday morning in February, and you'll have a relatively short wait to get into the Louvre and may find that you can simply waltz up and closely inspect *Mona Lisa*'s famous smile and probing eyes, and which will leave you hours to wander through the museum's vast and numerous galleries.

King Louis XIV's vast Château Versailles was built in the early 18th century. On a day-long visit, you can explore the many interior rooms as well as the extensive surrounding gardens.

Although there are nominal facilities for checking bags, the museum advises visitors not to bring their luggage with them owing to security concerns. The Louvre is open from 9 a.m. every day (except Tuesday) with extended hours on Wednesdays and Fridays. On first Sundays between October and March, the Louvre opens its permanent collections for free. Metro lines 7 and 14 serve the Palais Royal-Musée du Louvre Station, which incidentally has exhibits from the museum's collection on its platforms (behind glass, of course). (For more information, see **louvre.fr/en**.)

If your hankering for old world art finds you in Paris on a Tuesday, when the Louvre is shut, head across the Seine, where art is grandly displayed in the repurposed fine Gare d'Orsay railway station (see sidebar on page 164). The museum is served by RER route C. It is open from 9:30 a.m. daily except Mondays and late on Thursdays (**musee-orsay.fr/en**).

The serious museum connoisseur should consider the Paris Museum Pass that allows holders unlimited access to more than 50 area museums and is available for 2, 4, or 6 days. (Learn more about the Paris Museum Pass at **en.parismuseumpass.com**.)

A Eurotram navigates the cobblestone-paved Place Broglie in central Strasbourg. Of the six Strasbourg tram routes, lines B, C, and F serve Broglie, before diverging to reach outlying points. Route C runs west to serve Gare Centrale (Central Railway Station).

VERSAILLES

The Château Versailles is the vast and elegant 18th century palace and surrounding parks and gardens built by King Louis XIV. This is a huge place with lots to see, including the opulent Hall of Mirrors, Battles Gallery of large paintings, its fountains, and palatial well-manicured grounds. A visit can easily occupy a day or more. Versailles is located in suburban Paris near its namesake town and is reachable by train. The easiest route is taking RER line C to Versailles Château-Rive Gauche Station and walking 10 minutes to the palace gates. Both Mobilis and Paris Visite passes are valid on this route. Alternatively, SNCF trains from Paris Gare Montparnasse run to Versailles Chantiers and from Gare Saint Lazare to Versailles Rive Droite. These options require slightly longer walks. (See **en.chateauversailles.fr**.)

Strasbourg

Board an SNCF high-speed train at Paris Est (Gare de l'Est) and be whisked eastward at 200 mph toward the Alsace region on the border with Germany. The fastest express

Strasbourg's Reformed Church Saint Paul is located near the Pont de Auvergne east of the city center.

trains reach Strasbourg in just 1 hour, 45 minutes. SNCF's Strasbourg Station is situated on the northwest side of the city and is well connected to the city center by way of a modern tram network. Board trams underground in a subway below the station or at street level out in front (to the left of the main entrance). Strasbourg's seven tram lines weave their way through this delightful French metropolis that blends the medieval with the modern, and a self-guided tram tour is one of the most pleasant ways to explore the city. (For details on trams and buses, see **cts-strasbourg.eu/en**.)

Central Strasbourg is ringed by the channelized Ill River that offers picturesque views from bridges over the water. This is a very walkable city famous for its universities, architecture, and being the seat of the European Parliament. (For Strasbourg tourist and visitor information, see **otstrasbourg.fr/en**.) Attractions include the Cathédrale Notre Dame (de Strasbourg)—a medieval Gothic church made of pink stone famous for its astronomical clock, the nearby Musée Notre Dame that displays original sculptures that were part of the Cathedral, and the Musée Alsacien (Alsatian Museum) with displays of local interest. If museums are on your agenda, consider a visit to Palais Rohan that contains three museums, including the Musée des Beaux-Arts. If you want to learn more about

171

local history, visit the Musée Historique at 2 Rue du Vieux-Marché-aux-Poissons, 67000. For a change of pace, try a bit of shopping or a casual walk and aim for Place Gutenberg (named for the famous printer and inventor of moveable type) located at the very heart of the medieval city (which in Gutenberg's time was a German principality). A statue of Gutenberg is on display in the square. Strasbourg hosts many festivals and celebrations, and it is famous for its annual Christmas Market held from the end of November to Christmas Eve (**noel.strasbourg.eu**).

Bordeaux

Ringed by vineyards and known for its namesake wine, Bordeaux is now closer to Paris by train than ever before. In July 2017, SNCF officially opened its LGV Sud Europe Atlantique to Bordeaux, which has a top speed of 320 km/h and combines with other high-speed routes to cut the travel time from Paris Montparnasse to Bordeaux Saint-Jean Station to just 3 hours.

As a UNESCO World Heritage Site that was deemed the best city in the world to visit in 2017, Bordeaux is an exceptionally pleasant French city with lots of 18th century architecture faced with characteristic beige-colored limestone. This is a city of winding alleys and broad boulevards, beautiful fountains, fascinating museums, an impressive riverfront quayside, a classic French Gothic church with an unusual freestanding 15th century bell tower, and a state-of-the-art tram network.

Visit Bordeaux's Musée of Beaux-Arts and the adjacent Gallery of Beaux-Arts to view a world-class collection of European paintings from the Renaissance to the 18th century, including collections of Dutch, English, and Italian artwork as well as those from France. The museum is located at 20 cours d'Albret and is open daily, except Tuesdays.

Among the city's dozen museums is the Wine and Trade Museum at 41 Rue Borie, which tells the story of Bordeaux's wine industry and its close relationship with Great Britain. Be sure to participate in one of the museum's free wine tastings, where expert guides explain about the region's 10,000 assorted wine variations.

Bordeaux is among nearly two dozen French cities that have embraced modern light rail, with an impressive three-route (A, B, and C) tram network that crisscrosses

Bordeaux's Basilique Saint-Michel is an unusual French Gothic church that features a separate freestanding 15th century bell tower.

Belgium

Traveling by train in Belgium is easy, fun, and comparatively inexpensive. Belgium has lots of trains, dozens of routes to explore, and some of the finest railroad stations on the Continent.

The Belgian national railroad is commonly known by its abbreviations SNCB/NMBS, reflecting its name in French and Flemish (Belgium's two primary languages). The system offers some of the most efficient rail transport in Europe, while its reasonably priced tickets make it one of the most affordable countries to explore by train. The railroad also serves as an international high-speed railway hub, with fast trains running to Paris, London, Rotterdam, Amsterdam, and various German cities.

SNCB/NMBS

SNCB/NMBS is one of the densest railroad networks in the world and one of the busiest. The system's 3,500 miles consist of parallel mainline routes with two or more electrified main tracks. Weekdays, it handles an estimate 4,000 passenger and freight trains. Some 229 million ticketed passengers traveled the network in 2014. The top speed on high-speed lines is 186 mph, but domestic trains travel at more conservative speeds.

The network serves more than 540 stations, many of which have both French and Flemish names (which can be confusing to visitors, especially when these names are dissimilar). Liège is the French name for Belgium's eastern conurbation while it is known in Flemish as Guillemins. Matters are additionally confusing when the common English spelling matches neither of the two preferred Belgian names. You'll need to pay attention, or you might miss your stop!

Most SNCB/NMBS lines use a regular interval clock-face timetable in which trains operate at the same times every hour between 6 a.m. to at least 10 p.m. Many primary routes enjoy at least an hourly stopping service in addition to InterCity express trains. Some of the busiest routes host four InterCity trains each way every hour and more frequent service during peak periods.

Many Belgian towns are within a short walk of a railway station. SNCB/NMBS operates as a hub-and-spoke system. Lines radiate out from Brussels and Antwerp

---

Noted Spanish architect Santiago Calatrava has designed several modern railway buildings including SNCB/NMBS's stunning new station at Liège/Guillemins in eastern Belgium.

Charleroi Sud is the main station for this southern Belgian city. Trams connect the railway station with Charleroi's city center via a tram subway.

and smaller secondary hubs. Through express domestic InterCity trains connect Brussels with smaller Belgian cities.

Connections to change trains range between 8–20 minutes. Although for some travelers, changing trains may seem like an inconvenience, frequent schedules mean that if you miss your connection you rarely have to wait more than hour for the next scheduled service. Moreover, since Belgium's domestic trains are unreserved, there isn't a penalty for taking a later train. Changing trains allows passengers the opportunity to get some fresh air, purchase a snack, or take photos.

InterCity trains between Brussels Nord (north station) and Antwerp take 35–45 minutes and operate four times per hour (every second train runs via Brussels Airport at Zaventem). Brussels Nord-Brugge train takes less than 1 hour, 15 minutes with three InterCity trains hourly, Brussels Nord-Ghent is 41 minutes with four trains hourly, Brussels Nord-Liege/Guillemins is 52–54 minutes twice hourly (plus additional higher fare reserved international trains), and Brussels Nord-Mons and Brussels Nord-Namur runs both take about an hour with twice hourly trains.

SNCB/NMBS makes it easy to buy tickets, as large stations have both manned ticket windows and automated machines. You may also buy tickets using a smart phone.

International runs include hourly services to Amsterdam and Luxembourg, plus SNCF's TGV high-speed services from Brussels Midi Station (south station) to various French cities; Eurostar trains via Lille and the Channel Tunnel to London; Thalys high-speed trains to Paris, Rotterdam, Amsterdam, and Köln; and a handful of ICE trains to German cities.

The most intensive local passenger services are focused around the Brussels metropolitan area and, to a lesser extent, Antwerp. Brussels has been developing multiple-track lines to allow for even more frequent local and express suburban services modeled after the Parisian RER network.

TICKETS

Except for international high-speed trains (including Eurostar services to London, and Thayls trains to Paris, Amsterdam, and Köln), Belgian passengers trains, including domestic InterCity trains, are unreserved. SNCB/NMBS's favorable ticketing policy encourages domestic travel by providing a variety of low-cost travel options for residents and visitors. Although SNCB/NMBS generally requires passengers to purchase tickets prior to boarding a train, it is still possible and acceptable to purchase your ticket from the conductor after you board. However, this is not advised because it is unnecessarily expensive and requires a €7 ($8.25) surcharge in addition to the ticket price. But if you board at a station without ticket facilities, the surcharge is waived.

Buying tickets is comparatively easy. Many stations have ticket machines, and larger stations are staffed with agents. Presently, traditional paper tickets are being phased out in favor of various electronic options, including travel cards and E-tickets. You may purchase tickets online or using the SNCB/NMBS app on your smart phone. (Download the SNCB/NMBS mobile app from iTunes Apple Store.)

In addition to ticket sales, SNCB/NMBS's electronic interfaces offer journey planning including up-to-the-minute scheduling, timetables, and information about station services, such as which stations offer luggage storage. (See SNCB/NMBS's website at **belgianrail.be/en**. For international tickets, go to **b-europe.com/en**.)

One-way tickets are reasonably priced when purchased prior to boarding trains. Examples of ticket prices: Brussels to Brugge second class €14.70 and first class €22.60; Charleroi to Antwerp second class €15.40 and first class €23.60. Round-trip fares are typically double the one-way price.

Discounted fares are available for regular travelers, members of the military, families, and students. Pregnant women are allowed first class travel at no extra charge. One of the best bargains for visitors is the Railpass ticket: second class sells for €77 and first class for €118. Unlike a typical open pass with unlimited travel within a specified time frame, this really is a low-cost, flat-fare, multiple-journey ticket that allows the purchaser to make 10 individual one-way journeys between any two stations on the SNCB/NMBS network during the course of one year. This is especially useful if you are traveling without a fixed agenda and simply want to explore by rail. You are required to mark the end points of your journey and date the ticket before you board your train.

In general, SNCB/NMBS requires ticketed passengers to take the shortest or the fastest journey between end points. However, a break in the journey at a midpoint is permitted, provided it is on the accepted shortest/fastest route. Domestic travelers are allowed to carry up to three pieces of luggage, and most trains have ample luggage storage at the ends of the passenger cars.

Brussels has one of the most extensive city streetcar systems in Europe. Brussels tram routes 92 and 93 work along cobblestone streets through the 18th century Place Royal (Royal Square).

Brussels

Brussels is Belgium's capital, its largest city, and the center for European Union and European Commission bureaucratic functions. The administrative offices for the North Atlantic Treaty Organization are also located there. It hosts one of Europe's most extensive streetcar (tram) systems and has numerous museums and attractions for visitors.

BRUSSELS STATIONS

Brussels is served by several principal railway stations. Unlike London and Paris, which are ringed by stub-end terminals that lack direct rail connections between them (except by underground transit), Brussels' main stations are linked directly via the SNCB/NMBS railway network using a north-south tunnel through the center of the city.

The Maison de Roi, or Kings House (left), is among the impressive ornate buildings lining Brussels Grand Place.

Brussels Grand Place

The famous Grand Place is less than a 10-minute walk west of Brussels Central. This opulent cobblestone, automobile-free space is one of Europe's finest city squares; it is ringed by ornately decorated buildings and dominated by Brussels' Gothic Hôtel de Ville (old City Hall) with an imposing 315-foot-tall (96 meters) tower. The square is popular and often crowded with visitors; consider an evening visit when the buildings are illuminated with lights that give the Grand Place a magical feel.

Among the attractions are highly decorated guild houses. Visit the Brewers House on the south side of the square. The Maison du Roi (opposite the Hôtel de Ville) looks older than it is—built in the 1870s but based on a Gothic design. It displays artifacts, paintings, and memorabilia relating to Belgium.

Take time to wander the narrow streets and alleys and explore and soak in Brussels' old-world charm surrounding Grand Place. On a

short walk, you'll find delightfully quirky neighborhoods, as well as dozens of shops, cafés, restaurants, and pubs. There are numerous outdoor restaurants and lots of places to sample widely diverse Belgian beers. The Galeries Royales-Saint Hubert is a brightly covered arcade dating to 1846 that today houses a variety of high-end shops and is bisected by the Rue des Bouchers. It is among the antecedents of the modern-day shopping mall and makes for a nice interlude to get out of blazing midday sun or the all too common North Sea wind and drizzle.

Walk for 3 minutes from the southwest corner of Grand Place along Rue Charles Buls to Rue de l'Etuve to reach the city's most enduring icon: the beloved Manneken Pils fountain that features the bronze statue of a young boy perpetually urinating into a basin. The original 17th century bronze was sadly destroyed, with the present statue being a replica recast in the 19th century.

Located near its namesake square, SNCB/NMBS's Luxembourg Station in Brussels features a modern entrance at street level, while the tracks and platforms are below ground.

southward mainline trains stopping at Brussels Nord continue into the tunnel to Brussels Central and Brussels South.

Brussels Nord has a full range of services, including ticket offices (open 6:45 a.m. to 10 p.m.), luggage storage, and restaurants. Underground trams 3 and 4 continue south toward central Brussels. Rogier is one underground tram station to the south, and it is the interchange with metro lines 1 and 5. Continuing south on the tram to De Brouckére gives you easy access to tourist sites and shopping areas in the vicinity of Grand Place.

Brussels Shuman Station is a moderately busy station on the east side of the city with tracks and platforms below street level. It's near the Residence Palace complex that houses European Union offices and other bureaucratic institutions as well as the Berlaymont—headquarters for the European Commission.

Brussels Luxembourg Station is near Luxembourg Square and is also situated on the main line running south toward Luxembourg. Like Schuman, its tracks are situated below ground and just a short distance from European Parliament buildings. Nearby attractions are Parc Léopold (Leopold Park) that is southeast of the

Tram experience—rolling gourmet restaurant

On of the most unusual ways to tour Brussels is over a six- or seven-course gourmet meal on a specially transformed tram advertised as the Tram Experience.

This articulated PCC (Presidents Conference Committee) car functions as a rolling restaurant with tables for two or four and serves meals prepared by prestigious Belgian chefs or occasionally by foreign guest chefs.

Meals start at €210 for two people. Seating is limited, and midweek services are often given priority to corporate clients, so advance booking is required (**visit.brussels/en/sites/tramexperience**).

station; farther south is the acclaimed Royal Belgian Institute of Natural Sciences (entrance at Rue Vautier 29). Ideal for children of all ages, this natural sciences museum includes one of Europe's finest displays of dinosaur bones, and its Biodiversity Hall features a wide selection of taxidermic (stuffed) animals and fossilized remains. It is open 9:30 a.m. to 5 p.m. Tuesday to Friday and 10–6 Saturday and Sunday but closed on Mondays. (See **naturalsciences.be/en/museum/practical-information**.)

TRAIN WORLD

While Belgium's national railway museum has the English name Train World, it is so much more than a world of trains. It is ideally situated in suburban Brussels in the restored railway station buildings at Schaerbeek on the oldest railway route in Continental Europe (it commenced service between Brussels and Mechelen in 1835). Schaerbeek is a major junction that has been described as a crossroads of Europe.

Train World is among Europe's best interpretive railway displays, which tell the history of Belgian railways from their beginnings in the steam age right to the present day. Belgium, like the United States and Canada, has exceptional national ties to the development of the railway. Belgian independence from the Netherlands was granted in 1830, and diminished economic ties with its neighbor resulted in the unanticipated consequence of encouraging railroad transportation.

Wonderfully restored locomotives include *Le Belge*—the first new engine built in Belgium. Take a look at engine 12004, a sleekly streamlined 4-4-2 steam locomotive designed in the 1930s to whisk express passengers at speed, similar to Milwaukee Road's famous *Hiawatha*. There are an array of railway artifacts, photographs, and

186

Train World is Belgium's national railway museum and is located in the old Schaerbeek Station. Among the exhibits is this streamlined Atlantic-type steam locomotive built in 1939.

memorabilia. Exhibits include a display of railway signals, mockups of modern European trains including the latest variety of Eurostar, and a demonstration focused on the importance of heeding grade crossing signals.

You can purchase a combined museum admission and domestic train ticket to Schaerbeek. SNCB's platforms are just a short walk from Train World with frequent service to Brussels and outlying areas. Alternative transport includes tram route 92 that terminates in front of the museum and offers frequent service to urban points and connections in Brussels. (For information and tickets, go to **trainworld.be/en**.)

ATOMIUM

A prominent vestige of Brussels' 1958 World's Fair is an enormous silvery monument that rises 335 feet (102 meters) into the sky. The Atomium represents the structure of an iron atom, and this iconic freestanding building can be seen on the horizon for many miles. It is among the emblems of Brussels and a major tourist attraction. Originally, it was intended as a temporary World's Fair exhibit but was completely renovated between 2003 and 2005. The glistening metallic

Located to the north of central Brussels, the Atomium towers above the trees and offers magnificent views of the city. This view is from Level 6.

surface is impressive on the outside, but while the interior appears dated, it conveys the sense of optimism prevalent in the late 1950s. Each sphere is 62 feet (19 meters) in diameter and offers different exhibitions, some permanent and others temporary.

Views from the Atomium are worth the price of admission although there can be long lines to enter. Check out Level 6, located at a height of 118 feet (36 meters) for a 150 degree view of Brussels, and even more impressive is the panoramic view on Level 7, which is 301 feet (92 meters) high.

At the top is a panoramic restaurant with the best views. The meals are expensive, even by Brussels' standards, but where else can you enjoy lunch or dinner with such a tremendous view? To reach the fairgrounds take metro line 6 northern terminus at Heysel, or ride tram line 51 toward Heysel (Esplande). The metro may be faster, but the tram ride is more interesting.

Atomium admission is €12 ($14) for adults, €9 ($11) for children 12–17 and seniors, and €6 ($7) for children 6-11. Hours are 10–6 daily. (See **atomium.be** and **ticketing.visit.brussels/en/ato**.)

The moated Beersel Castle is open to the public for a small charge. The castle features narrow spiral staircases that bring you to the tops of the towers, where you'll have some wonderful views of the surrounding countryside.

KASTEEL VAN BEERSEL (BEERSEL CASTLE)

The remarkably well-preserved, moated, medieval Kasteel van Beersel is a historic treasure of Belgian's Flanders region, located less than 10 miles from central Brussels. Despite the ravages of war and time, this castle has largely retained its 15th century structure and features three prominent semicircular towers. Visitors cross the moat on a bridge and enter the walls through a fortified castle gate.

Much of the structure is open for exploration, including steep, narrow, winding circular staircases with century-worn triangular steps. From the tops of the towers are views of the countryside and railway line. Under restoration since 2003, it is open to the public from March to November. (It is closed Mondays with variable seasonal hours.) Admission is €3 ($3.60) for adults, €1 ($1.20) for children, and € 1.50 ($1.80) for those 65 and over. (See **en.visitbeersel.be/kasteel-van-beersel**.)

The castle can be viewed from SNCB/NMBS's S5/S7 suburban trains (running from Mechelen south toward Halle-Merode)—one of the nonradial services avoiding central Brussels. To reach Beersel from one of Brussels' main stations, you will need to travel south to Halle and change for the S7 train running northeasterly toward Mechelen. Running time from Brussels Midi/Zuid with the change is about 30 minutes. If you are traveling from Antwerp, take an InterCity train south and change to the S7 or S5 either at Mechelen or Vilvoorde and continue south toward Halle-Merode; journey time is just under 90 minutes. From Beersel Station, it is just a short walk to the castle.

Antwerp

Antwerp developed around maritime trade. It is one of the three largest European ports, and the city enjoys an unusually dense railway network that accommodates heavy volumes of rail freight moving to and from destinations across Europe. Most rail passengers arrive at Antwerpen Centraal (Antwerp Central Station), the city's elegant main railway terminal. This late 19th century masterpiece has been substantially augmented in recent years with new lines and modern facilities.

Centraal's magnificent station building is credited to architect Louis de la Censerie. Today, it's seen as a palace with tracks behind it, but at the time of its opening in 1898, this elaborately and elegantly adorned building was decried by critics as being overly ostentatious for its utilitarian function. A capacious iron and glass balloon-style arched train shed spans the first of three levels of track. Historically, all the trains served tracks beneath the shed but to expand capacity and improve access, the station was remodeled and reopened in 2007 with two additional track levels located below the original lines under the shed. The lowest level provides direct access to points north of Antwerp via a long tunnel, which serves domestic local trains as well as high-speed services operating to the Netherlands.

Prior to these improvements, Dutch through trains serving Antwerp either had to change direction and reverse out of the station before continuing their journey or skip Antwerpen Centraal altogether.

Ticket offices are open from 5:45 a.m. to 10 p.m. The station offers luggage storage and other amenities, including a paid parking area and restaurant. It is well connected with local transit including trams and buses. De Lijn transit tickets and an information desk are located in the station arcade near the Pelikaanstraat entrance.

Architect Louis de la Censerie's elegant Antwerpen Centraal opened in 1898. Top-level platforms are up the stairs under the vast balloon-style train shed.

De Lijn's Coastal Tram connects coastal resorts along the North Sea, such as Koksijd pictured here.

(Off-season half-hour intervals are common, while at peak times, there may be up to eight services an hour on a mix of long- and short-distance runs).

As expected, summer is the peak season when the beaches (and trams) are jammed with Belgians aiming to escape the heat of Brussels, Antwerp, and other cities. Off-season, the beaches are quiet but may be inhospitable when cold North Sea winds blow.

Explore the coastal towns. Koksijde-Bad is a popular resort about a 20-minute run north from De Panne. Typical of Belgian North Sea towns, it features high-rise holiday towers that line the beach for miles. In town are a variety of shops and pricey places to enjoy a leisurely lunch or a long dinner. If the prices shock you, consider traditional beach food: hot dogs, hamburgers, and a Belgian specialty: pommes frites (french fries) with mayonnaise.

Nieuwpoort is a lineside interlude that presents a contrast to the more modern resorts. If the beach overwhelms you, walk inland into the village, find a handy pub or restaurant, and relax over a refreshing Belgian beer. Maes Pils is a local favorite. North of Nieuwpoort toward Oostende, the line passes through beautiful

One of the last classic interurban electric lines in Belgium is De Lijn's Coastal tramway that runs the length of the Flemish North Sea coast. Here, tram tracks reflect a rosy sunset at Blakenberge.

windswept dunes best enjoyed in the warmer months, although largely free of visitors in the winter. (You might want to carefully check the tram schedule before getting off if the weather looks inclement).

Oostende has long been a Belgian holiday destination. In the 19th century, it was developed as an easy-to-reach beach resort for British holiday-makers owing to the frequent ferry service between Oostende and the English port of Dover across the English Channel. The tramway works its way through Oostende streets, where it makes a variety of local stops, serving resort hotels, shops, and beaches. Oostende ferries are of diminished importance since the opening of the Channel Tunnel between Calais and Dover in 1994.

Blankenberge is another vacation hot spot where a broad sandy beach seems to stretch for miles, and the tram makes several stops to serve resort destinations. Get off at Belgium Pier where the long pier runs out into the North Sea, featuring the Storms Expo theme park and Pier Brasserie restaurant (with stunning views of the sea and coast). Additional restaurants can be found along the boardwalk, just a short walk from tramway stops. From the station, a 10-minute walk or a tram ride to

Gent (Ghent) is a classic Flemish city featuring charming architecture and canals with lots of restaurants and pubs. Trams operated by De Lijn connect the Gent-Sint-Pieters Station located on the outskirts with the historic city center.

Sea Life-Floreal takes you to Sea Life aquarium, where you can enjoy watching a variety of underwater creatures.

De Lijn tickets and travel

De Lijn operates various tram and bus systems across Belgium, including Antwerp and Ghent city trams and the Coastal Tram (but not the city trams in either Brussels or Charleroi). It offers a variety of different ticketing options. (For details, see **delijn. be/en**.) If you buy day passes, they are valid on trams and buses across the De Lijn network, which will allow you to ride the Coastal Tram and city trams in Ghent and Antwerp on the same ticket during the validation period.

While tickets may be purchased from drivers on many transit vehicles, it is typically cheaper to buy them in advance of boarding. You must validate your ticket when boarding by inserting the ticket into the automated yellow validation machine (located near a vehicle entrance). Day passes need to be validated every time you get on and off a transit vehicle (except when you buy the pass from the

Lijnwinkels (transit shops)

Antwerp Central Station
Near Pelikaanstraat entrance
Open Monday-Friday 7 a.m. to 7 p.m. and
Saturday 8 a.m. to 4 p.m.

Antwerp Head Office
Grote Hondstraat 58
2018 Antwerp
Open Monday-Friday 8:10 a.m. to 12 p.m. and
1 p.m. to 4 p.m.

Antwerp Metrostation Groenplaats
Open Monday-Friday 8 a.m. to 6 p.m. and
Saturday 8 a.m. to 12 p.m. and 1 p.m. to 4 p.m.

Gent-Sint-Pieters Station
Open Monday-Friday 7 a.m. to 12:15 p.m. and
12:45 p.m. to 7 p.m. and Saturday 10 a.m. to
12:15 p.m. and 12:30 p.m. to 5 p.m.

Gent Zuid (Gent South)
Open Monday-Friday 7 a.m. to 7p.m.

Additional Lijnwinkels are located at Brugge,
Brussels Nord, Kortrijk Tikstraat, Leuven,
Oostende (Ostend), Ypres, and other central
locations.

bus/tram driver when the initial validation isn't required). The validation period for each day allows for travel up to 3:59 a.m. the following morning, so if you are out late you can continue to travel on the same pass.

Single tickets cost €3 and are valid for 60 minutes from the time of validation.

Electronic single tickets may be bought via SMS text using a mobile device (tablet or smart phone) at a reduced price (€2 plus a 15 cent processing fee). De Lijn has arrangements with two dozen European mobile phone operators. In addition to the 60-minute SMS ticket (SMS code DL), there is a 120-minute option (SMS code DL120). The Ljin Card is a reduced price ticket that provides 10 single 60-minute journeys for €15.

Day passes offer the best value if you plan to make wide use of De Ljin transit and will save you the hassle of procuring new tickets for each journey. Keep in mind that passes still require validation every time you get on and off a vehicle.

A single day pass advance purchase cost €6 for adults and €5 for children. A 3-day pass is €12 and a 5-day pass is €17. While valid on most De Ljin transport, day passes are not accepted on Limburg Express buses.

There is also a 7-day pass for travel on the Coastal Tram.

De Lijn tickets are sold at thousands of outlets across Belgium including select SNCB/NMBS railway stations, lineside automated ticket machines, newsagents, supermarkets, and at transit shops called Lijnwinkels.

Luxembourg

Southern Luxembourg consists of bucolic rolling agricultural lands. A local train from the German border works the double-track electrified main line toward Luxembourg City on a warm April evening.

The Grand Duchy of Luxembourg is one of the smallest European Union member states that operates its own national railway. At just under 1,000 square miles, Luxembourg would fit into neighboring Belgium almost a dozen times.

Its compact railway network, the Société Nationale des Chemin de fer Luxembourgeois (known by initials as CFL), is a minor European crossroads strategically located between railway systems in Belgium, Germany, and France. Two lines reach from Belgium, with one major route running east toward Trier, Germany, and beyond into the Mosel valley (see Germany), while other routes run south and west into France. In addition, there are several branch lines.

A southward CFL passenger train approaches a tunnel near Clervaux on its way toward Luxembourg City. This view was made from the path leading to Clervaux's Abbaye de Saint-Maurice.

Luxembourg City is rich with history and classic architecture. The city center is compact and readily explored on foot.

Tickets

CLF benefits from a remarkably simple fare structure, and riding trains is inexpensive. There are only a few types of tickets useful to visitors, and tickets are cheaper when purchased in advance from CFL station ticket offices, designated shops, and post offices, or from automated ticket machines on platforms. Tickets purchased onboard trains have a €1 ($1.20) euro surcharge. Basic tickets are valid for second class travel; however, passengers may upgrade to first class with payment of a nominal supplement (either beforehand or on the train).

The most basic fare is a short timed ticket called a **Kuerzzäitbilljee** that costs €2 ($1.40) and is valid on all domestic trains and buses across Luxembourg for 2 hours from the time of validation. Day tickets called **Dagesbilljee** cost €4 ($4.80) and are valid for unlimited domestic train and bus travel from the time of validation until 4 a.m. the following morning. Booklets of 10 tickets are available at reduced prices. Other types of tickets include day-return tickets from Luxembourg to cross-border destinations in Belgium, France, and Germany, plus the German Rheinland-

Luxembourg is a small scenic country that enjoys excellent cross-border rail services with its neighbors. At Wasserbillig, a German InterCity train rolls eastward across the Sûre River that marks the border with Germany.

Pfal-plus LU ticket aimed at unlimited travel with the specified German region plus Luxembourg. (For tickets and scheduling, see **cfl.lu/espaces/voyageurs/en**.)

Luxembourg City

Luxembourg's only large city is its namesake capital located in the south of the country. This colorful and scenically spectacular small metropolis is also the primary destination for many tourists visiting by train. Luxembourg Gare Centrale (Luxembourg Central Station) is situated just north of a major junction and about a 20-minute walk south of the historic city center. Buses run every few minutes and take about 11 minutes to reach the center.

Most of the historic city is scenically situated atop a high bluff over bends in the Alzette River. This once-fortified city is small and walkable with many sites close to one another. Spectacular views of the Alzette Valley can be seen from the 17th century ramparts at Rocher du Bock located along Rue Sigefroi and Montée De Clausen on the eastern edge of the old city. From here, you can watch trains

Weekdays, CFL serves Clervaux with hourly Regional Express and InterCity trains that provide half-hourly departures to Luxembourg City. Travel time is about an hour.

cross a magnificent multiple-arch viaduct on their approach to Luxembourg Gare Centrale. (See **visitluxembourg.com/en** and **lcto.lu/en**.)

Among interesting sites is the Grand Ducal Palace, which serves as the city residence for Luxembourg's Grand Duke—the hereditary head of state. This impressive structure, located on the Rue de la Reine, is famous for its Flemish Renaissance façade. It is open for guided tours from mid-July to September.

Nearby is the Place Guillaume II, Luxembourg's classic medieval public square, often host to seasonal open-air concerts. South of the square is the Cathédrale Notre-Dame, which was built in the 17th century in a blend of Gothic and Renaissance styles.

Clervaux

The cross-border line from Liege/Guillemins to Luxembourg City follows the Clerve River through the Ardennes region of northern Luxembourg. Clervaux is a picturesque village built on a strategic highpoint at a bend in the river. Clervaux is laid out in a

The 12th century Clervaux Castle is situated on small hill above the town and houses several popular museums.

horseshoe shape along the curved Rue Ley. The CFL station is a 15-minute walk north of the village. Just beyond the station, the line enters a tunnel that misses the town.

Sitting high above is Clervaux Castle, the primary tourist attraction and focal point of the town. It dates from the 12th century, although the present structure is largely a 17th century construction that required intensive rebuilding following World War II. An American tank is displayed out in front. The castle hosts a variety of exhibitions, including a Battle of Bulge museum (the battle badly damaged the castle and surrounding town) and the famous *The Family of Man*—iconic world photographic exhibition of the 1950s directed by Luxembourg-born American photographer Edward Steichen, which displays the work of some of the most talented photographers of the period.

The castle opens at 10 a.m. To reach the castle, follow Montée de l'Église, which winds around the village to the west. The Abbaye de Saint-Maurice is up the hill from the castle. It's worth the hike, as you'll find some stunning views of the valley from the trails around the old abbey, including some interesting views of CFL's railway line.

The Netherlands

The Dutch love their bicycles, and at most railway stations, there are impressive bicycle storage facilities.

Traveling across the Netherlands by train is the most interesting and efficient way to see the country. You can relax as you glide across fields of tulips with old windmills and modern wind turbines scraping the sky. Amsterdam, Rotterdam, Breda, and Maastricht are among the historic places interconnected by one of Europe's busiest railways. Local trains are unreserved and operate on frequent intervals, so you rarely have to worry about waiting long for a train. (For tourism, see **discoverholland.com**.)

The Netherlands is relatively small, but it is the most densely populated country in Europe. Most people live in high-density housing in cities and large towns. It features an unusually flat landscape with large portions of the country consisting of land reclaimed from the North Sea and protected from flooding by systems of dikes. The Dutch railway is heavily used and functions similar to a huge rapid transit network with major routes served by at least two passenger trains each direction every hour; the busiest lines offer even more frequent service.

Nederlandse Spoorwegen provides an intensive and largely electrified passenger network. An NS double-deck electric multiple unit train pauses for its station stop at Den Bosch.

Dutch passenger trains are among the most distinctive in Europe. The Koploper (*Headwalker*) is the common nickname for one of several types of electric multiple units.

The majority of Dutch trains travel less than 100 miles between terminals, so it is difficult to spend more than 2½ hours on any one train. The great operational frequency with its crisscrossing of lines allows for a hub-and-spoke system connecting secondary points. Most station platforms are protected with automatic barriers such as those used on urban metros, and passengers must have tickets to gain access to platforms. The Netherlands also benefits from excellent urban public transport with cities and towns tightly connected with trams and buses that logically interface with the railway network at multiple nodes. This makes transfer between modes as simple and straightforward as possible. The Dutch love their bicycles, so trains and railway stations are bicycle friendly: you'll notice thousands of cycles neatly parked at major stations.

Nederlandse Spoorwegen (NS) is the national railway operator. The railway network is largely electrified using direct current overhead catenary. Dutch passenger trains are among the most distinctive looking in Europe: in addition to the occasional locomotive-powered train assigned to some express or longer-distance services, you'll find a variety of electric multiple units working NS passenger services.

Dutch trains are clean, convenient, and functional. An all-stops local train called a Sprinter, destined for the Hoek van Holland (Hook of Holland), pauses at Rotterdam Centraal.

In terms of appearance, one of the more unusual types is the Koploper, which translates to *Headwalker*, and features a high-mounted cab at each end.

In general, trains are clean and functional. Most trains carry both first and second class accommodation, indicated by a large numeral 1 or 2 near the entrance of the carriage. In addition to national services provided by NS are international high-speed services operated by Thalys and DB (German Railways) ICE sets.

NS tickets

Dutch transport systems have embraced modern fare collection systems and traditional paper tickets haven't been used on the railway for several years. Many passengers are daily riders and use OV-Chipkaarts, which are preloaded with electronic tickets, or download E-tickets to their mobile devices (iPhone or Android smart phones). E-tickets are passenger-specific and require your birthdate on the ticket and must be presented with a valid identification, such as a passport. Unfortunately for most visitors purchasing E-tickets using the NS Reisplanner Xtra app (loaded from the iTunes site) or online requires an electronic bank account with one of several preapproved Dutch banks, and as a result, the more practical means to travel is single-use smart cards which may be purchased at railway stations from NS ticket windows or automated ticket machines. In many instances, NS's fare collection requires passengers to both tag on and tag off when using electronic tickets. (For details on the latest varieties of single-use smart cards, OV-Chipkaarts, the various types of tickets and their respective costs, plus how and when to tag on or off, see the NS website at **ns.nl**.)

NS offers several types of tickets as single-use smart cards, so it pays to decide in advance what ticket may be the most appropriate for you. The simplest, most straightforward ticket is the **Single** ticket that is intended for a single one-way journey. Passengers may break their journey en route, but travel must be completed on the same day. This type of ticket is only cost effective if you are planning one trip by rail or if you are traveling to your destination on one day and returning on another.

When planning a day round-trip journey it is nominally cheaper to buy a **Day Return** single-use smart card. (The train fare is the same, but there is a charge for each single-use card, so a Day Return will save you being charged this fee twice). However, you must complete your round-trip journey on the same day.

The **Railrunner** ticket offers a discounted fare for children 4–11 years old. Children less than 4 years old may travel free. When traveling on express services, such as InterCity direct trains or German ICE trains, a flat €2.40 ($2.90) supplement must be purchased in advance of travel in addition to your ticket.

If you are planning several journeys for a single day or hoping to explore the Dutch Railway network without a fixed plan, you should consider buying one of several varieties of day pass tickets. While the types offered appear similar, it is important to pay attention to ticket validity and for what types of transport it covers. The **NS Day** ticket (available as single-use smart card as well as electronic ticket) is designed for one-day's unlimited travel across the NS railway network, with first class selling for €89 ($106) and second class for €52.60 ($62.70) This ticket is valid on InterCity Direct and ICE trains with the necessary €2.40 ($2.90) supplement but may not be used on Thalys high-speed trains.

Similar are the **Off-peak Holland Travel** ticket (€39/$46.50) and **Holland Travel** ticket (€59/$70.30), which may be used on all forms of public transport. Significantly, the Off-Peak Holland Travel ticket may not be used between 6:30 a.m.

Rotterdam Centraal is a large modern station offering ample platform space, detailed scheduling and train arrival/departure information, and frequent service to points across the Dutch railway network.

and 9:30 a.m., while the full Holland Travel ticket may be use at anytime during the selected day of travel (defined as midnight to 4 a.m. the following morning).

Other types of passes are intended for regional transport and may be purchased for more than one-day's travel. An **Amsterdam Regional** ticket is good on both trains and other forms of public transport in the defined region; this is sold for 1, 2, or 3 days. Similar and slightly cheaper is the **Amsterdam Travel** ticket, which includes journeys to and from Schiphol Airport and unlimited travel on Amsterdam's trams, buses, the metro, and public ferries but is not meant for unrestricted rail travel.

Journeys

By and large, the NS network functions on a regular-interval timetable and trains typically work 30-minute frequencies throughout the day, seven days a week. One of the longest journeys is from Amsterdam via Utrecht and Eindhoven to Maastricht, which is located in the far southeastern part of the Netherlands near the Belgian

An NS locomotive-powered push-pull passenger train accelerates away from Lage Zwaluwe, heading toward Breda in southwestern Holland.

and German borders. This 136-mile (219km) run takes just 2 hours, 24 minutes on a fast train.

Holland's two best-known cities, Amsterdam and Rotterdam, are 51 miles (82km) apart and enjoy some of the most frequent rail service of any two city pairs in Europe. InterCity Direct trains operate every 15 minutes and take just 42 minutes. For passengers looking to save the €2.40 ($2.90) supplement and don't mind a slower pace, stopping local trains called SPR Sprinters fill the gaps between the InterCity direct services, but they take 1 hour, 15 minutes for the same journey.

THALYS HIGH-SPEED TRAINS TO BRUSSELS AND PARIS

Through high-speed service from Amsterdam via Rotterdam to Brussels and Paris is jointly operated by Dutch (NS), Belgian (SNCB/NMBS), and French (SNCF) railways under the marketing name Thalys (which doesn't convey any significant meaning). The trains are essentially specialized multi-voltage French TGV high-speed sets designed for uniform operation across Belgium and the Netherlands, and may be quickly distinguished by their striking burgundy red and silver livery with Thalys

A Thalys high-speed train running from Amsterdam to Paris sails across the modern span over the wide channel of Hollands Diep, an important estuary and shipping channel that flows into the North Sea. Seen below is an older railway bridge that is still used for conventional-speed railway traffic.

printed in stylized letters across the front of the train. Thalys is a premier service and a showcase example of European international high-speed rail. It features all-reserved trains and was based on the French TGV services.

It is more akin to airline travel than traditional train travel and feels like flying on the ground—but with greater comfort and flexibility. All seats are equipped with electrical sockets, and the train is completely equipped with WiFi Internet. There are two basic classes of service: **Comfort 1** equates to first class and includes an extra spacious seat, meal service at your seat, a complimentary newspaper, plus assistance with booking taxis in either Brussels or Paris. **Comfort 2** is essentially second class without the frills offered in Comfort 1.

One of the special features introduced on Thalys trains is its Le Salon a semi-private area situated at the ends of trains that can accommodate up to four passengers. Aimed primarily at business travelers, Le Salon provides ample work space with a large meeting table and is advertised as a meeting room on the train.

levels you won't be able to appreciate the station's wonderful architecture), and then be gliding along at speed again. After Brussels, the train makes rapid progress crossing into northern France, arriving below the Victorian shed at Paris Gare du Nord.

Amsterdam

Amsterdam, an eclectic melting pot, is the most popular city in the Netherlands. This waterfront medieval metropolis is ringed by five tiers of canals, populated with leaning, gabled houses and cobblestone streets, interconnected by trams, and famous for its curious blend of old world art, architecture, and culture with unusually liberal attitudes toward sex and drugs that has made it popular with youthful travelers and bohemians since the 1960s. For an inexpensive tour of central Amsterdam, consider a trip on tram route 2.

Centraal Station is the major transport hub centered in a waterfront facility located on reclaimed land adjacent to the harbor and immediately north of the medieval center. The core of the station stems from a dramatic mid-1880s redesign by Pierre Cuypers (architect of Amsterdam's famous Rijksmuseum). The impressive double-shed covering the tracks isn't as old as it seems, as it was built in 1922.

Four parallel north-south streets—from west to east: Nieuwezijds Voorburgwal, Nieuwendijk, Damrak, and Warmoesstraat—connect the station with the city's famous 17th century square known simply as the Dam, (a name that infers the whole of the city, as historically the site was occupied by a dam across the Amstel River). For many people, this is the very heart of Amsterdam. On the east side of the large open public space is the National Monument, a World War II memorial, while on the west are two of Amsterdam's most famous buildings: the Koninklijk Palace, originally intended as city hall, and Nieuwe Kerk, a 15th century church that was largely rebuilt following a 17th century conflagration.

Southeast of Central Station and northeast of the Dam is Amsterdam's infamous DeWalletjes—what Americans like to call a red light district.

Among Amsterdam's chief tourist attractions is the Rijksmuseum in the southwest area of the city on Houders Kade and Museumstraat. The Anne Frank House,

---

Amsterdam has 15 tram routes, with many lines focused on serving Centraal Station. Visitors may opt for hourly or day tickets, which can be purchased from automated ticket machines or local vendors across the city.

Rotterdam is Europe's largest port and ranked as the world's ninth largest in terms of traffic. You can take a boat tour of the port and get a sense of its vast size.

where the young Jewish diarist recorded her impressions hiding during World War II, is located in the Grachtengordel (Canal Ring) area on Prinsengracht.

Rotterdam

Rotterdam is the Netherlands' second largest city and Europe's largest port, and it is a great urban contrast with Amsterdam. Situated on the shores of Nieuwe Maas waterway, this is a showcase example of European modern architecture. The old city was virtually erased as result of massive war damage during World War II. Rotterdam is a fascinating place worthy of exploration; unfortunately, the city is too often unfairly dismissed by visitors seeking quaint old world charm.

Among the chief attractions is the port itself where you can see some of the world's largest container ships and mountains of 20- and 40-foot boxes that deliver goods to and from points around Europe. Spido harbor tours are a popular means of seeing the port; 75-minute and day-long boat cruises can be booked at the waterfront (**cityguiderotterdam.com/things-to-do/attractions/spido-rotterdam**).

A Rotterdam tram passes below the famous Cube Houses. The Cube Houses are near Station Blaak; take tram route 21 or 24, Rotterdam metro lines A, B or C, or NS trains one stop from Rotterdam Centraal.

Rotterdam's architecture is like an enormous Lego set on steroids. Architects have applied creative solutions using modern materials and unusual designs. Among the most impressive recent structures is the new Rotterdam Centraal Station, a massive asymmetrical structure and the city's main railway terminal and shopping mall. The iconic tilted Cube Houses are among the examples of the city's most unusual and most progressive modern architecture. They are centrally located at Overblaak 70 3011MH Rotterdam, near the Blaak railway station. Visitors can explore the Show Cube Museum. (See **holland.com/global/tourism/destinations/ rotterdam/rotterdam-cube-houses.htm**.)

Nearby is the enormous enclosed Market Hall shopping plaza and food hall, located south of Blaak Station at the intersection of Binnenrotte and Blaak Streets.

Rotterdam's Hoogstraat is a central pedestrian shopping district. The impressive cable-stayed Erasmus Bridge spans the Nieuwe Maas channel connecting neighborhoods north and south of this dividing body of water. Take a walk across for stunning views of the city and harbor. Visit the prominent waterfront Hotel New York, located on the south bank of the Nieuwe Maas at Koninginnenhoofd 1, for a beer and meal.

Rotterdam takes pride in its distinctive modern architecture, and its new asymmetrical Centraal Station building is among its most impressive civic structures.

Museum Boijmans Van Beuningen displays its vast collection of Dutch and Flemish paintings as well as Italian paintings and examples of modern art. It is open year-round but closed Mondays. It is located at Museumpark 18-203015 CX Rotterdam (**boijmans.nl/en**).

Rotterdam is well served by modern public transport. In addition to buses, trams serving 10 routes glide along streets and on grass-covered central medians, while a sleek 5-route metro rail system swiftly carries passengers below ground in the city center reaching far into the suburbs, with route E providing a direct link with neighboring Den Haag Centraal Station. (For information, see **ret.nl**.)

Den Bosch

This quaint medieval town is properly known by the confusing name 's-Hertogenbosch but more easily by its contracted name Den Bosch. It is most associated with its most famous son, painter Hieronymus Bosch (1450–1516), known for his elaborate macabre fantasy paintings featuring surreal panoramas filled with grotesque and mythic

An old stone lion juxtaposed with a NS Sprinter shows the contrast between modern transport and historical architecture that exemplifies the Netherlands today.

creatures that blend man and beast. A museum for the artist in the town center is more of a tribute than a showcase of his original paintings, which can be found in art museums elsewhere in the Netherlands (notably in Rotterdam at the Museum Boijmans Van Beuningen). A statue of the painter is displayed in the central market square.

The main attractions are the town's 13th century buildings built around the triangularly arranged central village, and the Sint-Janskathedral, which is a stunning example of a large Dutch Gothic church (constructed between the 13th and 15th centuries) that contains 48 bells.

Den Bosch's station features some classic iron sheds and blends historic and modern station design elements. It is on the main north-south line from Amsterdam via Utrecht to Maastricht, 1 hour, 25 minutes from Amsterdam by fast train, and also served by a busy nonradial route running from Zwolle via Tilburg and Breda to Roosendaal. Both routes feature half-hourly services throughout the day. The station is about a 15-minute walk west of the city's old town. Leaving via the eastern entrance, follow Stationsweg east, cross the Dommel River to Visstraat, and then bear right onto Hoge Steenweg, keeping your eye on the cathedral, which is hard to miss.

A downhill Jungfraubahn train approaches Kleine Scheidegg. The Alps are a formidable environment, and it can be blindingly bright on Switzerland's snow-crested peaks. Bring sunscreen and sunglasses or pay the price!

Swiss engineers found ways to build railways through seemingly impossible terrain that reach places that appear to be beyond the range of normal railroading by employing clever combinations of exceptionally steep alignments with spirals, long tunnels, and towering viaducts. Swiss operations put many other railways to shame. Steeply graded, single-track, mountain narrow gauge lines routinely accommodate three to four trains an hour and maintain precision punctuality, despite difficult winter conditions—circumstances that leave mere mortal railways in desperate shape and unable to maintain even basic schedules on double-track lines.

Not all Swiss journeys are equally impressive though and simply gazing at a map does not necessarily point you to the most impressive lines. Keep in mind that by virtue of the difficult terrain, many of the most stunning railway journeys are accomplished in a comparatively short distance. Yet very steep ascents and outstanding engineering can yield amazing, breathtaking vistas in just a few miles.

In general, the most scenic Swiss railways are in the southern portion of the country, where the mountains are the highest. To best experience the Alps by rail, travel from west to east, rather than from north to south. The primary north-south

BLS is a standard gauge Swiss railway that operates a 261-mile (420km) network focused on the important Lötschberg and Simplon Passes from which it takes its name. This BLS electric multiple unit approaches the Spiez Bahnhof.

railway arteries are the most heavily engineered and tend to use the lowest crossings of the Alps that now feature long base tunnels, which by design miss the most spectacular scenery.

Base tunnels were built to increase line capacity, while shortening journey times, and reduce the amount of energy required to move trains through the mountains, which is a fine accomplishment for pure transport but of little value to the casual traveler. Thankfully, Swiss railway companies have retained older lines that feature more impressive scenery specifically for the purpose of entertaining visitors and serving local communities along these lines.

Tickets

Buying tickets in Switzerland is easy. Most stations feature straightforward ticket machines with English language options, while larger stations have helpful, efficient and well-trained ticket sellers, who are often fluent in English and very polite. You can also buy tickets online or with your smart phone. The SBB mobile app is free

An SBB Class ETR 610 Avelia Pendolino races along Lake Geneva near Rivaz. These modern seven-car tilting trains allow speeds 35 percent faster through curves than conventional equipment by counteracting the effects of centrifugal forces.

to download and handles most Swiss railways, while supplying an easy-to-use trip planner as well the ability to purchase tickets for most domestic journeys.

However, great things do come with a price. Switzerland isn't a cheap country, and just about everything is more expensive there than in neighboring countries or the United States. Switzerland's walk-up rail fares are among the priciest in Europe. Consider that a second class Geneva to Zurich ticket can cost you 89 CHF ($90) for a journey just under 3 hours, while first class will be 156 CHF ($158)— prices comparable to European plane journeys.

The trick is to avoid buying full-fare single tickets at the time of travel. Instead consider more cost-effective options. The most cost-efficient way to travel by rail in Switzerland is to buy one of several rail passes.

The Swiss Travel Pass is the most versatile and offers some of the best value, but it is only available to non-Swiss residents. (See **swissrailways.com** for full details.) The pass can be purchased for first or second class travel over fixed periods of validity: 3, 4, 8, or 15 days. Adult, Youth (16–26), and Child (6–16) passes are available. You may purchase the tickets in advance online or when you arrive in

Golden Pass Route is a supremely scenic narrow gauge line operated by Compagnie du Chemin de fer Montreux Oberland Bernois (MOB). The extra-fare Golden Pass Panoramic approaches the resort at Gstaad.

Switzerland from most large railway stations. The pass will save you money if you are planning to make a number of journeys, and it offers great flexibility by allowing you to change your travel plans without needing to rebook or waste time buying new tickets. Just jump on a train and go. This is especially useful in Switzerland, where the large numbers of railway routes combined with regular interval scheduling makes for a very versatile network.

In addition to unlimited travel on the SBB intercity railway network, the ticket is also valid on most buses and boats, plus the majority of local transit systems (city tram and buses) while providing admission to many museums. However, it is not a blanket ticket to all transport; several of the more spectacular mountain railways, notably portions of the Wengernalbahn or the Jungfraubahn, are not fully covered by the pass. It also offers a 50 percent discount on some mountain lines and many cable car (aerial tramway) routes.

Regional passes tend to offer more economical options within narrower but clearly defined travel areas (**swissrailways.com/en/products/regionalalpspass**). Visitors to Lake Geneva may consider the Regional Pass Lake Geneva-Alps. It is ideal

Spring is a wonderful time to visit Switzerland. The days can be clear and bright, trees and flowers are in bloom, yet the distant mountains are still covered in snow. The winter tourists have departed and the summer tourists have yet to arrive, which leads to bargains at hotels and restaurants and shorter lines for attractions.

for visitors to any of the area's resorts or for travelers interested in exploring this supremely scenic region. It covers a wide variety of transport including boats on the lake and some rack railways, and it spans the area from Geneva to Montreux and east toward Villars, Gstaad, and Zweisimmen. A map, which is also available online, comes with the pass and highlights the routes covered.

Other regional passes include the Regional Pass Bernese Oberland that covers its namesake area and the Tell Pass Central Switzerland (as in William Tell) that covers rail travel in this region and notably does cover travel on mountain lines that are not covered by other passes.

Eurail Pass holders may find good value in Switzerland, especially when traveling on high-speed trains to and from other countries. Eurail is accepted by many of the local and regional railways including the popular Glacier Express and MOB's Golden Pass trains; however, several of the high-profile smaller lines do not accept it, and pass holders should carefully check the list of approved Swiss lines before traveling (**eurail.com**).

On a brilliant but cold February afternoon, a northward SBB train bursts forth from the Gotthard Tunnel at Göschenen. Inside the tunnel, the old Gotthard Route crests the Alps at 3,786 feet (1,154 meters) above sea level.

Swiss Federal Railways (SBB)

The Swiss Federal Railways, generally known by its initials SBB, is by far the largest and most-traveled railway in Switzerland. It operates the majority of the country's standard gauge trunk routes and numerous standard gauge secondary lines. SBB's intercity and international trains are comfortable, spacious, and clean and generally come with large side windows to afford passengers superb views of the scenery. Local trains are excellent, although many of the most modern trains have comparatively stiff seats, owing to the need to comply with fire-retardant requirements.

Many visitors avail of SBB between major cities, as frequent fast trains make for the most convenient and pleasant means of travel. Swiss rights-of-way and track maintenance standards are some of the finest in the world, so gliding along on an SBB intercity train is like floating on a sea of glass. Tilting ICN trains are assigned to several of the more sinuous domestic intercity runs, including the journey from Zurich to St. Gallen, and from Zurich over Gotthard Pass. SBB assigns its modern tilting Pendolino trains (easily identified by their long streamlined snouts) to fast international services from Geneva, Basel, and Zurich to Milan. Many other intercity trains are conventional push-pull sets with a locomotive at one end and a control cab at the other. Some of the newest trains are comfortable double-deck electric multiple units. On double-deck trains, riding upstairs offers better views.

SBB is one of the state railways in western Europe that doesn't require reservations on its domestic intercity trains. This may seem like a small convenience, but it is one of the great joys of traveling on SBB's long-distance trains. SBB typically aims to supply more than ample seat capacity on long-distance runs while offering abnormally frequent service. Furthermore, SBB runs additional trains during peak times. Light loading on average runs means that passengers have more space to spread out, which results in a more pleasant travel experience. Providing longer trainsets also helps SBB soak up patronage during peak periods when larger numbers of passengers show up without the extra planning required for reserved seats.

Consider the midday frequencies of intercity trains on major routes in each direction (not including the slower interregional and local services): Basel-Bern, Bern-Zurich, and Geneva-Zurich—two trains per hour; Zurich-Luzern and Zurich-St. Gallen—three trains per hour; and Basel-Zurich—five trains per hour. On these and other major routes, passengers rarely have to wait more than 30 minutes between trains. On secondary routes and branch lines, trains running at the same time every hour are more common.

SBB is comfortable, convenient, and efficient but does not operate many of the most famous scenic Swiss journeys. For the truly jaw-dropping Alpine climbs, you need to explore some of the narrow gauge and rack railway journeys covered later in this chapter. Yet in many countries, even the most prosaic SBB trips would be deemed fairly scenic, and several SBB trips are among the most interesting mainline journeys in Europe. And venturing off the well-beaten path on select SBB secondary lines allows you to explore some impressive-looking areas.

SBB'S GOTTHARD PASS

Among SBB's busiest routes are its lines over Gotthard Pass. Historically, the Gotthard route was one part of the most important long-distance European rail corridors. It was planned as an international connection from Germany, Belgium, the Netherlands, and northern France with Italy in the north and the Adriatic states in the south. It is the older of the two Swiss mainline north-south Alpine crossings. The comparatively low saddle of Gotthard Pass has made it a centuries-old trading route.

SBB Stadler Flirts working a southward InterRegio service approach the station stop at Flüelen. Perched on the hill overlooking the line is the town's 17th century Catholic church.

Where Switzerland's early railways were largely built on low-lying routes along river valleys, the Gotthardbahn (Gotthard Railway) route took Swiss rail-building high into the mountains. Yet the decision to tackle the mountains didn't come easily, and it was only after years of discussion that construction was finally initiated in 1872. Key to this route is the original Gotthard Tunnel that opened in 1882. This was among the earliest truly long tunnels and the crowning achievement of the Gotthard's highly engineered Alpine crossing. The line was engineered to maintain a maximum gradient of just 2.7 percent (a climb of 2.7 feet for every 100 traveled) even through rugged mountainous topography by clever use of tunnels, spirals, and tall viaducts.

Historically, the Gotthard Route began at Lucerne; however, in the modern configuration, SBB's main lines running from Lucerne and Zürich join at Arth-Goldau to begin the ascent of the Alps via the Reuss valley and then over Gotthard Pass. Intercity trains travel both routes offering connections beyond to other Swiss cities. Two other lines also connect with SBB at Arth-Goldau: one is the Sudostbahn (Southeastern Railway) that runs toward St. Gallen, and the other is the famous Rigi Bahnen, a standard gauge rack railway that terminates above the SBB's Arth-Goldau Station.

SBB has 19 Alstom-built Class ETR 610 Avelia Pendolinos that it assigns to EuroCity services on its Gotthard and Simplon Routes. Traveling north from Milan, a Zürich-bound EC train tilts through Flüelen on the Gotthard Route.

Running southward toward the Alps, the SBB Gotthard line winds its way through a lush picturesque valley and follows the eastern shore of Lake Lucerne. At Flüelen, the line emerges from a tunnel and passes the village that is comfortably nestled into the mountainside where sheep graze above on precipitous slopes. Flüelen offers a connection to ships crossing Lake Lucerne, and it was historically a popular place to begin a Gotthard journey. Today, it is a nice scenic interlude. Consider a layover at Flüelen and a trip across the lake's crystalline waters. Docks are on the west side of the SBB station, and in addition to scheduled boat services, boat taxis are available for hire.

Before reaching the Erstfeld station, SBB's line divides where the route through the new Gotthard Base Tunnel diverges from the historic 19th century route. (See Gotthard Base Tunnel sidebar on page 233). Although the base tunnel is one of the world's great railway engineering feats, a visiting tourist may instead wish to travel the old route over the mountains which, although slower, makes for a far more interesting journey.

Historically, Erstfeld was an important station for operations where most freights paused to take on helper locomotives for the stiff climb to the summit. Now, most

Nestled on the picturesque southeastern shore of Lake Lucerne, the Swiss village of Flüelen makes for a wonderful interlude on a trip over Gotthard Pass.

through trains bypass Erstfeld via a new tunnel. South of Erstfeld Station, the line begins its steep ascent and over the next 18 miles rises 2,080 feet to reach the south portal of the original Gotthard Tunnel. On its way, it navigates the most scenic portion of the line, including the famed tunnel spiral at Pfaffensprung, where the line loops to gain elevation within the confines of the narrow valley. A few miles higher, the line reaches its most famous location at Wassen, where it traces two horseshoe zig-zags through the village and allows your train to pass the town's iconic white church three times during its ascent.

The line levels out at Göschenen 3,638 feet above sea level (ASL), the station is at the north portal of the original Gotthard Tunnel, and it also serves as the junction with Matterhorn-Gotthard Bahn's steeply graded narrow gauge branch line to Andermatt, where it connects with the east-west route of the Glacier Express.

Although much shorter than the modern base tunnel, SBB's old Gotthard Tunnel is still among the world's longest tunnels, and you'll be in darkness for several minutes as the train hurtles through cool tunnel air and crests the Alps at 3,786 feet (but thousands of feet lower than the old road over the top of the pass). The tracks

Passengers interested in traveling the traditional Gotthard Route should take the hourly RegioExpress Gotthard Panorama trains that run from Erstfeld via Göschenen to Bellinzona, departing southward from Erstfeld at 30 minutes past the hour and northward from Bellinzona at 51 minutes past the hour.

In addition, there are a few InterRegio (Inter Regional/IR) runs that start at the Zürich Hbf (main station) that use the traditional route, such as the 7:40 a.m. train.

Schedules are subject to change, so it's best to consult either the SBB app or website for up-to-the-minute times. Be aware that SBB's travel-planning software tends to route you the fastest way regardless of scenery, so make sure the train you select is in fact running over the mountain and not below it.

exit the mountain at Airolo and then descend through the rugged and rocky Ticano valley, navigating four more spiral tunnels, which make it one of the most thrilling parts of the journey.

Perhaps most famous are the double spirals at Biaschina, a remarkable engineering achievement that is difficult to fully appreciate from the train, which circles its way downgrade through the overlapping tunnels. Ride on the right-hand side and remember that, as you gaze out the window, the tracks you see far below running along the river at the bottom of the valley are the very same tracks you'll be traveling on in a few minutes! Farther south, the line reaches the town of Bellinzona, where ancient castle walls flank both sides of the line. This is an ideal place for an overnight layover with several hotels available within walking distance of the SBB station.

Lake Geneva

As one of Switzerland's most diverse playgrounds, the Lake Geneva region features dozens of impressive railway lines including incredible mountain rack railways with nose-bleed ascents, lakeside main lines with Alpine vistas, scenic narrow gauge interludes, and some of the country's best-run urban rail transit. It would take the ardent railway rider weeks to make a thorough survey of all the railway lines here while remembering that the railways are merely a gateway to the scenic splendors of this wonderful area.

GENEVA-LAUSANNE-SIMPLON ROUTE

SBB's principal east-west route from Geneva runs along the north shore of the lake. From the south side of the train, you'll find numerous captivating views of

An FS Pendolino high-speed train navigates curves on the climb over Gotthard Pass. Since the opening of the Gotthard Base Tunnel, through InterCity trains now take this faster route beneath the mountains.

Gotthard Base Tunnel

SBB operates a steady parade of regional and InterCity/EuroCity trains via the Gotthard Route; however, following the December 2016 opening of the Gotthard Base Tunnel, approximately 50 trains per day skip the most scenic part of the historic Gotthard crossing because the new line offers substantially quicker transit time through the Alps, 30–45 minutes less than the old route.

Considered to be one of the world's greatest engineering feats, the 35.4-mile-long Gotthard Base Tunnel cost an estimated $12 billion and required 17 years to complete. It passes 1.5 miles below its namesake mountain, making it the world's deepest tunnel, as well as the longest (at date of completion). It is expected to ultimately accommodate up to 350 trains daily (mostly freight).

the clear azure water against snowcapped Alpine peaks. SBB's tracks are entirely in Switzerland, while the south shore is largely French territory served by an SNCF stub-end route.

Once by the urbanized suburbs east of Geneva, you'll pass palatial estates with expensive houses and lush green lawns that reach down to the railway line. Although not a super high-speed line, the railway is well built with trains moving along reasonably fast on smooth track.

Secondary railway lines connect with SBB's main line at stations along the lake. These probe northward into the hills above the lake. At Morges, there's a cross-platform interchange with the Morges Bière Cossonay (MBC) narrow gauge line, which traverses the relatively low rolling hills northwest of Lake Geneva that presents a sharp contrast to the extremely mountainous settings farther east. The MBC runs northward to Apples, where the line divides, with one route going to Bière and the other to L'Isle-Mont-la-Ville. The MBC is unusual among Swiss narrow gauge lines. In addition to its narrow passenger trains, it also accommodates standard gauge freight wagons interchanged from SBB moved to online customers using narrow gauge sleds (narrow gauge wheel sets placed beneath standard gauge trucks). You can see this equipment from the platform at Morges.

GENEVA

Located at the far western reaches of its namesake lake, bisected by the Rhône River which flows west from the lake, Geneva is Switzerland's second largest city, a popular destination, and an ideal gateway to Swiss railway travel. The city is close to the French border and predominantly French-speaking.

International trains to and from France, including TGV runs from Paris and frequent cross-border suburban trains to nearby French communities, serve Geneva Cornavin (the main railway station), located in the city center just a short walk from the lake. International passengers transit a customs control area served by platforms 7 and 8, while SBB domestic trains use platforms 1 through 6.

Geneva Airport (Gèneve-Aéroport) is well served by SBB InterRegio (Inter Regional/IR) and InterCity (IC) services, which originate and terminate at the

---

On a misty April morning, an SBB InterRegio train crosses the Fiume Ticino on an arched bridge at the lowest level of the famed Biaschina double spirals on the south side of Gotthard Pass. The viaduct at the top is on the highest level.

An SBB local train consisting of a new Stadler railcar glides along the north shore of Lake Geneva between Rivaz and St. Saphorin, where terraced vineyards rise high above the railway and the lake.

airport station located below the main terminal. Geneva is among Swiss cities that actively encourage visitors to use public transport. When arriving by air, visitors may obtain a free 80-minute ticket covering Geneva transport (including SBB trains into the city). This must be acquired in the baggage area prior to passing customs. An innocuous-looking vending machine near the SBB ticket machine dispenses these 80-minute free transport tickets, with just one per visitor allocated on the honor system.

Public transport tickets are available from machines at most major stops, although many hotels supply free passes for public transport. Geneva's wonderfully integrated public transport network includes trams, trolley buses, buses, and boats. Railway enthusiasts should be impressed by the tram network, which blends historical routes with modern construction. Sophisticated planning has produced parallel routes that cross the city center, allowing for unusually good frequency at peak times with minimal interference from road traffic while serving a variety of city center nodes. You may be quickly spoiled by Geneva's surface transport when you compare its exemplary service with that offered in cities in other countries.

Chillon Castle is beautifully situated on the east shore of Lake Geneva between Montreux and Villeneuve. This is a short walk from the Veytaux-Chillon SBB station, but it is also served by lake ferries as well as city bus route 201.

Geneva's attractions include its famous fountain located in the lake and visible from miles around. Old Town is worth a visit. Take tram route 12, which runs near the historic area via Rue de la Croix d'Or, or more directly by bus 36. Characterized by its network of narrow streets focused on Bourg-de-Four, and an ancient square dating to Roman times, Old Town is popular with tourists seeking classic European charm.

Most famous is St. Peters Cathedral where John Calvin preached his protestant theology. Calvinist austerity seems to have shaped Geneva's architecture, which exhibits a restrained style that is less ornate than in many historic European city centers.

The city is also home to United Nations' agencies occupying the Palais des Nations, erected to house the defunct League of Nations in the 1920s. The UN receives more than 110,000 visitors annually. Tours are normally available daily, but may be suspended during UN events. For times and prices, see **unog.ch**.

LAUSANNE

Lausanne is a popular destination that features classic architecture. Its central rail station is impressive with a solidly built main building and a traditional cantilever-style

Place de Neuve is a Geneva transport interchange south of Old Town, which is located adjacent to Parc des Bastions, one of the city's larger parks.

shed covering several platforms. This is a major stop for SBB, as several railway routes converge. Through and connecting services run to Bern, Basel, Lucerne, Zürich, and beyond.

Lausanne is served by a two-line metro system. One route is steeply graded, partially underground, and connects the waterfront at Ouchy with the railway station (access available from the main station by exiting on the north side), and continues up hill to the north side of the city, and terminates at Croisettes. The second route terminates at Flon (one stop north of Gare Lausanne on the Ouchy-Croisettes line) and reaches northwest with some roadside single-track running. There's also an electric interurban railway that runs from Flon to Bercher (in the mountains above Lausanne) using modern Stadler railcars.

SBB TO MONTREUX

Between Lausanne and Montreux, SBB passes stunning scenery where steeply terraced vineyards reach down among stone retaining walls toward Lake Geneva. The area around St. Saphorin is especially beautiful. Vevey is a moderate-sized

Geneva's tram route 12 runs south of the lake through largely pedestrian-friendly shopping areas, including Rue de la Confédération and Rue du Marché as pictured.

station where the main line interfaces with the Réseau Express Vaudois, which operates several branch lines. You can take le Lavaux Wine Train that operates hourly to Chebrex through the region's terraced vineyards. Dating to the 11th century, this is an UNESCO World Heritage Site that covers some 2,050 acres. Self-guided vineyard biking tours are a popular way to explore the area (bicycle rental is available at Vevey Station).

Montreux is the popular lakefront resort nestled against steeply rising mountains, famously frequented by 19th century Romantic poet Lord Byron, 20th century filmmaker Charlie Chaplin (the Chaplin World museum can be reached from Vevey Station), and Freddy Mercury, the late singer from the band Queen who is recalled with a large lakeside statue.

This a regional railway hub serving SBB local, InterCity, and EuroCity trains, as well as MOB. Montreux's station is a gem designed by Eugene Jost and built during 1901–1902. MOB has its ticket counters and a small gift shop in the mezzanine below track level.

Lausanne is a busy station with mainline trains operating every few minutes to various destinations across Switzerland.

MOB–Golden Pass Route

Among the great Swiss narrow gauge journeys is the Golden Pass Route between Montreux to Zweisimmen, operated by MOB. These initials don't imply a nefarious underworld organization, but rather the Compagnie du Chemin de fer Montreux Oberland Bernois, which literally describes the railway's territory. Unlike some Swiss mountain railways that provide comparatively spartan equipment, MOB offers a variety of upscale and themed train options to maximize their tourist appeal, as well as more ordinary trains for local travel (**goldenpass.ch**).

Among MOB's premier trains is its uniquely designed Golden Pass Panoramic, which makes several daily trips over the MOB main line. This distinctive modern streamlined train with large windows all around not only features an observation car in the middle of the train, but by situating the operating cab above the passenger compartment, it provides passengers an exemplary forward view of the tracks normally exclusive to train crews. To avail of this view, you will need to purchase Reserve VIP forward-facing seats. These are popular and require a 15 CHF supplement.

A panoramic view of Lake Geneva from near Caux, as the famous Montreux to Glion and Rochers-de-Naye incline train ascends the steeply graded rack from Montreux with luggage wagons at the front.

Although it is not required, it is advised that you book this (and other popular MOB trains) in advance. An onboard café car offers a variety of hot and cold drinks, including cappuccino, hot chocolate, hot tea, beer, wine, champagne, and soda, plus snacks and small meals.

Passengers looking for a retro experience, or who would like to try a different type of train distinct from the modern Panoramic, should consider MOB's Classic, advertised as the Belle Époque and decorated in the early 20th century luxury train style associated with trains typified by Wagon Lits' Paris-Istanbul Orient Express. The ornately decorated interior with paneled-wood veneer and teal-colored seats features large side windows for unobstructed views of the mountains. The train features a wine-tasting coach. Carrying both first and second class passengers, it runs on a limited-stop schedule between Montreux and Zweisimmen, only serving stations poplar with tourists including Château-d'Oex and Gstaad.

Another alternative is Le Train du Chocolat (the Chocolate Train) that works weekends and select days May through October (daily during July and August) using the Belle Epoque consist between Montreux and Gruyères. Tickets include road transport to the chocolate factory at Broc. Advanced reservations are required on this popular excursion. A similarly themed MOB train is the Cheese Train running from Montreux and Zweisimmen to Château-d'Oex.

Despite the tourist draw of its themed trains, unquestionably the finest attributes of MOB are its beautifully engineered mountain line and the surrounding magnificent Alpine scenery. The adventure begins the moment your train departs Montreux and ascends a steep ramp to rapidly gain elevation, soon passing into the inky gloom of a short tunnel—the first of many. When you emerge, there's a panoramic elevated view of Lake Geneva on the left.

By taking an early morning train, you can enjoy the painterly effect of mists on the deep blue lake with orange rays of the rising sun dappled on the snowcapped Alpine peaks on the far side of the water—all of which is viewed past the rolling silhouette of Montreux rooftops. Before long, sloping vineyards enter the tapestry as you get higher and higher. The line twists and loops, and the view on the left becomes the view on the right, but with a more spacious sky and a greater viewing distance made possible by the elevation.

More than just a scenic train ride, MOB is a fully functional passenger railway with local services and small stations. Short passenger runs out of Montreux and Zweisimmen serve the local population. MOB operates branches from Zweisimmen to Lenk, Montbovon to Bulle, and the MGN rack railway from Montreux to Rochers-de-Naye.

MOB's locomotive and equipment sheds and repair shops are located at Chernex, just 10 minutes from Montreux, where a variety of active and inactive relics can been seen among more modern trains.

Sonzier is a small station and a turn-back for short suburban runs, but it is also served by some long-distance trains that travel past fields of grazing sheep that seem oblivious to the stunning natural beauty of the Alpine meadows and the vast blue expanse of Lake Geneva below. Like many smaller stations on the MOB, Sonzier is a request stop for through trains. A button inside the train allows passengers to signal for a stop. On the station platforms, a machine is used by passengers who wish to signal a train for boarding. It is important to select the direction of travel, which is indicated by the end destination: southward trains go toward Montreux and northward ones toward Zweisimmen.

The MOB line runs through hills and forests, interspersed with rolling panoramas of alpine meadows. Chamby is a connection with the seasonal Blonay-Chamby

Among MOB's premier trains is its home-built and uniquely styled Golden Pass Panoramic that makes several trips a day over the line, seen here negotiating the curves above Gruben on its way toward Zweisimmen.

preserved railway, which takes visitors on a rides with historic equipment from May to October (**blonay-chamby.ch**).

While farther north, at Les Avants, the line passes a beautiful old station. Nestled in the shadow of a high cliff, this station is three stories tall, which is typical of those found in larger towns along the line. In general, MOB's stations are more attractive and interesting than those on SBB and other strictly more functional Swiss railways.

Not far from Les Avants Station is a steeply graded, meter gauge funicular railway on the left side of the line that rises up to Sonloup and serves a ski area and offers spectacular views. (See **lesavantsfuni.ch**.)

MOB dips into a short tunnel immediately after Les Avants, and then a few miles later, it enters a long tunnel at Jor. This passes below a range of higher peaks and leaves the train in darkness for several minutes.

Upon exiting at Les Cases, the line gradually descends through rolling hills and meadows into a deep river valley and crosses a rocky gorge. Montbovon is a junction station with MOB's branch toward Bulle, a common passing point for trains heading back toward Montreux.

MOB's Belle Époque from Montreux crosses a viaduct above the posh resort village at Gstaad. Belle Époque carries cars specially decorated to re-create the aura of classic deluxe railway travel. At the front are cars for passengers traveling on ordinary tickets.

Château-d'Oex is an attractive village with a church situated on a prominent free-standing hill east of the railway line. Located at about 1,000 meters above sea level, this is a popular resort for winter sports, but it also attracts visitors year-round and offers an idyllic layover point. Summer tourists may enjoy a variety of mountain trails ideal for exploring on foot or by bicycle, while nearby gorges offer whitewater rafting, kayaking, and other adventurous water sports. The town features the Etivaz cheese cellar, a hot-air balloon museum, and the Silhouettes Museum (Musée du Vieux Pay-d'Enhaut), which is open afternoons except Monday.

Forty minutes down the line is Gstaad, another popular sports resort town that features a variety of upscale shops and plush chalet style hotels. Immediately beyond the Gstaad station, the railway curls around a tight horseshoe curve (giving passengers on the left a view of the town and the line just traveled) and then crosses a viaduct on its way up to Gruben on its way over the mountains to Zweisimmen. Take a spin on branch up the valley to the resort at Lenk or connect with the standard gauge BLS line to Spiez, where connections can be made for Bern, Interlaken, Lötschberg Pass, and beyond.

A view of Château-d'Oex from MOB's Golden Pass Route. On the hill is a 15th century church that was rebuilt several times and features a 19th century bell tower.

MOB's Rochers-de-Naye

Among the railways operated by MOB is the famous MGN rack incline from Montreux to Glion and Rochers-de-Naye. Considered by many to be one of Switzerland's most impressive short railways, this exceptionally steep line ascends immediately from Montreux Station, climbing 5,164 feet within an hour while covering just 6.5 miles. In addition to giving travelers a nosebleed view of Lake Geneva, it serves mountain resorts as well as skiing and rock-climbing areas. The midway point at Caux offers a mountain interlude and layover point. This features panoramic views across the whole of the Lake Geneva region and is the location of the famous palatial Caux-Palace Hotel perched on the mountainside. The railway comes up through the hotel grounds on its way to the station. To reach the summit station at Rochers-de-Naye, the line curls through a curved tunnel and snow sheds and exits at a mountain plateau. At the top is a restaurant and observatory, plus hotels and campsites. Attractions include Alpine gardens and a marmot colony.

Although covered by the Regional Pass Lake Geneva-Alps, travel on the MGN is not included with other rail passes. The full adult round-trip fare booked on the day of travel is among the most expensive in Switzerland mile for mile, typically costing 35 CHF. Trains depart hourly but can quickly fill up during peak seasons.

Narrow gauge railways radiating from Aigle

Aigle is a charming medieval town nestled in the Rhône valley east of Lake Geneva, and a 10-minute train ride from Montreux. The town developed around Aigle Castle—a 12th century fortress built to control the gateway to the Rhône valley and travel to the Pays d'Enhaut district to the north. Aigle is famous for its vineyards. Today, the restored castle hosts the Vine and Wine Museum, which features a variety of displays relating to regional wines and the culture of its producers. Aigle is located immediately north of the railway station where you can enjoy restaurants, hotels, and wine bars in a classic continental setting. Other attractions are the World Cycling Center, a nearby forest adventure park, and a variety of annual festivals.

SBB's Aigle station is on its main line connecting Geneva, Lausanne, and Montreux with towns in the eastern Rhône valley, including Martigny and Brig, and via the Simplon Tunnel to Domodossola and Milan, Italy. Adjacent to the main station on the north side of the SBB are platforms serving three distinct interurban electric narrow gauge lines operated by Transports Publics du Chablais (TPC).

TPC's Aigle-Leysin (AL) is a short route that extends for 3.2 miles (5.2km) in a westerly direction high into the mountains. In town, TPC's small trains first cross the Place de la Gare and work single-track street trackage up Rue de la Gare at a conservative 9–10 mph (14–16 km/h). The bright green and yellow trains contrast with the town's comparatively sedate architecture. Upon reaching AL's Aigle depot, trains change direction and join a steeply graded rack section, where trains ascend through terraced vineyards on a dizzying 23 percent ruling grade (representing more than 1 foot climbed for every 4 traveled). To enjoy stunning views, sit on the right side of the train as it makes its slow ascent of the mountain. Below, Aigle Castle and surrounding vineyards make for a fairytale vista against a panorama of the Alps looming to the south. Trains operate hourly, departing at 55 minutes past the hour, and the journey takes about 28 minutes.

Switzerland offers railway travelers seemingly endless lush mountain vistas and pastoral scenes. Here, cattle graze in an Alpine meadow near Gruben.

Leysin, situated at 4,147 feet (1,264 meters) ASL, is a popular year-round resort community that offers a wide range of winter sports, including skiing, snowboarding, dog sledding, and tobogganing, as well as summer activities such as self-guided explorations of elaborate networks of hiking and bicycling trails. It is home to the Leysin American School and other educational institutions. Visit the revolving restaurant for stunning 360-degree panoramic views of the Alps. (For more on Leysin tourism, see **leysin.ch**.)

TPC's Aigle-Sépey-Diablerets (ASD) trains depart Aigle in a northeasterly direction, leaving town on Avenue de Loës street trackage before entering a private right-of-way. ASD's depot is just north of town near the castle. Ascending into the mountains, this railway curls through series of impressive loops above the castle that provide impressive views into the Rhône valley. After rising above the open rolling vineyards, the line enters a steep forest where there's a request stop for Aigle's Forest Adventure Park. Immediately afterwards, the line dips into a short tunnel and continues its climb through trees and past several small stations toward the junction at Les Planches, 3,094 feet (943 meters) ASL.

A two-car TPC electric train climbs the AL rack line toward Leysin, passing through the terraced vineyards above Aigle. Trains operate hourly in both directions and take 22 minutes.

ASD's operating arrangement is unusual and involves minimal infrastructure with just a single switch in the road where the Le Sépey branch diverges from the line to Les Diablerets. Ascending trains first head to the resort at Le Sépey, running across a bridge shared with the local road, and then up a steep grade to Le Sépey Station. Then the train reverses to return back down for a second stop at Les Planches junction and takes the other leg of the switch to begin its uphill climb toward Les Diablerets.

TPC's Aigle-Ollon-Monthey-Champéry (AOMC) is a wonderful little railway that is too often overshadowed by better known mountain narrow gauge lines in a nation saturated with spectacular railways. It begins as a low-lying interurban electric line connecting Aigle with Monthey to serve intermediate stations using a pastoral single-track line that wanders through the greenery of the Rhône valley. At St. Triphon, TPC's AOMC line crosses above SBB's immaculately built tangent double-track line to Brig and an autoroute expressway and then over SBB's single-track branch to St. Gingolph (that follows the southeastern shore of Lake Geneva). Approaching Monthey, TPC follows the side of the main

Aigle Castle is situated on a scenic hill surrounded by vineyards north of the town. Inside, you can view historical implements used in wine-making as well as explore the wall walk and several towers.

north-south road called Route de Collombey in the manner of a classic light inter-urban electric line.

At Monthey En Place, a roadside junction connects tracks leading into the main TPC AOMC station at Monthey-Ville with the line that continues up the mountain to Champéry. Monthey is located in a deep valley, and trains from Aigle continue to Monthey-Ville, where they reverse for the run to Champéry. Monthey is billed as a festive city and features a charming old town that hosts cultural events including theatre. It is also a jumping-off point for regional winter sporting resorts, with numerous hotels and other accommodation.

The railway line up the mountain from Monthey En Place is a treat for railway enthusiasts. After crossing Route de Collombey at grade (and pausing for a request stop), the rack portion of the line begins and climbs steeply into the Vièze valley. Trains slow to about 5 mph to engage the rack, which can be heard as a muffled clattering below the floor. TPC's modern Stadler railcars enable travelers to get a nice forward or trailing view by standing at the ends of the car, while the best side views are on the left side of the train.

A TPC interurban car climbs away from the Alpine junction at Les Planches, Switzerland, on the way from Le Sépey to Les Diablerets.

The line hugs the valley as it climbs, crossing the Vièze on an impressive viaduct at Troistorrents and continues southward along the Illiez valley. The village of Val-d'Illiez is a scenically stunning resort near the high end of the line. In view of an impressive limestone massif, TPC's railway terminates at Champéry. Located at 1,050 meters ASL, this is a large ski resort in the Les Portes du Soliel area with ample (but pricey) accommodations, much of it within walking distance of the station. You may continue your journey via an aerial tramway that ascends another 1,000 meters to a nearby ridge. Access to the tramway is just off the station platform.

Railways of the Jungfrau Region

The towering Alpine region of the Jungfrau south of Interlaken is among the world's most sublimely scenic settings, among Switzerland's best-known winter playgrounds and a popular tourist area year-round. It is well connected by a distinctive network of colorful railways that are some of the most famous in Europe.

TPC's lines radiate from Aigle in three directions. The climb to Le Sépey and Les Diablerets snakes through vineyards around Aigle Castle.

TPC's newest equipment includes Stadler-built electric railcars, which feature nice interior décor and amenities such as this location display.

Among the stunning Swiss panoramas on the Wengernalbahn route is the view back toward Grindwald nestled in the shadow of the majestic Mattenberg where spring meets winter.

INTERLAKEN

Idyllically located on a strip of land between Lake Thun and Lake Brienz, Interlaken is a relatively small city that serves as a gateway to regional tourism (**interlaken.ch**). In addition to being a perfect place to explore the lakes, Interlaken is a popular starting point for tourist exploration of the Jungfrau Region, which is focused on three high Alpine peaks: the Eiger (ogre), Mönch (monk), and Jungfrau (maiden).

Interlaken offers tourists a variety of attractions. The regional tourist museum showcases two centuries of the area's tourist attractions which have been fundamental to the economy (**tourismuseum.ch**). Flowing through the city are the rich turquoise waters of the Aare River that connect the two lakes and are controlled by prominent sluice gates. Nearby, visit Interlaken Monastery & Castle, which began in the 12th century as a monastic center and features a 15th century Gothic cloister gallery.

Interlaken has two railway stations, Interlaken West and Interlaken Ost (east). The latter is the more important of the two stations, as it functions as

The Zentralbahn skirts the northeastern shore of Lake Brienz at Neiderreid on its way to Interlaken Ost. In any other country, Zentralbahn would be a scenic highlight, but in Switzerland, it is eclipsed by nearby railways that reach mountain summits.

a regional hub that enables passengers to transfer between standard gauge mainline services and regional narrow gauge lines. In addition to BLS and SBB InterRegio and InterCity services that operate up to three times per hour, Interlaken is also directly served by German premium Intercity Express services (DB-ICE) to and from major German cities, including Karlsruhe, Mannheim, Frankfurt, and Berlin.

ZENTRALBAHN

Interlaken Ost is the southern terminus for the historic narrow gauge Brünigbahn, a meter gauge network now operated by SBB as the Zentralbahn. It runs north-easterly along the scenic north shore of Lake Brienz and then via a connecting rack line over Brünig Pass to Luzern. Modern trains are well appointed with comfortable seats and large windows affording panoramic views along the line. An end-to-end journey takes about 2 hours, with stunning scenery all along the route. The northern terminus is at Luzern's main station, where Zentralbahn's narrow gauge tracks are intermingled with SBB's standard gauge lines.

RIDING THE BOB

The Bernese Oberland Bahn is a meter gauge (narrow gauge) railway network extending from Interlaken toward additional connections to the Jungfrau Region. Trains depart Interlaken Ost, mostly on half-hour intervals, and proceed southward through the broad level valley toward the towering peaks beyond. BOB's older carriages still have opening windows, which provide a fresh-air experience and offer serious photographers better conditions as exposing through glass tends to produce distracting reflections, gives the photos an unnatural tint, and reduces sharpness.

At Wilderswill, passengers can change to the seasonal Schynige Platte Bahn, a colorful rack railway that climbs steeply to reach its namesake, which at 3,500 feet (1,067 meters) offers spellbinding views of the Jungfrau Region. SPB trains run from end of May until October (**jungfrau.ch/de-ch/schynige-platte**).

Beyond Wilderswill, the valley narrows, and at Zweilütschinen, BOB's lines divide, with one route climbing east to Grindenwald and the other to Lauterbrunnen. Both routes feature stunning mountain scenery, involve steep rack sections, and meet branches of the wondrously scenic Wengernalbahn. Before boarding your train, be sure to select the correct carriage based on your final destination, as BOB trains split shortly after reaching the Zweilütschinen station. Where on some railways dividing a train would be a time-consuming process, BOB executes it with Swiss efficiency, and the first section heads toward Lauterbrunnen within a minute of its arrival at Zweilütschinen. The longer of the two runs is up the valley to Grindlewald. If you are traveling this way, consider a seat on the right side of the train to take in the best scenery. After an ascent of a series of steep inclines, the grade rapidly levels out on

A BOB train ascends a rack section on the final leg of its run from Interlaken Ost to Grindenwald, where passengers can make a cross-platform transfer to Wengernalbahn for the run up to Kleine Scheidegg.

arriving at the Grindlewald terminus. Visitors will be awed by the cosmic mountain views here, while the best train rides are yet to come, but at a suitable Swiss price.

WENGERNALBAHN AND JUNGFRAUBAHN

The Wengernalbahn is an electric mountain narrow gauge rack railway that uses carriages painted yellow and green and passes some of the most impressive scenery viewed from a railway window anywhere in the world. Together, the Wengernalbahn and Jungfraubahn offer one of the greatest Swiss railway journeys: from Alpine snowfields and green meadows to vertical cliffs and towering mountain waterfalls, while following a sinuous steep alignment and passing through tunnels and quaint mountain towns.

Wengernalbahn connects with BOB at both ends, allowing travelers to make a circular journey, which is both cost effective and provides wondrous panoramas. Be aware that travel on these lines typically involves a special fare. Before boarding the Wengernalbahn at Grindenwald or Lauterbrunnen, check to make sure your ticket or pass covers the Wengernalbahn and Jungfraubahn portions of your journey.

A Jungfraubahn train ascends from Kleine Scheidegg toward its namesake summit. This short, steep railway is an unusual example of three-phase overhead electrification that requires two separate sets of powered wires.

MGB is a rack railway that ascends steep Alpine grades with magnificent views. The western terminus of the line is at Zermatt, the connection between the Glacier Express route and the precipitously steep (and stunningly expensive) Gornergrat Bahn that runs above 10,200 feet with stunning panoramas of the famous Matterhorn. (It's best to make this journey on a clear day or the mountain may be obscured by clouds.)

Running east from Zermatt, the MGB drops down through a rocky gorge to the open Rhône valley near Visp. Here, narrow gauge tracks run parallel to SBB's standard gauge route from Geneva that is joined by the BLS base tunnel route over the Lötschberg Pass from Spiez. Both lines run east to Brig, an important junction and a moderately sized town offering reasonably priced accommodation.

East of Brig, MGB begins its ascent of the high Alpine Furka Pass; among the highlights is a climb through a spiral tunnel. Historically, the railway crossed the pass on a spectacular route across the Rhône Glacier that was closed seasonally to avoid the threat of avalanches. Today, the MGB line transits the Furka Pass via a long base tunnel. A portion of the original route is now operated seasonally by a preserved steam railway called the Furka-Dampfbahn (**dfb.ch**).

The narrow gauge Rhätische Bahn is a largely single-track line with strategically placed passing sidings. A train descending from Disentis passes an uphill train.

After crossing a broad Alpine plateau, MGB reaches Andermatt, a junction station, resort, and location of one Europe's most expensive hotels. Consider a side trip down the short branch that descends precipitously through tunnels and snow sheds to reach Göschenen, which is the spectacularly situated junction with SBB's original Gotthard Tunnel Route. While on MGB's main line, the amazing ascent of the Oberalp Pass begins immediately east of the station at Andermatt. After crossing a street, the trains grip the central rack and the line curves up and climbs through a series of step-like loops to an elevation of 6,667 feet (2,032 meters) ASL. Take a look back as you climb the mountain to gaze upon one of the great railway sights of southwestern Switzerland: from this towering vantage point, you can look down on Andermatt and trace your progress back along the line toward Furka Pass.

MGB hands over the Glacier Express to the RhB at Disentis, and this equally spectacularly engineered railway continues east through the Alps. However, there's a significant technical difference between the two railway lines: MGB uses central racks to ascend very steep gradients, and RhB is strictly an adhesion line, relying upon conventional steel wheel on steel rail friction to lift its trains over the mountains.

Brig is the junction between MGB's narrow gauge line and the standard gauge BLS and SBB routes. Narrow gauge trains serve street-level platforms adjacent to the mainline station (right).

RhB's line is one of the most impressive through-running Swiss mountain railways, featuring scenic highlights and engineering marvels at every turn, including 55 tunnels and more than 190 bridges. Most famous of these is the often-pictured Landwasser Viaduct, a curved structure with six towering stone arches running directly into a tunnel cut into a sheer rock face.

Perhaps the most impressive part of the journey is RhB's ascent of rugged Albula Pass between Bergun and Preda using triple spirals where the line corkscrews up through a scenically sublime rock gorge. As you climb, look back to review your progress on the line as the train loops and winds its way through tunnels and crosses and recrosses its own path. You may find it difficult to fully comprehend this ascent without the aid of an interactive map. This circuitous line is even more impressive when viewed from trackside: with the spirals appearing

Göschenen is at the summit of SBB's original line over Gotthard Pass but at the base of MGB's exceptionally steep branch to Andermatt, where its main line continues to climb to higher summits over the Furka Pass in the west and Oberalp Pass in the east.

Austria

An ÖBB Bombardier-built Talent electric multiple unit speeds through the snow-covered valley of the Salzach River near Werfen south of Salzburg, serving as a Regional Express (REX) to Wörgl.

Picture rolling panoramas of Alpine vistas featuring picturesque villages dotted with low-pitched Tyrolean chalets and punctuated by classic needle church spires set in lush mountain meadows with rocky ridges and distant silhouettes of snow-covered peaks. These features combine to make Austria one of the most beautiful countries in Europe that you can explore by train. Sit back, sip a rich coffee, and take in the shafts of light filtering over the mountains, piercing deep valleys, as your train winds its way along a river swollen with melting snow. The hillsides are topped with fairytale castles and rolling fields are filled with sheep or cattle blissfully grazing as your train rolls along with effortless grace.

Although Austrian railways don't boast a network of super high-speed lines on par with other large European railways such as those of France, Spain, or Germany, they do benefit from an excellent network of intercity main lines improved through significant investments and numerous modern upgrades that have contributed to it being one of the finest networks in central Europe and a joy to travel upon.

The sun rises over the Alps at St. Jodok on Austria's Brenner Pass Route.

Austria's historic railway network stems from traditional lines established prior to World War I when the Habsburg-ruled Austro-Hungarian Empire extended across much of central Europe, encompassing not just the modern Austrian nation-state, but also all of Hungary, Czech Republic, Slovakia, Slovenia, and Croatia, as well as territory now in parts of Ukraine, Italy, and Poland. Railways of the Habsburg Empire extended from Vienna south to Trieste (now in Italy), north to Prague (Czech Republic), Krakow (Poland), and east to Lviv (Ukraine), as well as west to Germany and Switzerland.

Today, many of Austria's trunk routes are defined by the Alpine passes they cross. The four principal standard gauge Austrian Alpine crossings are north-south routes over Brenner, Semmering, and Tauern Passes, while the route via the Westbahn and Arlberg Pass is a scenic east-west thoroughfare. These lines have remained as important corridors despite significant 20th century changes that resulted in the break up of the Habsburg Empire and the redrawing of international boundaries.

Alpine mountain grades present railways with operational challenges, but for passengers, these are the most scenic lines with towering viaducts, tunnels both long and short, and seemingly endless spectacular mountain scenery. The combination of superbly engineered lines and stunning scenic panoramas with high-quality locomotive-powered intercity trains make Austrian railways an enjoyable, relaxing, and supremely civilized way to travel.

Mainline journeys are operated year-round on regular interval schedules and in all weather. Consider traveling in late winter when deep, fluffy snow covers Alpine slopes. The effect looks like marshmallow poured over trees, rocks, and mountainsides, making for a winter wonderland comfortably viewed via large glass windows in the warmth of a passenger carriage. If all that marshmallow makes you hungry, consider a trip to the dining car where you can enjoy prepared meals as your train rolls through the frozen tapestry of the Austrian Alps.

Trains, schedules, and tickets

Railjet is ÖBB's brand of limited-stop, fast, long-distance trains that have largely replaced older InterCity (IC) trains. These consist of specially painted long-distance carriages in a push-pull configuration with a Siemens Taurus locomotive at one end. They may travel up to 143 mph (230 km/h) on select high-speed routes. Although

The pride of the ÖBB fleet are its Railjets. These luxurious trains provide both domestic and international service from Vienna to cities such as Graz, Salzburg, Zürich, Prague, and Budapest.

not the fastest trains in Europe, ÖBB's Railjets are among the most comfortable intercity trains in Europe; they offer free WiFi and onboard web-portal entertainment, a full-service dining car as well as a food-service cart, plus extras such as a children's cinema.

There are three grades of Railjet service: **Economy class** offers spacious accommodation, ample luggage storage, and an outlet for each seat pair. **First class** has leather seating with more leg room, and passengers are offered a free newspaper or magazine and have the option of at-seat delivery of meals. **Business class** is ÖBB's deluxe first class that provides finest and most comfortable grade of travel, offering passengers a quiet working environment, better seats with adjustable headrests, and a free drink in addition to other first class amenities. Business class requires a supplement in addition to first class fare (but passengers may opt for the upgrade onboard if space is available).

ÖBB's Railjets serve most intercity routes, connecting major Austrian cities as well as those in neighboring countries. Railjet routes include Munich-Salzburg-Vienna-Budapest, Prague-Vienna-Graz (via Semmering Pass) with some trains serving

Pictured is the main entrance to Wien Hauptbahnhof, Vienna's new central station. In addition to platforms serving intercity, regional, S-Bahn, and U-Bahn lines, the station also houses an extensive shopping mall.

VIENNA STATIONS

Wien Hauptbahnhof (Vienna Central Station) is a massive modern station built on the site of the old Sudbahnhof. The architecture represents a stunning and effective example of modern station design with long broad platforms and plenty of capacity for human and railway traffic. In addition to InterCity/RailJet/EuroCity, plus regional and S-Bahn passenger services, freight trains pass through without interfering with ÖBB's tight passenger timetable.

Like other modern stations, Wien Hauptbahnhof is a transport hub integrated with a shopping mall, where you can find almost everything you need for a trip. ÖBB supplies ample train information with numerous arrival and departure boards listing train and platform details. The station is well served by public transport via U-Bahn line U1 at the Hauptbahnhof stop, trams 18 and O to Belvedere Hauptbahnhof stops, and tram D to the Hauptbahnhof Ost stop.

If there is a downside to Wien Hauptbahnhof, it is the exposed nature of the platform area. Although covered by a massive stylish roof, the design tends to funnel in the wind and rain, making it an unpleasant place to wait in inclement weather.

A German ICE (InterCity Express) train stops at Wien Hauptbahnhof. These trains provide connections between various German cities and the Austrian capital, with some continuing on to serve Vienna's international airport.

WESTBAHNHOF (VIENNA WEST STATION)

Westbahnhof is among the major Vienna stations and was the historic terminus for the Westbahn route and related lines. Today, most ÖBB long-distance trains serve the new Hauptbahnhof; however, this is the terminal for open-access operator WESTbahn's Salzburg-service as well as suburban and regional services including trains to Amstetten and St. Polten and those serving S-Bahn routes. Westbahnhof buildings are postwar structures that were largely refurbished in recent years and feature an array of shops and restaurants. Take U-Bahn lines 3 and 6 or tram route 5 to reach the station.

If you are looking for places to watch trains on the move, consider a visit to Wien Praterkai, a smaller station with a good view of passenger and freight trains rolling off the Stadlauer Brücke over the River Danube, which also offers views down onto the freight lines paralleling the river along Handelskai. It is accessible via Regional and S-Bahn trains. The station at Kaiserebersdorf has good views of InterCity/RailJet/EuroCity long-distance trains plus regional and S-Bahn passenger trains running toward the airport and Wolfsthal, as well as freight on the line to the Danube docks. You can reach this station via S-Bahn S7.

Take S-Bahn S45 to Penzing or Handelskai to experience station design by Otto Wagner, the famous architect and urban planner whose Secession style can be found around Vienna. His works include stations at Ottakring, Hernals, Gersthof, Krottenbachstrasse, Oberdöbling, and Heiligenstadt.

PUBLIC TRANSPORT

Wiener Linien is Vienna's primary public transport operator. Wiener Linien offers a comprehensive range of transport tickets and passes, many of which are most useful for daily commuters and/or residents. (For Wiener Linien transport tickets, maps, and information, see **wien.gv.at/english/transportation-urbanplanning/public-transport**.) Discounted fares and passes are available for children, students, and seniors. (For details, prices, and an interactive trip planner, see **wienerlinien.at**. You can also download Wiener Linien's mobile app for smart phones and tablets at **shop.wienerlinien.at/mobile.php**.)

Single tickets called **Einzelfahrscheine** (for one-way journeys) allow for continuous one-way journeys with transfers between modes. These must be validated at the time travel begins and may be purchased in bundles, which are most useful for travelers making infrequent trips. There are also 2-journey and 4-journey tickets that lower the cost of an individual trip but must be purchased in minimum quantities of 5 at a time. However, if you plan a lot of urban travel, it's more cost effective to buy one of several varieties of day passes.

The best transport value for visitors is **Vienna's Travelcard**, sold in 1-, 2-, and 3-day denominations. This allows for unlimited travel on trams, buses, U-Bahn, and S-Bahn systems within Vienna's Zone 100 (that covers most of the attractions in the central city but doesn't reach the airport, which still requires a separate ticket). The Vienna Travelcard requires initial activation by inserting it into a blue validating machine found at U-Bahn stations and on trams and buses.

For additional value, consider buying the Vienna Pass, which has all the benefits of a Travelcard, plus free entry to more than 60 of Vienna's top attractions, including the ferris wheel, Schönbrunn Palace, and Spanish Riding School. The **Vienna Pass** can be bought for periods up to 6 days and is available for both adult and child passes. Children less than 6 years old may travel with an adult carrying a Vienna Pass free of charge. Passes may be purchased online and can be refunded if unused. (For a list of benefits and prices, see **viennapass.com**.)

In September 1960, at Kennedybrücke in the Hietzing area of Vienna, a Kriegsstrassenbahnwagen (Wartime Tramway Car) works route 58, which ran from Babenbergerstrasse to Unter St Veit. The view in Hietzing has changed: Kennedybrücke is now much wider and there is an entrance to the U3 metro station on an island in the center of the road and much more road traffic. The buildings in the background remain and one on the left now houses a McDonald's. *Richard Jay Solomon*

U-BAHN AND S-BAHN

Vienna's U-Bahn rapid transit is both a vital means of transport and a historic attraction in its own right. Today, there are five U-Bahn routes numbered 1 to 6 (but no number 5). The modern system has its origins in Vienna's Stadtbahn (city railway) that began operations at the end of the 19th century. The network covers more than 50 miles (80km) and serves more than 100 stations. Highlights of this highly developed network include U-Bahn line 2 (Karlsplatz-Seestadt) elevated between Krieau and Seestadt. Some of its underground stations, including Rathaus, feature staggered platforms that allow you to gain excellent angles to photograph trains paused at stations. U-Bahn line 4 (Heiligenstadt-Hütteldorf) has elegant stations designed by Otto Wagner at Friedensbrücke, Rossauer Lände, Stadtpark, Karlsplatz Stadtbahn, Kettenbrückengasse, Pilgramgasse, Margaretengürtel, Schönbrunn, Hietzing, Ober St.Veit, and Hütteldorf.

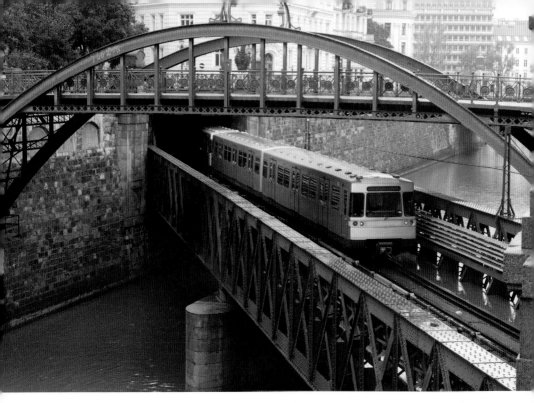

A metro train on Vienna's U4 line emerges into daylight to cross the Wien River on an Otto Wagner-designed bridge. Wagner was also responsible for the Zollamtssteg pedestrian bridge above the train and railings alongside the river.

U-Bahn line 6 (Siebenhirten-Floridsdorf) incorporates portions of the Stadtbahn on a largely elevated section between Längenfeldgasse and Nussdorfer Strasse with Otto Wagner architecture at Gumpendorfer Strasse, Burggasse-Stadthalle, Josefstädter Strasse, Alser Strasse, Währinger Strasse-Volksoper, and Nussdorfer Strasse. Wagner also designed the line's Wien River span located between Längenfeldgasse and Gumpendorfer Strasse Stations.

The S-Bahn network augments other urban rail transport by providing regular-interval suburban service connecting central Vienna with outlying towns on the traditional heavy railway lines, often sharing tracks with long-distance and regional trains.

TRAMWAYS AND LIGHT RAIL

Tram enthusiasts will delight in Vienna's extensive streetcar, tram subway, and electric interurban network. This system is among the most varied and extensive in the world. Wiener Linien operates no less than 29 different tram routes. You'll find numerous photo locations on the Ring, where you can place trams with

A line 5 tram on a rainy evening at Julius-Tandler-Platz near Vienna's Franz Joseph Bahnhof—a terminal station on the northside of the Austrian capital for regional trains heading toward Krems and intermediate points.

Vienna icons including Stadtpark, the Opera, Maria-Theresien-Platz, Parliament, Burgtheater, Schwarzenbergplatz, and Julius Raab Platz. Other noteworthy locations include Löwengasse (line 1) with trams passing the Hundertwasser House, and Schwarzenbergplatz (lines 71 and D).

Travel on line 60 where there are especially photogenic locations between stops at Maurer-Lange-Gasse and Breitenfurter Brücke and at the Rodaun outer terminus.

The tram subway has 6 underground stops; system highlights include Südtiroler Platz and Eichenstrasse on lines 6/18, plus a short branch below Wiedner Hauptstrasse from Kliebergasse to Laurenzgasse covered by lines 1 and 62 and cars of Lokalbahn Wien-Baden, and a southern ramp at Matzleinsdorfer Platz (lines 1 and 6).

Badnerbahn (Lokalbahn Wien-Baden) is an interurban light rail line that runs for 18.9 miles (30.4km) between Vienna Opernring and Baden bei Wien. It shares tracks with city trams for about the first 4 miles (6km) and then runs on its own private right-of-way.

Visit the Transport Museum of Wiener Linien located in the halls of the former Erdberg depot at Erdbergstrasse 109. This houses a collection of trams, buses, and

If you are hungry, head to the Naschmarkt. This vast market, with 16th century origins, features more than 100 food stalls plus adjacent restaurants. Take U-Bahn line 4 to Karlsplatz or Kettenbrückengasse.

Schönbrunn Palace (Schloss Schönbrunn) was the Habsburgs' 18th century summer palace. This complex is to Vienna what Versailles is to Paris. Take the time to tour Schönbrunn's lavish rococo ceremonial rooms, and don't miss the palace gardens and its outdoor maze. Take U-Bahn line 4 to Schönbrunn or Hietzing or trams 10, or 60 to Hietzing.

Not far from Schönbrunn is the Technisches Museum Wien at Mariahilferstrasse 212. The museum owns the most valuable railway collection in Austria. Take U-Bahn line 3 to Johnstrasse or line 4 to Schönbrunn or take trams 52 or 60 to Penzinger Strasse.

Go for spin, literally: a permanent fairground attraction is Vienna's Giant Ferris Wheel at Riesenradplatz. The wheel was built in 1945 with wooden cabins, and was featured prominently in Orson Welles' *The Third Man*, a 1949 film about Cold War espionage in postwar, divided Vienna. Take U-Bahn lines 1 or 2, trams 5 or O to Praterstern stop, or regional and S-Bahn trains to Wien Praterstern Station.

The Belvedere (Schloss Belvedere) at Prinz Eugen-Strasse is a baroque, 18th century palace, which is now an art museum with a range of exhibits from the Middle Ages to the present, including the notable Klimt collection. Take tram D to Schloss Belvedere or Quartier Belvedere, trams 18 or O to Quartier Belvedere, tram 71 to Unteres Belvedere, or regional or S-Bahn trains to Quartier Belvedere Station.

Grinzing is noted for its vineyards and numerous heurige—wine taverns serving wine and grape juice known as "must." Take tram 38 from Schottentor at Schottenring or bus 38A from Boschstrasse in Heiligenstadt. For some wonderful views of Vienna and surrounding countryside continue on the 38A bus from Grinzing to the top of the Kahlenberg, where on a clear day, you can see all the way to Bratislava (capital of neighboring Slovakia).

House of the Sea (Haus des Meeres) is an aquarium with some 10,000 creatures on display including snakes, crocodiles, and sharks. Don't miss the tropical house. This is another place for great city views from the observation platform. Take U-Bahn line 3 to Neubaugasse.

Central Cemetery (Wiener Zentralfriedhof) is a vast, multidenominational parkland cemetery housing the tombs of many famous Austrians, including Johannes Brahms (composer), Carl von Ghega (engineer), Karl Kraus (writer), Karl Renner

The magnificent Schloss Schönbrunn (Schönbrunn Palace), former summer palace of the Habsburg monarchy is situated in the western part of Vienna. Tours of the lavish rococo ceremonial rooms and gardens are available.

(statesman), Franz Schubert (composer), Johann Strauss I and Johann Strauss II (composers), and Kurt Waldheim (UN Secretary-General). Take trams 6 or 71 to Zentralfriedhof 2 Tor or S-Bahn line S7 to Wien Zentralfriedhof Station. A public bus line operates within the grounds to take you around.

Semmering Pass Route

Austria's oldest, and one of its busiest mountain lines, is ÖBB's route across the Semmering Pass. As constructed, Austria's Südbahn was an 1830 plan intended to serve as a unifying trunk route between Vienna, Graz, Ljubljana, and the key Adriatic Port at Trieste, a line that when built was entirely within Habsburg territory but now spans three nations: Austria, Slovenia, and Italy. The most scenic portion is less than an hour from Vienna.

After a century of steam operations, the Austrian sections of the line were electrified. Today, the Semmering route running from Vienna to the junction at Bruck an der Mur is one of the busiest Alpine rail crossings. The intense volume of traffic and

An ÖBB InterCity train rolls through Semmering station en route to Vienna. Seen at the top of the slope on the extreme right is one of the hotels for which the Semmering region is famous.

anticipated growth has led to the construction of a 17-mile-long (27.3km) base tunnel planned to bypass the most difficult historic portions of the climb by 2026.

Begin your Semmering journey at Vienna's Airport Station or Vienna's Hauptbahnhof (main railway station), where there's a choice between InterCity trains heading toward Graz or Villach (and beyond) that use this historic mountain crossing. The first 30 minutes aren't special as the train glides through heavily populated lowlands toward Weiner Neustadt. This large station is served by most InterCity trains as well as Vienna suburban runs. However, for local travel on the Semmering Pass, you may wish to either change here or farther south at Payerbach-Reichenau Station. Keep in mind that local trains make numerous short stops, and don't move as fast, so this slower pace allows for better opportunities to take in the scenery. Consider getting out at one of the following mountain stations and explore the mountains on foot.

South of Gloggnitz, the railway enters the most scenic part of the old Südbahn as it winds its way up toward the Semmering summit. For the best views, take a seat on the left. The railway initially hugs the Schwarza River running up the valley to

An ÖBB regional train calls at Eichberg am Semmering Station. Here you will find amazing views looking into Schwarza River valley and the surrounding, often snowcapped mountains.

Payerbach. This quaint scenic mountain village has some excellent accommodations and offers an ideal place to stay for extended exploration of the mountains. On the south side of the tracks, you'll notice a preserved 2-10-2T steam locomotive, which was typical of the large tank engines for heavy service on the Semmering before it was electrified.

Railway enthusiasts may be interested in the seasonal Höllentalbahn Payerbach-Hirschwang narrow gauge railway that connects with the main line near the Payerbach station. This is a short 760mm gauge line that employs diminutive diesel and electric trains to bring tourists to Hirschwang and operates on Sundays and public holidays from June to mid-October. (See **lokalbahnen.at/hoellentalbahn/ timetable-e.html**.)

The main line makes a sweeping horseshoe curve to the left immediately after departing Payerbach-Reichenau Station and loops around the town crossing a multiple-arch viaduct. It climbs sharply and doubles back on the valley. You'll see the station and village below, and as you gain elevation, there are some fine views back down the Schwarza valley. If you have a sharp eye, you may glimpse a following train.

A train shuttling a set of locomotives crosses the Adlitzgraben Viaduct on the northern ramp of the Semmering railway.

Südbahn history

The historic Südbahn running from Vienna to Trieste via the Semmering Pass is the best known of Austria's mainline Alpine crossings. Planned as early as 1838, and largely constructed between 1848 and 1852, it was the earliest European mountain mainline railway.

It benefited from early American railroad practices; its engineers traveled to the United States to study mountain railroading, and Philadelphia locomotive builder William Norris supplied several early engines including an aptly named 4-2-0 type called *Philadelphia*.

The Semmering crossing faced complicated engineering including tunnels and tall, curved stone-arch viaducts exemplified by the famous Kalte Rinne Viaduct near Breitenstein that resembles a Roman aqueduct. The crucial Semmering Tunnel opened in 1854, completing the original route. In 1952, a second tunnel opened parallel to the original bore. The line was finally electrified in 1959.

Mountain running is relatively slow. Local trains will halt at Eichberg, a small station situated on a tight bend. The line loops sharply southward as it continues its ascent. After passing the short Weinzettefled Tunnel, the line levels at Breitenstein, which is a small station favored by hill walkers. Here, you can follow trails for excellent views down on the line as it makes its torturous climb through the curves and over 19th century arched viaducts to reach the summit. Breitenstein is also the location of a passing siding, so it's common for through trains to overtake uphill freights and local trains paused here.

Preserved locomotive 1040.01, in ÖBB's early green livery and with the company's original logo, is seen at the Mürzzuschlag's Südbahn Museum.

Semmering summit is an Alpine saddle where a classic stone station has been built to serve nearby winter resorts. Immediately beyond the platform, the line divides and enters parallel bores to begin a long descent on the south slope.

On the south slope, visit Mürzzuschlag's Südbahn Museum. This is a UNESCO World Heritage Site that displays a variety of equipment and railway memorabilia. It is open from March to October (**suedbahnmuseum.at/english/home**).

Beyond Mürzzuschlag, the line descends toward Bruck an der Mur traversing pleasant mountain scenery, which while characteristic of eastern Austria didn't require the same degree of extreme engineering that was necessary on Semmering's north slope.

At Bruck an der Mur, the line divides, with one leg following the traditional Südbahn route toward Graz and beyond into modern-day Slovenia. The other leg runs in a southwesterly direction via Klagenfurt to Villach with connections to Italy and the Tauern route. A secondary main line route connects at St. Michael running through the Alps via Selzthal to Bischoshofen (to travel on this line, change trains at either Bruck an der Mur or Leoben).

The present border is the result of post World War I changes that mandated Austria cede portions of southern Tyrol to Italy. Although the international boundaries changed, many people in this area have retained their culture and continue to speak German.

The Italian side of the pass may be less interesting to modern travelers since immediately south of the summit the railway enters a line relocation built to reduce curvature featuring a long tunnel. It rejoins the traditional alignment at a lower elevation. At Fortezza, the line navigates a deep rocky gorge.

Innsbruck

Innsbruck is the capital of Austrian Tyrol and is considered to be the Austrian "capital of the Alps." The city, characterized by elegant architecture, is ringed by Alpine peaks and divided by the Inn River that lends the city its name. Its main station is well served—ÖBB's Railjet services connect Innsbruck with Salzburg, Vienna, Bregenz, and Zurich, while EC international long-distance trains continue to other destinations in Italy, Germany, and Switzerland.

Innsbruck is an aesthetically placed urban Alpine playground offering a variety of attractions. (For general Innsbruck tourism, see **innsbruck.info/en**.) Its public transport system is operated by IVB and includes three tram lines: routes 1, 3, and 6. Route 3 serves the main station connecting it to the city center. Route 6 connects at the southern terminus of route 1 at Bergisel. This exceptionally scenic line, known as the Forest Line, winds its way into the hills above the city, offering panoramic views of the area. In addition to IVB's urban tram routes, an interurban tram called the Stubaitalbahn (Stubai Valley Railway) runs southward to Fulpmes, and a funicular runs north from Congress across the Inn to Hungerburg.

Visitors may consider buying an Innsbruck Card that, in addition to covering the fare for most of the city's public transport (including trams, city buses, and the sightseer bus), also allows single entry to all of the city's museums, provides up to 3 hours free bicycle rental, and offers a host of discounts at area attractions. Cards cost €39 for 24 hours, €48 for 48 hours, and €55 for 72 hours. These may be ordered online from **innsbruck-shop.com**.

In addition to the modern trams that serve as public transport, the Tiroler MuseumsBahnen maintain and operate fleet of restored historic trams for the benefit of tourists and railway enthusiasts.

An ÖBB InterCity train, composed of modern air-conditioned carriages hauled by one of ÖBB's powerful Taurus electric locomotives, stands at Innsbruck Hauptbahnhof. The view is dominated by the Karwendel mountain range.

Among Innsbruck's major attractions is the famed Schloss Ambras, located south of the city on a picturesque rock plateau 325 feet (99 meters) above the valley floor. The grounds are open year-round (except November) from 10 a.m. to 5 p.m. Exhibits include the Habsburg Portrait Gallery (open April to October) that displays more than 200 period images of members of the Habsburg dynasty—rulers of the Austro-Hungarian and Spanish Empires, and the most powerful family in central Europe for centuries. The museum contains the Chambers of Armour with historic suits of armor worn by famous Habsburg military commanders, collections of Gothic sculpture, and the magnificent 143-foot-long (43.6 meter) Spanish Hall. To reach the castle by public transport, take tram 1 to its end and then transfer to tram 6 for the remainder of the journey. (For more information and admission prices, see **schlossambras-innsbruck.at/en**.)

The Museum of Tyrolean Regional Heritage is perfect for families. It exhibits a variety of regional arts and crafts, featuring farmhouse recreations, plus special exhibits for children and seasonal displays at Christmas. Open daily from 9 a.m. to 5 p.m., it is located in the Innsbruck historic district near Court Church. (See **tiroler-landesmuseen.at**.)

Westbahn

The historic Westbahn Route is among Austria's most important railways. It began in 1856 as the Kaiserin-Elisabeth-Bahn, built westward from Vienna. In later years, this route acquired the name Westbahn and was principally served from Vienna's Westbahnhof—one of the six historic terminals encircling the Austrian capital. Significantly, it functions as a domestic trunk route that connects Vienna with Linz, Salzburg, and Innsbruck, and with connections over Brenner and Tauern Passes to Italy and Arlberg Pass to Switzerland. It is also part of the busy Vienna-Münich Route with through trains operating west of Salzburg on DB (German railways).

In modern times, the Westbahn Route has been improved with massive investments aimed at speeding transit times by reducing curvature and raising maximum line speeds while improving line capacity. In addition to the historic alignment, new parallel lines have been built along level and more tangent alignments. This effectively gives the route four main tracks in many places although on different alignments. Express intercity trains, such as Railjet services, tend to be routed via the newer lines, while local services and some freights use the historic line. Frequent crossovers and connections between the two sets of tracks provide ÖBB with operational flexibility, so when the newer line is scheduled for maintenance, fast trains may be easily detoured onto the traditional line.

ST. PÖLTEN

St. Pölten is one of the larger towns along the historic Westbahn. The town's Hauptbahnhof (main railway station) is close to the center, making it ideal for day trips from Vienna (30 minutes by express train) or Linz (46–50 minutes). This is the provincial capital of the Lower Austria region which flourished in the 17th century and offers wonderful period architecture, including several quaint town squares. Attractions include the Festspielhaus—a modern concert hall well known for its music and dance, and the Museum Niederösterreich that has been praised for its regional exhibits on history and nature.

St. Pölten Hauptbahnhof serves as the junction station for two interesting secondary lines. There's a 19-mile (31km) standard gauge branch that extends northward to Krems an der Donou (the junction with an east-west secondary route that serves the north bank of the Danube). More interesting is the 53-mile (85km) narrow gauge Mariazellbahn that runs along the scenic Pielach valley into the

A WESTbahn double-deck Stadler electric multiple unit arrives at Vienna's Westbahnhof with a scheduled service from Salzburg.

WESTBahn service

Since December 2011, the private company WESTBahn has offered through express passenger services on the Vienna-Linz-Salzburg portion of the Westbahn route in competition with ÖBB's Railjet. It was among the first passenger companies in Austria to take advantage of EU railway liberalization policies.

WESTBahn operates a small fleet of low-floor Stadler double-deck railcars that carry up to 501 passengers and travel up to 125 mph. These are comfortable trains featuring adjustable leather seats and free WiFi.

WESTBahn offers hourly service departing Vienna Westbahnhof westbound 40 minutes past each hour from 6 a.m. to 8 p.m. and east-bound from Salzburg at 52 minutes past each hour (with an express that departs at 7 a.m.). Running times are typically 1 hour, 19 minutes from Vienna to Linz, and 2 hours, 28 minutes from Vienna to Salzburg.

WESTBahn offers competitive fares that may be booked online. Its standard adult fare between Vienna and Linz is €19.60, with a restricted advance purchase "best price" fare of €14.99, and the Vienna to Salzburg standard fare is €26.50 with a best price fare of €19.99. There is a variety of other low fares available including WESTspar tickets, student tickets, senior tickets, multiple journey, and travel passes. (See **westbahn.at**.)

mountains to reach its namesake terminus. Regular services are provided by gold-and-white electric railcars. In the summer, some trains carry panoramic observation cars, and there is also an historic consist hauled by a vintage class 1099 electric locomotive billed as the Ötscher Bear Train, and a very limited seasonal steam service. (See **webshop.noevog.at**.)

West of St. Pölten is the Melk Abbey (open May to October), which can be seen from the train perched on a hill over looking the Danube. Take a REX (regional express train) from St. Pölten to Melk, with a travel time of 18–21 minutes. Then walk up the hill to the north. Surrounded by steep terraced vineyards, this vast baroque architectural masterpiece dates from the early 18th century. It houses a beautiful church and an expansive 12-room library (**stiftmelk.at/englisch**).

Arlberg Pass

Continuing west from Innsbruck is the main trunk route and the historic western end of the WestBahn running through the upper Inn valley, then over the rugged Arlberg Pass. Traveling west of Innsbruck, the broad open valley gradually narrows as it gains elevation. On the tops of the mountains to the south, you'll see picturesque castles and fortresses, some precariously perched—making you wonder how their builders ever managed to organize their construction.

Landeck is an important station and most trains stop here. This moderate size town is located at the confluence of the Inn and Sanna Rivers. Today, it offers visitors a base for regional winter sports or hiking. Nearby are the romantic ruins of Burg Schrofenstein. Situated on a rocky promenade above the town is Landeck Castle, a 12th century stone fortress that houses a regional museum focused on local history. In addition to art displays, it serves as a cultural center hosting concerts and other activities. Open from the end of April until mid-October, it has limited opening hours in December and January (**tyrol.tl/en/highlights/castles/landeck-castle**).

Continuing west, the railway crosses a bowstring viaduct over the narrow craggy Trisanna gorge located below Wiesberg Castle (Schloss Wiesberg).

The railway works upgrade through stunning mountain scenery along the Rosanna River gorge. Near the top of the pass is St. Anton am Arlberg Station that serves nearby ski resorts. Despite modern operations, the Arlberg route remains treacherous and may be closed due to avalanche threats after heavy winter storms. The railway transits the pass via the 6.4-mile-long (10.3km) Arlberg Tunnel that was completed in 1884 by engineering genius Julius Lott.

An ÖBB Railjet on the Westbahn Route heading from Vienna to Salzburg passes Eugendorf.

An ÖBB Taurus electric leads a westward InterCity train through heavy snow on Arlberg Pass near St. Anton, Austria.

West of the summit tunnel, the line drops sharply through Bludenz toward Feldkirch near the three-way boundary between Austria, Liechtenstein, and Germany. Here the route divides, with one line continuing west through Liechtenstein (operated by ÖBB) toward Zurich, Switzerland, and the other running northward via Bregenz into Germany, with direct trains connecting Feldkirch with Lindau (located on the eastern shore of Lake Constance).

Through international long-distance (EC/Railjet) trains operate between Vienna, Innsbruck, and Zurich every 4 hours during the day, with overnight trains operated as ÖBB's Nightjet (**nightjet.com**).

Hourly domestic Railjet services between Vienna Hbf via Innsbruck to Feldkirch (and some to Bregenz) fill the gaps in the international service. Railjets to Feldkirch take about 6 hours, 15 minutes from Vienna, and about 1 hour, 55 minutes from Innsbruck.

Route S2 local trains between Innsbruck and Landeck operate hourly and take 1 hour, 15 minutes.

One of Zillertalbahn's more modern diesel locomotives leads a passenger train on the narrow gauge line that follows Ziller valley toward Mayrhofen.

Zillertalbahn

The independent narrow gauge Zillertalbahn offers a pleasant interlude through its namesake Alpine valley. This pastoral line uses very narrow tracks, just 2 feet 6 inches (760mm) between the rails. The line connects with ÖBB at Jenbach (located 22 miles/35km east of Innsbruck). Zillertalbahn runs southward up the scenic Ziller valley for 21 miles (32km) to Mayrhofen. You'll arrive at Jenbach on an ÖBB regional or IC train. This is Zillertalbahn's base of operations where it maintains locomotives and railcars. Although most trains are diesel powered, it also operates several fully functional steam locomotives for seasonal tourist trains.

Among the line's 18 stations are Strass im Zillertal, Schlitters-Bruck am Ziller, Fügen-Hart, Uderns, and Ried. Zillertalbahn spans the Ziller on an immaculate steel-arch truss bridge near Zell am Ziller. The terminus at Mayrhofen is a local transportation hub where Zillertalbahn's trains interchange with its regional buses that serve area winter sports and mountain resorts. In season, this is busy place, but it lacks the charm of the smaller towns in the valley. (For schedules and information, see **zillertalbahn.at**.)

Italy

Local trains bask in the sun between runs at Roma Termini—the largest and busiest station in Rome, which serves dozens of trains every hour.

FS Group is the holding company for Ferrovie dello Stato Italiane (Italian State Railroad, known by the initials FS), and Trenitalia is the FS passenger train operator. The FS network is a vast enterprise that annually handles an estimated 600 million passengers.

Trenitalia is the largest passenger operator in Italy, but there are also several regional rail networks and small railways. NTV (Nuovo Trasporto Viaggiatori) is Europe's first private open-access, high-speed train operator. It runs its Italo service on the national FS network in competition with TrenItalia's own frequent high-speed intercity Frecciarossa services.

Passenger operations and achievements

Italy was a European high-speed rail pioneer. Before World War I, the state railroad under the visionary administration of director general Riccardo Bianchi,

Italy's mainline railways are heavily built and largely electrified and provide frequent service. An FS local approaches Framura on the Mediterranean coast.

FS's Frecciarrossa 1000 is among newest, fastest, and most efficient types of high-speed train in Italy. Although presently limited to 186 mph (300 km/h), these are designed for a top speed of 220 mph (360 km/h).

who made Italy's trains run on schedule (a claim often incorrectly attributed to Benito Mussolini), began planning for new supremely engineered railway lines known as Direttissimas. The war delayed construction, but in 1927, under Mussolini's regime, a new, direct, low-grade, high-speed line opened between Rome and Naples.

At 135 miles long, this largely tangent line (requiring 21 miles of new tunnels) was nearly 36 miles shorter than the old, slow railway it supplanted. Maximum gradient was limited to just 1 percent. What had been an arduous 4-hour, 30-minute journey became a 2-hour, 45-minute trip. (In 2017, this trip was accomplished by TrenItalia's Frecciarossa high-speed trains in just 1 hour, 10 minutes, which offers up to four services per hour in each direction.)

The second Direttissima was opened by the King of Italy in April 1934, connecting Bologna and Florence via the 11.5-mile Apennine Tunnel (at the time, the longest in the world). World War II curtailed Italian high-speed developments. Then in the early 1960s, FS resumed investment in high-speed infrastructure, so rail could more effectively compete with highway and airline transport. Work on the Florence-Rome

The proliferation of automated ticket machines, such as these at Roma Termini, make it easier to buy tickets. Although multiple language options are offered, patience is required to navigate the machine's layered menus.

Direttissima began in 1969 but wasn't completed for nearly 20 years. Since then, there have been several important additions to the high-speed network, including the 24.6-mile section that opened on the Milan-Venice route in December 2016.

TRENITALIA TICKETS

For the most part, you don't need to buy Italian rail tickets from agents at ticket windows since many FS stations have modern ticket machines. These offer an English language option, yet to buy a ticket typically requires navigating more than a dozen steps, including continuing through various warnings that advise you about pickpockets, unauthorized persons supplying information, and reminders to validate your tickets (*You've been warned!*).

Be patient with the machines and eventually you'll reach the screen that prompts you to pay for your tickets. If you pay by credit card, you'll need to follow instructions on the separate keypad to the right of the main touch screen. If you are traveling via an InterCity or high-speed train that requires compulsory seat reservations and supplements, the machine will automatically prompt you to buy them.

An NTV's Italo Alstom-built Avelia high-speed train arrives under Milano Centrale's vast train shed. These trains are similar to the new Amtrak high-speed trains presently on order for its Northeast Corridor in the United States.

There's an Trenitalia mobile app available via Apple iTunes that features a trip planner and enables the sale of E-tickets. However, one of the easiest ways of ordering tickets in advance is using Trenitalia's website, which facilitates the purchase of regional tickets and passes as well as long-distance travel options.

The trip planner allows you to select and purchase E-tickets and then sends you an email confirmation and a PDF image of your ticket. The site is straightforward and you can use most credit cards (**trenitalia.com/tcom-en**).

Although paper tickets require validation (prior to traveling) by correctly inserting them into electrical stamping machines on platforms, this action is not necessary (or possible) with most E-tickets.

Italo high-speed trains

NTV's modern Italo services offer travelers an alternative to Trenitalia high-speed trains on key intercity trunk routes. Italo services use modern Alstom-built Avelia-series trainsets that were engineered for 225 mph (362 km/h) but are presently

A highlight of Milan's intense public transport system are its vintage Peter Witt-style streetcars, a classic type that originated in Cleveland around 1915 and used by many North American streetcar systems including those in Philadelphia and Toronto.

limited to 186 mph (300 km/h) on Italian high-speed lines. Alstom boasts that these are among the most energy-efficient high-speed trains. If you travel, check your Italo ticket, which highlights the estimated carbon emissions advantage of the train for your journey by comparing your Avelia high-speed trip to similar trips by automobile and airlines.

Italo offers four classes of travel, all of which have free access to the train's onboard entertainment system using a WiFi web portal to provide passengers a wide selection of movies, television, music, and games. You simply need to log on with a smart phone or tablet.

Milan

Milan is a large industrial center, famous as a premier European design and fashion complex. It is also a leading Italian banking hub. The city is a lively bustling place with lots of restaurants and shops, but it lacks the opulent Renaissance charm and plethora of ancient monuments, museums, and other tourist attractions associated with other Italian cities. Owing to its strategic importance as a railway hub, many visitors arriving in Italy by railway will need to change trains here and may find it a convenient layover point before venturing to other tourist destinations.

Milan is well served by tram lines, some of which still run vintage Peter Witt-style cars that date to the 1920s. It also features a three-line metro system and extensive suburban railways.

One of the best ways to explore Milan is by wandering on the tram network. Single tickets are cheap but time restricted. A better option is one of the day passes that allow for unrestricted travel over a designated period of time.

MILAN STATIONS

Milan is Italy's most important international railway hub and has several railway stations. Most significant and most impressive is Milano Stazione Centrale (Milan Central Station). This is a stunning structure with its monumental façade facing Milan's vast Piazza Andrea Doria—one of Europe's largest squares. It was among the last classic railway terminals completed in Europe, and although it was finished in 1931 during Benito Mussolini's regime, its design was much older, dating to a pre-World War I architectural competition won by Ulisse Stacchini. Despite civic interest in the project, the onset of World War I and postwar financial distress delayed construction until 1925.

Ticket counters and machines are located at ground level (below the concourse). Both Trenitalia and open-access operator NTV's Italo high-speed operations serve this station, among the busiest in Italy.

The station is fed by a complex network of railway lines that circle from every direction, entering the sheds from the north. Sidings and yards around the terminal can hold dozens of trains, and following the morning rush hour, you will find more rolling stock stored within sight of Milan Central than is owned by whole networks in smaller European nations (such as Ireland).

As with other large Italian terminals, you should mind your surroundings at Milan Central as the station harbors panhandlers, pickpockets, and petty criminals. At the risk of appearing rude, you should avoid disreputable characters and keep your valuables close at hand.

Milano Centrale (Milan Central Station) was completed in 1931. The scale of this massive station appears out of proportion with humanity. The entrance hall is decorated with Roia marble and travertine stone.

Principe and Genova Brignole connected by a long tunnel beneath the city. Its one metro line is one of Europe's shortest urban transit systems and offers an additional means of traveling between the two stations.

A scenic narrow gauge railway operated by Ferrovia Genova Casella runs from Manin Station (off Piazza Manin on the north side of the city) via a sinuous line into the hills to Casella using antique equipment. (See **ferroviagenovacasella.it/geca**; site is in Italian.) Genoa also has several urban funicular lines. (See **visitgenoa.it**.)

Genoa is most famous as the hometown of Christopher Columbus, and there's an impressive statue of the explorer near Genova Piazza Principe. Attractions include a world-class aquarium, some 20 museums including Museo di Sant' Agostino, Christopher Columbus House, and numerous urban palaces dating from the 16th and 17th centuries.

One of the most rewarding experiences in Genoa is simply to wander the narrow alleys of the old city. In many places, towering ancient buildings result in some streets never seeing direct sunlight, and most aren't wide enough for automobiles. Yet there's a full range of shops, markets, restaurants, bars, cafés, and bustling commerce in this warren of small streets. Remember that it is an active seaport with age-old traditions, not all so savory.

MEDITERRANEAN RAILWAY JOURNEYS

For a classic Mediterranean railway journey, travel in either direction along the sea from Genoa. If you go west toward France, you'll pass Sovona, Albenga, and San Remo. Historically, this route enjoyed some stunning sections of precarious seaside running; however, massive investment in line relocations has resulted in an improved railway inland from the old alignments. Ventimiglia is the last large town in Italy and the border crossing with France. Italian intercity and regional (*regionale*) trains terminate here, and you'll need to change to an SNCF TER (French regional) train to continue your Mediterranean journey. Transfer times vary, and you may need to take the time to procure SNCF tickets unless you are traveling on a pass or bought a through international ticket in advance.

GENOA TOWARD PISA

South and east from Genoa, the railway's heavily built main line serves towns and resorts of the popular coastal Italian Riviera and Cinque Terra. Trenitalia offers several types of service on this line, including fast Eurostar (ES) tilting Pendolinos

An FS train heading northward to Genoa runs along the rugged and sublimely scenic portion of the Italian Mediterranean coast known as Cinque Terra.

(not to be confused with the Eurostar trains of the Channel Tunnel route) and semi-fast locomotive-hauled InterCity (IC) trains, both of which offer great comfort and require supplements. An ES train runs from Genoa (Genova Brignole) to Pisa Centrale in just 1 hour, 45 minutes, gliding rapidly along and overtaking slower moving trains, while a typical IC train takes 2 hours, 30 minutes for the same trip. Regional trains are slowest, and as you would expect, also the cheapest, and take nearly 3 hours to make the same run to Pisa, while requiring a change of trains mid-journey.

However, if you are interested in more than just a passing glimpse and plan to explore these stunning areas, a regional train is the best one. Regardless of the type of train you travel on, sitting on the right-hand side provides the best views, as there are many miles of seaside running, where you can gaze across the rich waters of the Mediterranean as palms and villas blur past.

The Portofino Promontory is among Italy's most popular coastal destinations, famous for its exclusive resorts and coastal hiking trails with stunning views of the Mediterranean. Yet you cannot buy a railway ticket to Portofino because the town

An FS train crosses the viaduct at Tende heading for Ventimiglia. Although service is sparse, the Col de Tende line connecting northwestern Italy and southeastern France is worthy of exploration. *Michael J. Walsh*

Col de Tende

One of the most spectacular and virtually unknown Alpine railways is the lightly traveled Col de Tende Line. This straddles the Italian-French frontier, and runs nearly 60 miles (100km) from Ventimiglia to Cuneo, with an SNCF branch extending from Briel-sur Roya, France, over the mountains to Nice. The route was conceived as a through line from Turin to Nice and built over a 40-year span between 1887 and 1928, with heavy work interrupted by World War I.

Operations have been complicated by the international nature of the railway. Not only do tracks cross the French-Italian border several times, but also as a condition of the Treaty of Paris, the border itself was shifted, transferring portions of Italian territory to France including key areas occupied by the Italian-built railway line. Despite politics and changes, the Ventimiglia-Cuneo section has remained largely an Italian operation run by Trenitalia (although some SNCF trains from Nice to Briel-sur Roya continue to Tende on the Italian

section). Trenitalia offers connections from Cuneo to Torino (Turin).

The line traverses stunningly rugged scenery, following the Roya River valley north from Ventimiglia and traversing 77 tunnels and more than 5 dozen bridges and viaducts on its sinuous passage to Cuneo. The most intensive engineering is on the French side of the border. North of Briel-sur Roya are three spiral tunnels as the line ascends the Alps. The railway route around Tende is most impressive. North of Tende, the railway crosses back into Italy via the 5-mile (8.1km) Col de Tende Tunnel under the mountains.

The SNCF route from Briel-sur Roya to Nice features impressive infrastructure with two dozen tunnels and almost as many bridges.

Politics have threatened to close or truncate the Col de Tende Line and in recent times, through services on the line have been limited to just two or three per day. (The line may be closed for modernization and maintenance until sometime in 2018.)

At Framura, an all-stops local accelerates southward, while a northward express, formed by a tilting Pendolino, blitzes the station, which is scenically situated between two tunnels on a narrow shelf above the Mediterranean coast.

isn't served directly by rail since the rugged nature of the coastline has necessitated construction of long tunnels and some inland running to maintain an even gradient while providing the shortest routes which miss the famous promontory altogether. To access the coastal promontory, get off at either Santa Margherita or Rapallo and continue your journey by bus or coastal ferry. (For ferry schedules and tickets, see **traghettiportofino.it/en**.)

The peak tourist season is April to September. Rapallo has more stopping trains, but Santa Margherita is a more interesting town. Rapallo's station is located on a relatively sharp curve with views of hillsides in both directions. The seaside is just a short walk through the old town. Visitors will find ample accommodation here.

Continue south along the coast to reach the Cinque Terra region.

Framura makes for a lovely quiet Italian interlude. The railway station is located between two tunnels with the tracks perched upon a ledge above the sea. From the station, you can access a coastal walk by crossing the footbridge and following the signs. This offers some stunning seaside vistas.

Traveling from Ventimiglia via Genoa toward Pisa, you'll be treated to expansive views of the Mediterranean Sea. When traveling southward, be sure to sit on the right side of the train for the best views.

Near the station, but high above it, sits the family-run Augusta Hotel, which requires a stiff climb up a staircase and a walk along a winding road (alternatively arrange to be collected in a car). The hotel has a restaurant, and the views over the Mediterranean at sunset are stunning. Local trains serve Framura nearly every hour. Historically, FS posed publicity photos here because of its classic scenic background.

Beyond Framura, the line seems to be in tunnels as much as it is out in the open. At Bonassola, the railway exits a tunnel immediately before the station. Notice the old viaduct between the station and the sea that shows the railway's older alignment. Upon departing the station, the line dives into another long tunnel.

This pattern is repeated at Levanto, while at Monterosso, a tunnel begins in the middle of the platforms.

After passing La Spezia, the line wanders inland. Change trains at Viareggio for the line to Florence via Lucca.

Belmond's iconic Venice-Simplon Orient Express is famous for recreating the aura of deluxe Golden Age railway travel by using period equipment on a supremely scenic route.

Belmond's Venice-Simplon Orient Express

Historically, the most famous deluxe European train was undoubtedly Wagons-Lits' international Orient Express that made its splashy debut back in 1883. Today, Belmond recaptures the spirit of classic early 20th century railway travel with its exclusive luxury cruise train marketed as the Venice-Simplon Orient Express (VSOE). Where Wagons-Lits' original Orient Express ran from Paris to Istanbul, the modern-day London-Paris-Venice Pullman-style train is designed as a romantic 2-day, 1-night excursion that recreates the style once offered by the interwar period Venice-Simplon Orient Express—so-named because it had favored the recently opened Swiss Simplon Tunnel (instead of the pre-World War I route across Germany and Habsburg domains).

Belmond's VSOE is a 16-carriage train consisting of restored vintage Wagons-Lits equipment decorated in traditional cream and navy and featuring authentically styled interior cabins opulently finished with plush fabric, varnished panel woods, and polished metal fixtures. Smartly uniformed attendants assist passengers. Like other

309

Belmond trains, this emphasizes the classic dining car experience, in which you leisurely consume gourmet meals served on fine china while enjoying a cocktail as a rolling panorama passes your window. Sleeping compartments consist of single cabins with lower berths, double cabins with upper and lower berths, plus deluxe cabin suites that join pairs of adjacent cabins to provide travelers with greater comfort.

Belmond assigns this train consist on several routes, with its namesake London-Paris-Venice service being one of the most popular. Begin in London and board restored British Pullmans at Victoria Station for the journey to the Kentish coast. After crossing the English Channel, you'll board the classic 16-car Continental train for the overnight run to Italy. If you desire to closely follow a route of the historic Orient Express, Belmond's VSOE operates its "Signature Journey," a 6-day, 5-night trip from Paris to Budapest and Istanbul. (See **belmond.com/venice-simplon-orient-express**.)

Venice

Venice (Venezia) requires little introduction—it is one of the most popular, most pictured, and certainly one of the most distinctive cities in Europe. It has been so often pictured in books and featured in films that when you arrive there, you may get a distinct sense of déjà vu. What may not be apparent from its many appearances is the vast scale of the canal network, which is dominated by the serpentine Grand Canal that serves as the city's main thoroughfare.

Venice consists of some 118 small islands in the Adriatic Sea a few miles from the Italian mainland. These are protected from the sea by a breakwater island known as the Lido. In addition to the primary Grand Canal, there are an estimated 150 smaller canals many of which are exceptionally narrow, and occasionally dead-end into ancient enclaves of buildings. By and large, the canals are not especially deep, but tend to be polluted, which lends to the city's unusual aroma.

RAILWAY STATIONS AND TRAVEL

The historic city is served by Venezia-Santa Lucia, a moderately sized stub-end terminal that connects with the mainland network via a long causeway. The station's architecture is disappointingly bland considering the historic nature of the city, but it is remarkably well situated in the northwestern corner of the islands, directly facing the Grand Canal. Visitors can easily reach vaporetto (water buses) from the station or set out to explore Venice on foot.

In Venice, a gondola ride at dusk is one of the great experiences you should treat yourself to while in Europe.

Venice is also served by Venezia-Mestre, a relatively large through station on the main line. While many of long-distance trains continue on to Venezia-Santa Lucia, there are also regional trains between the two stations that operate about every 5 minutes at peak times. The journey time is just 10 minutes and the fare is a little more than a euro. Venezia-Mestre has more long-distance options for connections across Italy. Keep in mind that Venezia-Mestre is a suburban station that isn't near the enclave of canals and islands in the old city.

Venezia-Santa Lucia is well connected with other Italian cities. Trenitalia's Frecciarossa high-speed trains to Milan take about 2 hours, 25 minutes; to Bologna in 1 hour, 25 minutes; to Florence in just over 2 hours; and to Rome in 3 hours, 45 minutes. It's cheaper but longer to use combinations of regional and slower long-distance trains.

VENICE ATTRACTIONS

The city's myriad canals filled with boats, colorful decaying architecture with narrow alleys, and numerous cafés, restaurants, and shops are the main attractions here. Every visitor will want to experience a boat ride along the Grand Canal and a gondola ride through the narrower side canals (best accomplished in the fading light of a warm evening). Walk across the world famous Ponte di Rialto (Rialto Bridge) that majestically spans the Grand Canal.

Visit Venice's largest public square known as Piazza San Marco, which is thronged with visitors during the day and plagued by pigeons (that are remarkably tame and may land on you!). The Piazza is lined with outdoor cafés and is home to several prominent museums. At the east end is the Piazza's namesake basilica and the adjacent Palazzo Ducale, once the seat of local rulers that presided over the Venetian empire centuries ago.

Venice is famous for its glass, lace, and masks, and artisans' shops abound, many tucked away in small alleys off the primary streets. The best known of Venice's museums is the Galleria del Accademia, which spans three ancient buildings. If you're interested in taking in the museum's wonders, get there early, as there are long lines throughout the day.

Too many visitors don't budget enough time to see Venice, let alone experience it properly, and so are faced with a hurried agenda that leaves them swimming in sensory overload (but better than swimming in the canals). While a few hours will give you a taste of Venice, you should plan to spend several days. Be warned—Venice is expensive and there are very few bargains. It's busiest in summer, so to get the most out of Venice, plan to visit in March or October. Winter can be less pleasant as high water can flood portions of the city. (For Venice tourism, see **in-venice.com**.)

PUBLIC TRANSPORT

As might be expected of a city surrounded by water and dominated by canals, the primary public transport in Venice is by boat. While private gondolas are plentiful and water taxis abound, the city is well connected by public water buses and operated by ACTV. ACTV is Venice's public transport provider and also operates rubber-tired buses to outlying areas including Venice's Marco Polo Airport.

Single tickets are expensive, so visitors should consider purchasing travel cards. These are available in 12-hour, as well as 1-, 2-, 3-, and 7-day denominations. (For details on public transport tickets and timetables, see **actv.avmspa.it/en/content/ water-bus-service-timetable**.) Another option is the Venice City Pass that covers public transport in addition to other features (**tripplanner.veneziaunica.it/en**).

A sunset in Venice—when old meets new and light meets shadow: as the sun slowly sinks into the Adriatic Sea, medieval buildings are silhouetted against the evening sky.

Florence (Firenze)

This gem of Renaissance Italy has more world-class opulent architecture, famous art works, and cultural attractions compressed into one beautifully laid-out compact city than can possibly be absorbed by a short visit. Everywhere you look are sights, sounds, and smells that will delight your senses. Even the chalked graffiti and painted wall decorations are executed with sublime style.

Unfortunately, because Florence is so beautiful and such a completely wonderful place that exudes old-world charm by the gallon, it is completely swamped with tourists at all times of the year. Visiting the most famous museums and main attractions often requires hours of waiting in lines. One of the best ways to get a flavor for Florence without the crushing hoards of fellow visitors is to wander the streets in the early morning before busloads of visitors arrive.

The city's main railway station is called Santa Maria Novella (or Firenze SMN on train schedules) and is in close proximity to central Florence, situated on the aptly named Piazza delle Stazione opposite the church of the same name. Reaching the city center is

It's no wonder that Italian sunsets have inspired generations of classic painters. A tapestry of color forms a backdrop over the Arno in Florence with the church of San Frediano in Cestello's baroque dome in the background.

a relatively short walk across the piazza and then following one of several main streets in a south/southeasterly direction. Considering this architecturally stunning city, it may amaze you that Florence has been bestowed with one of Europe's ugliest large railway terminals. The building's exterior is so nondescript and un-railway-like that it might be confused for a postal depot or an electrical substation except that, even in Italy, these utilitarian structures are more attractive. Appearances aside, Florence benefits from excellent railway service, and there are frequent and regular trains to all main cities, with as many as four trains hourly to Rome and Bologna.

Florence has many attractions. (The official Florence website is **firenzeturismo.it/en**.) The city is bisected by the Arno River and among the several bridges spanning the river is the medieval Ponte Vecchio, which now hosts high-end jewelry shops, owing in part to an endless parade of lovers hoping to propose and accept marriage here.

The Duomo is Florence's immense cathedral and among Italy's most impressive and memorable Renaissance buildings. The city has several phenomenal museums—perhaps best known is the Uffizi Gallery, which is filled with some of the world's finest Renaissance art, including works of Botticelli, Michelangelo, and Da Vinci.

314

The view from Boboli Gardens (Giardino di Boboli) features the dome and tower of the Duomo, Florence's cathedral completed in the 15th century, among numerous iconic Renaissance buildings.

Other museums include the Galleria dell' Accademia, Galleria Palatina, and Museo Archeologico. The Boboli Gardens (Giardino di Boboli) are located south of the Arno. From the top of the gardens are some stunning views of the city. However, the gardens close before sunset, so don't wait until late in the day to make the uphill trek and find that the gates have been shut. For a treat, position yourself along the banks of the Arno at sunset and watch as the golden glow bathes the city, before finding dinner in one of Florence's many restaurants.

Rome

The Italian capital is an expansive city that is home to millions of people, making it a thriving, congested metropolis that has an amazing blend of stunning ancient ruins and functional modernity. Rome wasn't built in a day, and you certainly can't expect to see it all in a day either—or a week for that matter. Many of the most interesting sights are near the city center, and the city may be enjoyed on foot.

Looking toward Rome's railway station at Trastevere (left), this view features a colorful sunrise. When visiting Rome, remember that it is also one of Europe's largest metropolitan areas, so while well supplied with public transport, trains, trams, and metro lines can be packed at peak times.

Rome is home to some of Europe's most visited tourist attractions, and like other popular Italian cities, it is thronged with tourists, especially during peak seasons. If you want to experience Rome's highlights, be prepared to get an early start and be patient as you work your way through long lines of similarly minded visitors.

While the city's iconic landmarks are worth seeing in person, Rome is also a wonderful place to wander around without a strict agenda. Take time to explore narrow streets and cobblestone lanes, sit down for a leisurely lunch of freshly cooked pizza with a tall cool beer or glass of wine and enjoy gelato in a cone or a rich cappuccino. Watch the bustle as it flows past you.

Rome also tends toward sensory overload, so take it easy or you may find yourself visually exhausted. Plan to spend an evening in the alleyways and small squares of the Trastevere area located near the Tiber River to the southwest of central Rome. Here you can find numerous small restaurants and bars where you can relax and simply enjoy the atmosphere.

Capitoline Hill (the smallest of ancient Rome's seven hills) hosts numerous antiquities of the Roman Empire, including this bronze equestrian statue of Marcus Aurelius located in Piazza del Campidoglio (Capitoline Plaza).

TRANSPORT

Rome has a complex weave of public transport including suburban trains, buses, trams, and a two-line metro system. Despite this, be prepared to walk your feet off, or hire taxis, which are plentiful. Be exceptionally careful crossing streets as Roman motorists are notorious for their disregard of traffic rules—details such as traffic lights, pedestrian crossings, and traditional conventions of direction on roads are all viewed by drivers as advisory! Don't be surprised if you see a Vespa mount a sidewalk at speed.

Rome public transport is provided by ATAC. Frequent service operates on most routes and tends to be well patronized. ATAC's two metro routes are focused on Roma Termini (the main railway station). Line A runs roughly east-west from Anagnina to Battistini through the commercial center and passes near the Vatican. Metro line B runs from Rebibbia in the north to Laurentina in the south with a stop called Coloseo near the Colosseum.

While you probably won't need to ride to the ends of the metro, it helps to keep the relative directions of terminal stations handy when trying to orient yourself at stations. Many metro stations don't have connections between platforms below ground, so you'll need to determine the direction you intend to travel before descending stairs or escalators and passing the turnstiles. The metro is a pulsing mass of humanity at rush hours that makes the London Tube seem tame; if you're traveling with luggage, it may be better to take a taxi. In addition, an urban railway that connects Roma Porta San Paolo Station with the Lido shares characteristics with other metro lines but is operated by FS.

Surface transport includes a variety of tram routes. Among the most useful for visitors are portions of lines 3, 5, 8, 14, and 19. Line 3/3B follows a partially circumferential route, running from a terminal loop in front of the FS station at Trastevere and sharing tracks with route 8 along Viale di Trastevere before turning southeast at Porta Portese, crossing the Tiber, and passing the transport hub at Piramide (with connections to metro line B and FS/Trenitalia). It continues by wandering northeast past the Colosseum to the tram junction at the old Roman city gate at Porta Maggiore (with connections with lines 5/14/19 plus the vestige of a narrow gauge interurban tram line that runs southeast toward Centocelli). Line 3 continues on the same tracks as line 19 providing connections to national museums on the northside of the city, including Galleria d'Arte Moderna and Museô Etrusco di Villa Giulia (near its terminal loop). This route offers a pleasant means of exploring areas outside central Rome.

Lines 5/14 run from a terminal loop at the southwest flank of Roma Termini and run through shopping areas to Porta Maggiore and then continue into the southeastern suburbs. These are useful to connect with other tram lines at Porta Maggiore.

Line 8 runs from Casaletto via the FS station at Trastevere to Venezia (Piazza Venezia), which makes it a useful line when visiting the south side of the city. Piazza Venezia is located near the center and is within walking distance to numerous attractions.

Line 19 variously shares tracks with lines 3/5/14, running from the southeast suburbs through the northern sections of the city ultimately turning southward and terminating near the Vatican at Risorgimento/S. Pietro. It briefly shares tracks with line 2 between Flaminia/Belle Arti to Ministero Marina. (Continue on line 2 to connect with metro line A at Flaminio, or stay on line 19 for connections with metro line A at Lepanto or Ottaviano). As of 2017, line 19 is one of a few tram routes that still uses vintage streamlined trams with opening side windows. Stand at the back of the tram and

---

A 1940s-era streamlined tram passes an arch of old city walls at Porta Maggiore. In the distance are the approach tracks to Roma Termini.

Tram route 3 follows a circumferential route east of central Rome and runs right by the Colosseum. However, metro line B may prove more useful to visitors since it is just two stops from Colosseo to Roma Termini (the main railway station).

give yourself a personal tour of Roman neighborhoods. Photographers will appreciate the ability to point cameras out the windows without reflective glass in the way.

Purchasing ATAC tickets can be challenging. In theory, many station platforms and terminal stations have automated ticket machines; however, in practice, these tend to be in bad order and, while you are attempting to use them, you may be targeted by panhandlers or pickpockets. Machines in metro stations tend to be in better repair, but often these have long lines of impatient passengers. A more practical option is to buy tickets from news agents and kiosks.

There is a great variety of different tickets covering both the city and greater Lazio region. For short journeys, ATAC offers an **Integrated Time** ticket for €1.50 that may be used across various transport modes (bus, tram, and metro) for up to 90 minutes. If you are staying in Rome for a day or more, it pays to invest in day passes. These are sold as **Roma** 24-hour, 48-hour, or 72-hour tickets. They allow you the freedom to get on and off bus, tram, and metro services (and some FS suburban trains) without the need to procure tickets for each trip, and if you travel often, they provide a significant cost advantage. Integrated Time and Roma tickets require

At Porta Maggiore, ruins of the old city wall and a 3rd century city gate make for a stunning backdrop to an important transport junction between tram routes.

validation at the time of first use. This is accomplished by passing the ticket through the turnstile slot at metro stations or by inserting it arrow-first in the slot on the yellow validation box (situated near doors on buses and trams). A computer-printed time stamp prints on the back of your ticket. Another option is the **Roma Pass** that is similar in concept to the Venice Pass described previously. (For tickets and day passes, see ATAC's website **atac.roma.it**.)

ROME STATIONS

Roma Termini is the city's largest rail-transport nexus and a vast virtual city in itself that includes a multilevel shopping mall with many name-brand shops. The present station is an eclectic mix of 1930s and 1950s architecture that was transformed into a modern multimodal center in the early 2000s and rededicated by the Pope in December 2006.

Nearly one-half million passengers pass through Roma Termini on weekdays. In addition to nearly 30 platforms that host suburban and long-distance trains operating all across Italy, it is the crossing point of metro lines A and B and a tram

News kiosks inside Roma Termini and elsewhere across the city are good places to buy transit tickets and passes. Watch for signs like these.

Dropping off your luggage

Roma Termini is among major Italian stations that offer a left luggage service, which can be found at track level on the western flank of the station.

Experience has shown that it can be slow and disorganized to drop and collect your bags, which can be frustrating if you are trying to catch a train. A cheaper and easier option is BAGBNB, which operates at numerous locations across Italy, as well as London,

Amsterdam, Madrid, Lisbon, and other European cities. In Rome, BAGBNB is hosted by Hotel Agorà and located across Via Marsala (the main street on the station's eastern flank).

It can be booked in advance online at **bagbnb.com/luggage-storage/rome/termini**. To enter the hotel, press the buzzer on the street, enter the building, and take the elevator to the first floor (in Europe the first floor is above the ground floor).

terminus. As a primary hub for high-speed trains operated by both Trenitalia and Italo, there are numerous daily departures to major Italian cities.

To Firenze SMN (Florence), Trenitalia offers 3–4 hourly trains and Italo 1–2 trains, with a travel time of 1 hour, 30 minutes; to Napoli Centrale (Naples), Trenitalia offers 4–5 hourly trains and Italo 1–2 trains, with a travel time of 1 hour, 10 minutes; and

Roma Termini's fronts Piazza dei Cinquecento. This is more than merely a railway station but a multimodal transit hub that also features a two-level shopping mall, where you can get everything from an espresso to the latest cosmetics.

to Milano Centrale (Milan), Trenitalia offers 2 hourly trains and Italo 1–2 trains, with a travel time of about 3 hours. Numerous high-speed services also connect Bologna, Torino, and Verona among other points.

Rome has numerous secondary stations serving both suburban and long-distance trains. Roma Tiburtina is located on the eastern side of the city adjacent to a main bus station. Many long-distance, high-speed trains on the Florence/Bologna/Milan/Venice routes stop here.

In the south of the city, Roma Ostiense is a busy suburban station. This is a useful station adjacent to the Porta S. Paolo terminus of the Roma-Lido transit line and Piramide station on metro line A and near a stop on tram line 3. Roma Trastevere is another important suburban station. This is near various hotels and numerous restaurants and can be readily accessed from the city center by tram line 8, while tram line 3 terminates immediately in front of the station building.

Frequent regional trains connect both Ostiense and Trastevere with Leonardo DaVinci Airport and Roma Termini, making these ideal points for visitors looking to stay in suburbs convenient to the city center.

Rome's Piazza di Spagna lends its name to an impressive flight of stairs popularly called the Spanish Steps.

ROME SIGHTS AND ATTRACTIONS

Few cities have as many ancient monuments sprinkled throughout their urban environs, which makes Rome a delight for the history enthusiast. Yet Rome has far more to see than the ever-present vestiges of its imperial grandeur. There are numerous statues, fountains, columns, churches, museums, and other structures that in any other city would scream for attention but are nearly lost in the visually intense maelstrom of Rome.

It's hard to miss the extravagant National Monument to Victor Emmanuel II, known colloquially as Rome's "Wedding Cake," located prominently between Piazza Venezia and Capitoline Hill. This powerful impressive symbol of national unity is dedicated to the first king of unified Italy. Although it draws from classic design and themes, the monument is relatively modern when compared to the antiquities that surround it. Constructed from white marble, it was designed by Giuseppe Sacconi and erected between 1885 and 1911. The monument is prominently situated near the terminus of tram line 8.

If you walk southeast of the monument, you'll pass the museums of Capitoline Hill; continue on and you'll see the splendor of the excavated ruins of the Roman

If you are traveling from Fiumicino Aeroporto (Leonardo DaVinci Airport) to central Rome or have intercity rail connections at Romi Termini, consider taking the direct Leonardo Express, which has space for luggage and skips intermediate stations.

Leonardo Express

Rome's primary international airport is known as both Fiumicino Aeroporto and Leonardo DaVinci Airport. It has direct rail connections to central Rome via both local trains and the sleek Leonardo Express, which runs nonstop between Roma Termini and the airport station every half hour with an advertised 32-minute travel time. This uses specially decorated modern electric railcars with ample luggage space.

Leonardo Express is considered a first class service so first class tickets are required. They may be purchased online or from Trenitalia ticket machines. At the time of your purchase, you need to select a travel time, but you are not required to travel on the specific train that you booked and may travel on any train during the day you specified. You will need to validate your ticket prior to boarding using one of the ticket validation machines near platform barriers.

Leonardo Express is a comparatively expensive service, costing €14 one way. If you are not in a hurry, you can save money by taking local trains (some of which require a change en route), although these are often not listed on the Trenitalia website, which encourages you to use the more expensive option.

Also, while Leonardo Express is well suited for travelers to central Rome, this may not be the most effective option if you are planning to visit a suburban location. Consult Trenitalia's website or mobile app to see if a local train from the airport serves your station directly.

Forum. The various colonnades, columns, arches, and ruins here were at the heart of the commercial and organizational center of ancient Rome. Yet for centuries it was covered over, forgotten by generations of Romans, and only rediscovered in the 20th century. You can see many of the structures from the sidewalks around Capitoline Hill; however, accessing the Forum itself requires a ticket. The most

Some of the best views of the Roman Forum—the heart of ancient Rome—are from the public street to the west called Via Monte Tarpeo on the way down from Capitoline Hill.

popular access is from the southwest side, where the Forum faces Rome's most memorable ruin, the immense and iconic Colosseum.

If you only have time to wait in one of Rome's many tourist lines, the queue for the Colosseum is one of your best choices. It is considered the symbol of Rome—equivalent to the Eiffel Tower in Paris and the Brandenburg Gate in Berlin. It is also one of the world's most-visited attractions, with more than 6 million annual paid visitors. If you don't have the time or the patience to wait in line, consider traveling by the Colosseum on tram line 3. The site also has its own metro station on line B (Colosseo) located to northwest of the famous amphitheater.

The Colosseum was built in the first century AD, the famous venue for staged battles between gladiators, lions, and other beasts. Although the stone vestiges remain, the structure was once far more elaborate and featured complex staging areas

Italian unification is symbolically celebrated in the ostentatious display of white Botticino marble facing Piazza Venezia designed by Giuseppe Sacconi called the Monument of Victor Emmanuel II and known colloquially as the "Wedding Cake."

Finland

Helsinki is a dynamic city with a mix of historical and modern architecture. Helsinki Cathedral is an iconic neoclassic church facing Hallituskatu (Senate Square). Take tram 7 or 7H from Helsinki Central Station.

Finland is a relatively large European country by size, 338,440 square kilometers, but small in population with just 5.5 million inhabitants. This wonderful country is off the European tourist path with many visitors viewing it as being on the edge of Europe. So while it isn't overrun by a great volume of tourists, and doesn't feature stunning mountainous scenery in sight of a railway, nor the range of antiquities associated with central Europe, it makes for an excellent holiday destination and an enjoyable place to explore by train.

Finnish is the primary spoken language, but Swedish is also an official language since there is a significant native Swedish-speaking minority, and many people also speak some English. Helsinki is the capital and largest city as well as an important cultural center. The greater Helsinki metro area represents almost a fifth of the Finish population and features well-developed public transport including a suburban rail

Finland's VR Group operates a national network of long-distance passenger trains. A VR class Sr2 Swiss-built electric locomotive glides along on perfectly maintained track with InterCity 48 destined for Helsinki.

During the long days of summer, when the sun shines late into the evening, a pair of Soviet-built Sr1 electrics lead overnight train 266 from Rovanemi to Helsinki near Oulu.

network, metro system, and light rail tram routes. Beyond Helsinki, Finland is largely pastoral, characterized by forests, rolling scenery, small farms, and hundreds of bucolic woodland lakes. Its northern reaches—well past the Arctic Circle—are beyond the extent of railways yet feature some mountains and the finest Finnish scenery.

Railway operation

Finland's railways were largely developed before World War I and are a legacy of Finland's domination by Czarist Russia. Even today, the tracks here are based on the Russian broad gauge width, which is sufficiently similar to allow through operations between the countries. (Finland uses 1,524mm track width compared to Russia's (1,520mm.) Russia is Finland's largest foreign connection for rail traffic.

Finland's modern network operates under the umbrella of the state-run VR Group (The initials VR infer Valtion Rautatiet, which means state railways). Outside of the intensively operated Helsinki suburban area, Finnish towns and cities are served by a well-maintained intercity network with clean, affordable, comfortable,

One of Helsinki's most unusual tours is the pub tram, on which you can see the sights and enjoy a Finnish draft beer as you glide along in a vintage Helsinki tramcar retrofitted with a bar inside.

Pub tram

Do you like exploring a city by tram? Would you enjoy a beer? Consider a spin on Helsinki's unusual Spårakoff pub tram that is aimed at tourists and makes a circuit through the city while serving beer and cider.

The trip takes under an hour, operates May to October, seats about 30 passengers, and departs near the eastern side of Helsinki Central Station.

The route uses one of the older nonarticulated trams in a distinctive red livery, and is unlikely to be mistaken for a service tram.

and well-appointed trains. Although most towns have multiple trains daily, Finland's intercity services are less frequent than those of more populated countries of central Europe but are generally adequate to serve the demands of the population. The passenger network is largely electrified, although many rural intercity lines are single-track with passing sidings.

VR's InterCity trains will delight railway enthusiasts. In contrast with the European trend toward standardized mass-produced multiple units, most Finnish intercity services largely employ locomotive-hauled passenger cars, with the exception of some fast runs employing tilting Pendolinos. VR's older traditional passenger cars are spacious, comfortable, and well decorated, while the newer cars use nicely fitted double-deck designs. Among the most enjoyable and interesting long runs are the

A VR Pendolino at Helsinki Central Station boards passengers for its trip north to Oulu.

overnight services between Helsinki and the Arctic, which carry sleeping cars and automobile carriers.

Buying tickets

Tickets are sold at staffed stations and automated ticket machines. Planning your journey and buying tickets is also easily accomplished in advance online. VR's Online Shop webpage has an English language option (**vr.fi/cs/vr/en/frontpage**). VR's downloadable mobile app for smart phones and tablets is called VR Mobiili, which is free and easy to use.

Eliel Saarinen's magnificent Helsinki Central is one of the most distinctive main stations in Europe.

334

Helsinki City Transport (or HKL/HST) operates 11 streetcar (tram) lines that crisscross central Helsinki, making this a convenient way to get around and explore the city.

Ticketing choices include single (one-way), round-trip, and multiple-journey tickets, as well as saver fares and passes. If you have a flexible trip, or can purchase tickets well in advance, try the Price Calendar option to search for the cheapest fares on popular routes. For example, a one-way intercity journey between Helsinki to Oulu, a distance of 559 miles (900km), can cost €30 ($36) or €56 ($67), depending on your dates of travel and how early you purchase tickets.

Buying tickets at least three weeks in advance tends to yield the best prices; however, bargains may be offered up to a day before (depending on the demand for specific trains). VR's Saver tickets typically have the lowest single-journey fares, but keep in mind that the low ticket price is tied to a specific journey. For a small fee, some Saver tickets may be exchanged in advance of travel. Long-distance tickets may be purchased using online services up to one minute before departure.

In additional to standard class tickets, VR offers greater comfort for its extra class seats with an extra fare supplement from €5–€17 ($6–$20.20), depending on distance. Alternatively, you can travel in upper-deck compartments in its DuettoPlus restaurant car.

In 2015, VR began its new airport service on a heart-shaped loop that begins and ends at Helsinki with the airport station (pictured) in the middle of the run, so wherever you board at the airport, you go to Helsinki Central.

Helsinki Airport Railway

The Helsinki Airport Railway opened in summer 2015. It's unusual in that it consists of two lines that loop northward from Helsinki Central to the suburbs and then converge at a new, purpose-built airport station. In addition, there are various new stops en route.

Modern Stadler electric railcars run every 10 minutes during peak periods and 20 to 30 minutes off-peak. Although the airport train is relatively quick, the airport bus is faster and runs directly to Helsinki Central. (See hsl.fi/en.)

Helsinki Centtral Station

Finland's railway icon is Helsinki's Central Station. Even if you have no intention of traveling by train, if you visit the Finnish capital, consider a visit to this famous railway station. It is among the great stations completed near the end of the golden age of European station building in the early 20th century. This art nouveau-style civil structure exudes Finnish nationalism and dates to a time when sophisticated architectural styles were used to make beautiful public buildings, and railway stations were seen as more than merely utilitarian transport hubs. Helsinki's main station exhibits traditional elements of European station design including its clock tower, broad concourse, and gateway arch. Yet the building's style has more in common with other Finnish civic architecture than with other European railway terminals.

Helsinki Central Station's architect Eliel Saarinen drew upon traditional Finnish rural architectural themes, blended with artistic ideals of the Vienna Secession and Arts and Crafts movements, to produce a reactionary style that contrasted with Russified architecture which had dominated Helsinki's public buildings. Although the basic plan was conceived by 1905 and construction began a few years later, the onset of World War I delayed completion and it was not inaugurated until 1919 (after Finnish independence from Russia). Best known is the bold frontal façade of Finnish granite exhibiting pairs of muscular globe-wielding statues.

Helsinki Central Station remains the focal point for VR's passenger operations and the place that many first-time visitors are likely to embark on an initial long-distance Finnish railway journey.

The larger portion of daily passengers using Helsinki Central are daily commuters, with frequent electric services on several routes (including the Airport Railway, see sidebar on page 337), but this is also the busiest and most important long-distance station in Finland. Word of warning: double-check the timetable if you plan to take one of the overnight sleeping-car trains since some night trains depart from Helsinki Pasila Station rather than Helsinki Central.

In addition to information desk, ticket counters, and platforms, Helsinki Central is integrated with a multiple-level shopping plaza having underground tunnel connections to other nearby shopping centers. If you're on a budget, consider an inexpensive breakfast on the go in the form of fresh pastry and coffee from one of the vendors below the station. You can find even cheaper food in a mini-supermarket and bring your breakfast with you on the train. But if you want to splurge, consider breakfast in a dining car, which are still carried on some Finnish intercity trains.

Helsinki transit

Helsinki Central Station is also the primary transit hub served by Helsinki City Transport's (HKL/HST) trams and buses, and a two-line heavy-rail metro. The metro's central station is located below the VR station, with trains running from 5:30 a.m. until 11:30 p.m. Monday to Thursday, extended hours Friday and Saturday, and a 6:30 a.m. start on Sunday. A variety of ticketing options are available (**hsl.fi/en/tickets-and-fares**). Single tickets may be purchased on trains, trams, and buses, but it is cheaper to buy them

Take the ferry from Helsinki across the Gulf of Finland to Estonian capital Tallinn. This compact city is a wonderful stop and may be a jumping-off point for exploration of the Baltic states.

from ticket machines in advance using your phone via SMS text messages or from the HSL mobile ticket app. Mobile tickets must be purchased before boarding a transit vehicle. Most single mobile tickets are valid for 80 minutes and may be used for a journey involving more than one vehicle within that period. If you are planning to explore Helsinki for one or more full days, 1- and 7-day tickets offer much better value and the freedom of being able to jump on and off public transport without the hassle of having to purchase individual tickets. Reduced-price tickets are available for children ages 7–16.

SUOMENLINNA

Suomenlinna is an 18th century fortification dating from Swedish control of Finland. Beautifully situated on the Susiluodot Islands near Helsinki, it is a UNESCO World Heritage Site and contains several popular museums, galleries, and restaurants. Activities including guided tours are available. You can reach the fortress by a ferry operated by HSL/HKL as part of the city's public transport. These run year-round from the docks at Kauppatori (Market Square) daily and from Katajanokka on weekdays. (See **hel.fi/hkl/en/by-ferry**.)

Ferries to Estonia

You can easily make a day trip from Helsinki across the Gulf of Finland to the Baltic republic of Estonia. Ferries to the Estonian capital Tallinn operate more than a dozen times daily. Most tourists to Estonia arrive by water, and fast crossings take about 1 hour, 45 minutes. Although four companies compete for traffic, it is advisable to book ahead as popular ferries often sell out (**laevapiletid.ee/en**).

Helsinki's passenger ferries depart the port from West Terminal 1, and to get there from the city center you can take trams 6T or 7. (For details on Helsinki's port and the ferry terminal, see **portofhelsinki.fi/en**.)

Tallinn makes for a wonderful place to wander around on foot as the old town is a picturesque maze of medieval cobblestone alleys with a large town hall square, fascinating architecture, ample restaurant and cafés, and interesting little shops. Tallinn operates a compact tram system. Additional travel in Estonia is possible by rail. Suburban and intercity trains operate from Tallinn's main railway station on the south side of the city.

Helsinki to the Arctic

For a unique adventure, consider traveling from Helsinki north to the Arctic Circle and beyond. The Arctic is a surreal destination: in high summer, points north of the Arctic Circle enjoy the famed midnight sun that stays above the horizon for weeks. By contrast, in winter the Arctic remains nearly completely dark for weeks, with only the faintest hint of twilight in the southern sky. Imagine riding by train through endless twilight or staring into the frozen darkness to catch a glimpse of a scintillating sky.

In season, VR operates three nightly sleeping-car trains from Helsinki; one terminates at Rovaniemi, another uses essentially the same route but continuing north to Kemijärvi, while a third runs to Kolari. The sleeping-car run from Helsinki to Kemijärvi is a 13-hour trip. If you want to enjoy the scenery, you may wish to make the journey in stages using daylight runs. For Helsinki trains to the Arctic, use the electrified line via Tampere, Kokkola, Ylivieska, Oulu, and Kemi. The view from the train is a rolling tapestry of trees and endless numbers of small lakes dotted with wooden summer cottages.

Rovaniemi is located on the Arctic Circle at the confluence of Kemijoki and Ounasjoki Rivers. It makes for an interesting place to discover and is a jumping-off

Overnight sleeping-car trains from Helsinki to the Arctic are among the longest runs in Scandinavia. A northward train greets the rising sun at Kempele south of Oulu. VR recently re-equipped its overnight trains with modern bi-level sleeping cars.

point for Arctic exploration. This is a cosmic place in winter when the Northern Lights dance across the heavens. The town was a World War II casualty and largely rebuilt after 1944; today it is advertised as the hometown of Santa Claus, which reflects the popular seasonal attraction called Santa Claus Village.

Rovaniemi's railway station is immediately south of downtown. The Arktikum is a museum and Arctic science center located at the Arctic Circle that offers an array of engaging displays that tell the story of the Arctic environment (**arktikum.fi**). Its 564-foot (172 meter) glass-lined corridor is designed to convey an Arctic gateway and is symbolic of Rovaniemi's relation to the Arctic and Lapland regions.

Kemijärvi is the end of the passenger railway and at the very edge of the European railway network. This hilly Lapland town is known for outdoor sports and being another gateway to the north. Keep in mind that by European standards, train services are sparse; most of the year, there's just a lone daytime train that runs to Rovaniemi. (For information on Swedish Lapland, see **swedishlapland.com**.)

Allegro service between Helsinki and St. Petersburg, Russia, uses specially outfitted broad gauge Pendolino tilting trains equipped to work on both Finnish and Russian lines.

Helsinki to Russia

Helsinki-St. Petersburg Allegro services operate four times daily by Karelian Trains (a joint venture between Finnish and Russian railways headquartered in Helsinki). Allegro uses custom-built Pendolino tilting trains to provide a deluxe through passenger service on a 3½-hour schedule between terminals with limited intermediate stops. Allegro trains are equipped with Finnish and Russian signaling systems that ensure safe operation on both sides of the historic frontier. These trains are rare examples of through services between an EU country and Russia without the need for gauge-changing equipment. Passport and customs control are conducted onboard the train.

Allegro trains depart from Helsinki Central and travel in a northerly direction before heading east. Once beyond the suburbs, the scenery largely consists of dense forest broken by occasional open pastures and natural lakes. After passing the Russian frontier, you cross the Republic of Karelia, historically part of Finland and forcibly ceded to Russia during World War II as a condition of its peace treaty.

The Tolstoi runs six nights a week between Helsinki and Moscow using Russian railway passenger cars. In this view, one of VR's Soviet-built class Sr-1 electrics leads the Moscow-bound Tolstoy at Helsinki.

The old Finnish city of Viipuri, now Russian Vyborg, once featured a significant Eliel Saarinen-designed railway station that was an architectural twin to Helsinki's. Arriving at St. Petersburg, Allegro trains use the famous Finland Station, which signified Lenin's entry during the Russian Revolution.

The more adventurous traveler should consider booking the Tolstoi, a sleeping-car train that runs nightly except Saturday between Helsinki and Moscow using heavy Russian equipment. From Moscow, you can continue your rail journey across Russia via the famed Trans-Siberian Route to Vladivostok or take the Trans-Mongolian Route via the Gobi desert to China. Each of these options require many days of rail travel. Moscow has a variety of main terminals and the Tolstoi arrives at Leningrad Station, while trains to the east leave from other stations.

American travelers will need to secure a Russian visa prior to traveling across the Russian frontier. Buying visas can be a trying process for the novice, so it's best to work through a travel agent experienced with the ins and outs of Russian travel bureaucracy.

Sweden and Norway

SJ's X2000 tilting trains provide comfortable moderately high-speed service on intercity routes. A northward X2000 departs Stockholm Central on a May evening.

Sweden's state railway, Statens Järnvägar (known by initials SJ), is the country's largest passenger railway operator, running an estimated 1,100 daily trains that serve 275 stations. In addition, there are a number of smaller Swedish operators.

SJ operates moderately high-speed service (up to 125 mph/200 km/h) using its X-2000 tilting trains, as well as more conventional SJ interCity and SJ night trains. Many of these runs require reservations in addition to a ticket, so passengers traveling on an Eurail or Interrail pass will still need to make reservations prior to traveling. Some routes also offer SJ regional services.

SJ night train routes include Stockholm to Sundsvall, Östersund, and Åre; Stockholm to Malmö, Stockholm to Luleå and Narvik, Norway. Most night trains also carry a bistro car that offers breakfast to passengers. First class sleepers feature compartments, while budget options include a choice of a couchette or traditional sleeping-car berths.

On a misty autumn day, a southward SJ local passenger train from Narvik, Norway, passes rugged Arctic scenery near the Swedish-Norwegian border. *Chris Guss*

The classic timber station at Gällivare, Sweden, is not only north of the Arctic Circle, it boasts to be 1,313 kilometers from Stockholm (where no one measures in miles, but in case you were curious it's 816 miles).

SJ's website features schedules, tickets, and general information (**sj.se/en/home. html**). SJ also has a mobile app for Apple iPhones and Android devices that may be downloaded via the website.

Arctic adventures

The journey from Stockholm overnight to the Arctic Circle and beyond to Narvik is among Europe's great passenger train rides and one of the longest. In the long days around the summer solstice, you'll experience continuous daylight, as the midnight sun crosses the northern sky. Equally surreal is the swirling effervescent glow of the Aurora Borealis in winter, when the long night reigns for weeks.

The railway to the Arctic Circle and beyond is known in Swedish as *Malmbanan*. It was built in stages primarily for the movement of iron ore from Swedish mines to ports. The Luleå-to-Gällivare portion opened in the late 1880s, while the northern section reached the ice-free Norwegian port at Narvik in 1902.

The Aurora Borealis makes ethereal green light swirls in the night sky above Stenbacken, Sweden, on the railway line to Narvik. *Chris Guss*

Aurora Borealis

Northern winter skies famously exhibit the northern lights, or Aurora Borealis, a mesmerizing natural phenomena that results when electrically charged solar particles collide with the earth's atmosphere above the northern magnetic pole. Scintillating nocturnal displays may last from a few seconds to several minutes. At times, the whole sky is lit with cosmic swirls of color. (For a northern lights forecast, go to **aurora-service.org/aurora-forecast**.)

Malmbanen connects with the rest of Swedish rail network at Boden. The south end of the line runs to Luleå, a port situated at Svartön Harbor on the Gulf of Bothnia (in the northern portion of the Baltic Sea). Luleå is a big town and a regional passenger terminus.

For a different experience, you can board a sleeping-car train at Stockholm Central Station and ride overnight through central Sweden, which allows you to enjoy the stunning scenery of the Malmbanan in daylight.

Gällivare is located north of the Arctic Circle, 104 miles (168km) from the junction at Boden. It features a classic wooden railway station on the east side of the line, and it is a junction with a secondary line running south to Östersund, which is a lightly traveled alternative to the more popular route from Stockholm.

The Malmbanan Route to Narvik had been the stomping ground for massive three-section Dm3 siderod electric locomotives that hauled ore trains. Although these leviathans have been retired, you can view one on static display at the Bothnia Railway Museum.

Kiruna is Sweden's northernmost city with a population of 23,000 and an important rail station. Ore mining is the primary economy here, and recently, the necessity to expand iron ore mines resulted in the wholesale relocation of the entire town, railway, and railway station. Notwithstanding this minor disruption, Kiruna is a tourist center catering to winter sports and adventure seekers and hosts dog sledding trips among other activities.

LKAB (Luossavaara-Kiirunavaara AB) is the primary mine operator, and you can tour LKAB Kiruna's mine (claimed to be the largest in the world). (See **kirunalapland.se/en/ see-do/guided-tours-to-lkabs-visitor-centre**.)

Ore is the lifeblood of Malmbanan. LKAB freights are among the heaviest in Europe. Most are hauled by massive and extraordinarily powerful purpose-built class IORE electric locomotives. Some trains run south to Luleå, but the majority run northward to Narvik for transshipment there.

To enjoy the finest views north of Kiruna, sit on the right side of the train. The line follows a man-made shelf above the expansive crystalline Arctic lake known as Torne Träsk. This is sparsely inhabited territory. Arctic tundra rolls to the horizon

An SJ local train passes snow sheds on the scenic climb from Narvik, Norway, toward the Swedish border at Riksgränsen. *Chris Guss*

for miles in each direction. With little more to see than scrubby trees and rocks (and mosquitoes), this is still a beautiful landscape largely untouched by the hand of man.

Other than the parallel highway and the occasional village, you see very little evidence of human activity. Notice the large disused substations along the line that are made of red brick and date from the original direct-current electrification in the early part of the 20th century.

Make a side trip and visit Sweden's Abisko National Park, served by the Abisko Turiststation. This popular Arctic park also features the Aurora Sky Station, Abisko Mountain Station, and views of Torne Träsk. Bus connections offer alternative transport to Kiruna. (For hotels, see **abisko.net**.) Consider a hike along the Navvy road that served as the primary artery to Narvik during the construction of the railway line. *Navvy* was the colloquial term for the migrant workers employed in the building of the railway, and both the trail and its history are infused with colorful folklore. The road runs from Abisko to Rombaksbotn, where in the summer there is boat service to Narvik.

At Narvik, views of scenic Ofotfjord seem otherworldly in the long twilight of midsummer when the sky never goes dark.

North of Abisko, the line enters a tunnel beneath Mt. Noulja and then crests at Rikgränsen Station, which is partially in a snow shed. Known in Norwegian as *Ofotbanen*, this railway line is isolated from the rest of the Norwegian rail network and only accessible through Sweden. Near the Swedish-Norwegian frontier is the world's most northerly ski resort, nearby Bjørnfell, Norway, a popular place to pick up the Navvy road. The railway follows an alignment on the Norwegian side of the border via twisting curves and snow sheds on its long descent to Narvik. Here, the line is on a high shelf with outstanding views of Ofotfjord.

Despite its Arctic location, Narvik's harbor is ice-free year-round and has flourished as result of its ore port. In April 1940, German forces seized the port to ensure its control of Swedish ore. Fierce battles raged in the fjord, with fighting extending on land to secure the railway line, and the railway's role in the war is well remembered. Narvik is still a major terminal for LKAB iron ore trains that unload into ships.

Narvik's curiosities include the unusually deep pedestrian tunnel below the harbor. Walking in the tunnel gives you the sense of a post-apocalyptic vision from

350

Among the 140 pieces of historic railway equipment displayed at the Bothnia Railway Museum is this vintage lightweight Swedish rail bus built by Hilding Carlsson in Umeå. It had a top speed of just 50 mph (80 km/h).

Railway museum

The Bothnia Railway Museum (Norrbottens Järnvägsmuseum), located near Luleå, is one of Sweden's largest historic railway attractions. It houses roughly 140 pieces of railway rolling stock that includes an impressive selection of vintage steam and electric locomotives, many of which once worked the Malmbanan. Indoor displays span 10 buildings with additional equipment outdoors. (For hours, directions, and transport, see **nbjvm.se**.)

a Jules Verne novel, where the perpetual sound of dripping water provides an uneasy sensation of what lies above.

A more popular attraction is the aerial tramway ride (June-August) that carries passengers to a mountain restaurant 2,150 feet (656 meters) above sea level and offers panoramic views of Ofotfjord. Arctic cruises of the fjord also take place in summer. (For Narvik tourism, see **visitnarvik.com**.)

SJ's Arctic Circle Pass is aimed at visitors and is valid for three consecutive days between Kiruna and Narvik. This flexible ticket allows unlimited travel on the line, with the caveat that there are only 2–3 trains in each direction daily. The Arctic Circle Pass is sold at SJ ticket agents and offers better value than purchasing single tickets. (For details, go to **sj.se**.)

Norway's Bergen Line

Norges Statsbaner (Norwegian State Railways) is known by the initials NSB. Today, the NSB Group is a Scandinavian transport company operating passenger and freight trains in Norway and Sweden. NSB group carries more than 60 million passengers annually with its four passenger subsidiaries. Its domestic services include commuter and intercity trains. In addition to ordinary seating, some NSB trains also offer Komfort class travel (aimed at business travelers), overnight Sove sleeping cars that have comfortable compartments with beds and blankets, Familie cars designed for passengers traveling with children, and Meny Kafé food service cars.

NSB Group's website (which has an English language feature) offers general company information, a journey planner, and up-to-the-minute on-time performance details (**nsb.no/en**).

Among Europe's great scenic railway journeys is the NSB route from Oslo to the historic port of Bergen on Norway's southwestern coast. It runs 306 miles (484km) over mountains on a tortuous line that required some of most intensive railway engineering in Scandinavia. It is noted for rocky terrain and having more than 180 tunnels, the longest being the 3.3-mile (5.3km) Gravehalsen Tunnel.

Many visitors opt to travel from east to west and then continue from Bergen by boat up the Norwegian coast. Through trains between Oslo and Bergen operate four times daily and require 7 hours to make the journey. In addition, there's an overnight service but this does not allow travelers to thoroughly enjoy the spectacular scenery for which the Bergen Line is famous, except in high summer when it never gets completely dark.

After departing Oslo, NSB's Bergen Line curls westward through forests and then climbs through rock cuts and tunnels to a summit above the snow line at 4,200 feet (1,280 meters) above sea level. Snow sheds and fences help keep the line passable in winter.

Myrdal is a mountain station situated at a high saddle while serving as the junction with Norway's famous Flåm Railway. You may wish to take the time and explore this unusually scenic and very steep mountainous line. Continuing west of Myrdal, the Bergen Line faces its most difficult geographical challenges. A line relocation in 1964 shortened the route on its approach to Bergen, although the old route is now seasonally operated at the Gamle Vossebanen. NSB terminates on the south side of

An NSB RegionTog (regional train) is ready to depart from beneath the arched train shed at Bergen, Norway. *Bonnie Gruber*

a rocky peninsula where the city's colorful port offers a picturesque setting on the fjord ringed by distant mountains.

Bergen's historic city center is famous for its antique wooden buildings and Viking heritage. Ardent railway travelers may wish to travel on the Fløibanen funicular railway that climbs high above the city for exceptional views of the fjord below.

Flåm Railway

Compared with other Scandinavian railways, Norway's Flåm Railway is a relative latecomer among traditional European railways, only being completed in the 1930s. Running northward from a connection with the Bergen Line at Myrdal, it descends precipitously into its namesake valley to the town of Flåm on Norway's Aurlandsfjord.

From end to end, this railway features difficult engineering on a steep alignment passing 20 tunnels, while providing stunning vistas of the Flåm gorge. Fascinating in the summer, it's even more impressive in the winter when frozen landscapes offer a wonderland of ice and snow.

Norway's Gamle Vossebanen (Old Voss Railway) seasonal steam excursion train is seen at its eastern terminus at Garnes. Leading the train is a restored Norwegian type 18c steam locomotive built in 1913. *Bonnie Gruber*

Gamle Vossebanen

The 67-mile (108km) section of the railway from Voss to Bergen was the oldest portion of the route between Oslo and Bergen. Originally a narrow gauge railway, this supremely scenic route followed a sinuous approach to Bergen. This was later converted to standard gauge and electrified. In 1964, when NSB completed a modern line relocation with long tunnels to shorten the run between Oslo and Bergen, the western portion of this colorful route was abandoned.

Today, an 11-mile (18km) section of the original line operates seasonally as Gamle Vossebanen (Old Voss Railway), a tourist line running from the station at Midtun (near Bergen) via Haukeland, Espeland, and Arna to Garnes. Trains run Sundays from mid-June to mid-September. (For schedules and connections, see **njk.no/tourist-information**.)

One of the premier attractions of the Flåmbanen (Flåm Railway) is the powerful Kjosfossen Waterfall that may only be reached by train via a special stop. *Bonnie Gruber*

Portugal

An overnight train from Lisbon pauses at Entroncamento to collect passengers. CP uses its electric locomotives to haul international sleeping-car trains consisting of Spanish-designed and operated low-profile Talgo sleeping cars.

Comboios de Portugal (CP) is Portugal's national railway, which operates a well-maintained intercity network providing passenger services to most major points. Its busiest intercity line offers nearly hourly timetable connections between the capital at Lisbon and the northern city of Porto. Numerous secondary lines and branches connect smaller cities and towns, including long-distance service to Algarve resort communities in the south.

CP operates passenger trains that are tailored to a specific type of service. Urban services work Portugal's suburban networks in Lisbon, Porto, and Coimbra. Regional trains are local runs that work main and secondary lines reaching smaller towns and communities. Intercity (*Intercidades*) trains provide limited-stop express services that require seat reservations (available when tickets are purchased). CP's Alfa Pendular (indicated on timetables as AP) are premier express services operated with Italian-designed Pendolino articulated tilting trains. These primarily operate on

Portugal's premier long-distance passenger trains are operated with Italian-designed tilting Pendolino trains and marketed as Alfa Pendular services.

A southward Intercidades train ascends the stiff gradient at St. Vincente de Paul on its run from Porto to Lisbon Santa Apolónia.

the Lisbon-Porto corridor with a pair of runs continuing south to the Algarve. Alfa Pendular requires an extra fare plus compulsory seat reservations and offers two classes: **tourist** (*turística*) class has two-by-two seating while **comfort** (*conforto*) class has larger seats in a one-by-two arrangement. An onboard cafeteria and minibar offer passengers a selection of drinks and food (including kid's meals) that allows passengers the opportunity to walk around the train and enjoy a light meal while watching the scenery roll by.

In addition, CP runs two types of international trains. Celta regional services connect Porto with Vigo, Spain. CP handles two regularly scheduled international sleeping-car routes run by the Spanish railway, Renfe, equipped with modern low-profile Talgo sleeping carriages. The Sud Express connects Lisbon with Hendaye and Irun at the Spanish-French border. The train's name and route are a legacy of the deluxe train historically operated by Wagons-Lits, the international railway car operator best known for the Paris-Istanbul Orient Express. The other route is the Lusitania, an overnight Lisbon-Madrid service.

A CP regional train passes lush scenery on the Lisbon-Porto route at Caxarias (north of Entroncamento). Many CP regional trains consist of self-propelled electric multiple units such as those pictured.

Tickets, timetables, and apps

Most CP long-distance trains offer both first and second class fares. In some instances purchasing tickets 5–8 days in advance may allow passengers to take advantage of special promotional fares (discounted up to 40 percent). Promotional fares are a bit of a gamble, as ticket prices are locked to a specific journey and nonrefundable, although depending on conditions some promotional tickets can be rebooked in advance of departure (depending on availability of seats).

Children up to age 3 may travel free provided they do not require a separate seat, while children 4–13 may occupy a seat and travel at half fare. On international trains, children are allowed a 40 percent discount.

Frequent travelers may consider purchasing one of several varieties of contactless cards used to store tickets. Among these are the **CP Card** and **Lisbon Viva Card** which are aimed at Portuguese residents and EU citizens. The **Lisbon Viva Viagem Card** is designed for infrequent travels on greater Lisbon transport, while the **Siga**

359

Card is for travelers in Porto. Cards are reusable but require a nominal, nonrefundable deposit. See CP's website for details (**cp.pt/passageiros/en**).

CP's website is in both English and Portuguese. For English, click EN in the upper right. Although most of the pages translate without difficulty, at the time of this writing, there were some glitches where key pages would revert to Portuguese without appearing to offer English options.

Fares can vary greatly depending on the distance traveled, the time the ticket is purchased, and preference of first or second class. For example, the ticket price for a journey between Lisbon and Porto can range from €42.40 for first class purchased at the time of travel to just €13.50 for a promotional second class ticket (a limited, train-specific, nonrefundable fare).

The CP app is available for download to Apple and Android mobile devices. It offers a simple straightforward interface that provide passengers with a variety of timetabling and ticketing options, including the ability to display tickets on the device (when delivered directly via SMS text message).

Lisbon

Lisbon is one of Europe's most impressively situated capitals and Portugal's largest city. It blankets seven steep hills that tower above the north shore of the Tagus River and its urban verticality has produced a variety of interesting mainline railway alignments, steeply graded tram routes (street car lines), a metro, and inclined funicular railways.

According to legend, Lisbon was established by Ulysses, the hero of Homer's *Odyssey*. The city was famously destroyed by a catastrophic earthquake in 1755 that left little standing. Today, the city's colorful architecture overlooks the Tagus estuary—the westernmost point in continental Europe. The popular Alfama district is its oldest and is characterized by narrow, winding alleys and inky dark streets.

LISBON STATIONS

Lisbon is served by three historic stub-end railway terminals. Some long-distance trains depart from Santa Apolónia located near the Tagus waterfront, southeast

Platforms at Lisbon's Rossio Station are protected by this lofty Victorian-era iron train shed. Although convenient to central Lisbon, Rossio primarily serves suburban trains so most distance rail travelers should to take the metro to Santa Apolónia to begin their journey.

Lisbon enjoys stunning weather and is a wonderful city to explore. Its urban verticality allows for great panoramas such as this view looking toward the Church of São Vicente of Fora (the twin-spired building at upper left).

of the city's commercial and administrative center. Cais do Sodré Station is on the southwestern waterfront. This small terminal serves electric suburban trains that run west along the north shore of the Tagus to Estoril and Cascais. Historically, this was the Estoril Railway that opened in 1895. Lisbon's Rossio Station is located at its namesake square in the city center, known for its elegant façade with a distinctive double-horseshoe-shaped entrance at street level; tracks are at a higher level, with trains arriving via a long tunnel beneath the ridge. Rossio primarily serves CP Lisbon-area commuter trains.

Lisbon Oriente is one of the city's most interesting stations. Unlike the historic stub-end stations serving the city center, Oriente is a through station serving suburban Lisbon. Designed by Spanish architect Santiago Calatrava, it was built to coincide with the 1998 Lisbon World Expo. Calatrava embraced an organic style to resemble a desert oasis with a modern train shed rising high above the platforms designed to look like giant white palms. Street access is well below the tracks, with station facilities, parking garage, and a multimodal terminal located below the platforms.

Lisbon's trams are popular with tourists, and tourists are popular with nimble pickpockets, so be mindful of your valuables.

Mind your pockets

Lisbon, a beautiful city popular with foreign visitors, is known for its nimble-fingered pickpockets—well-seasoned professionals who can spot a tourist a mile off.

A common technique used by stealthy thieves is mingling with the crowd and pressing against victims from behind. Beware unwelcome bumps in crowded places, and also avoid con artists who will try to engage you with a cheery smile while an accomplice skillfully robs you.

By the time you discover your loss, the thieves will be living it up on you.

Be wise, not paranoid, and don't let the latent hazard of petty crime dissuade you from exploring the city. Enjoy your visit, but mind your wallet and bags, and avoid exposing your valuables.

Estação do Oriente (Lisbon Oriente) is a suburban station several miles northeast of the city center and near the airport, which is an important multimodal transit hub. The unusual style is the work of Santiago Calatrava, an architect noted for his exceptional modern railway station design.

FERTAGUS SUBURBAN TRAINS

Fly across the Tagus by train and visit the historic seaport of Setúbal less than an hour from Lisbon. Setúbal enjoys some of the best railway service in Portugal. In addition to the traditional CP route running along the south bank of the Tagus, with ferry connections to Lisbon, Fertagus trains operate a modern suburban rail line that runs directly to Lisbon stations via the expansive 25 de Abril Bridge, a road-rail suspension bridge high over the Tagus named to commemorate the April 1974 revolution. This was Portugal's first privately operated passenger service.

Fertagus operates modern bi-level electric multiple units on hourly schedules between Lisbon Roma-Areeiro (located northeast of the historic city center) and Setúbal, with half-hourly rush-hour service running via Lisbon Entrecampos, Pragal,

Largo da Estação do Rossio (Lisbon's Rossio Station) is centrally located and famous for its double-horseshoe entrance. You pass through these doors and go up to reach platforms under the station's impressive iron train shed.

Lisbon's majestic 25 de Abril Bridge is the suspension bridge over the Tagus named to commemorate the April 1974 revolution that helped return Portugal to democracy following years of authoritarian dictatorship.

and Coina. End-to-end running time is under an hour. Fertagus offers numerous multimodal connections with CP heavy rail, Lisbon metro, tram, and bus routes as well as light rail lines south of the Tagus. (See **fertagus.pt**.)

LISBON TRAMS

Lisbon's famous antique electric trams are on par with San Francisco's cable cars as rolling iconic symbols of the cities they serve. While popular with tourists, these antique-looking cars are still operated as part of Lisbon's transport and used by residents when not swamped with visitors. The colorfully painted cars grind up and down steep grades through alleys and narrow streets on narrow gauge tracks. Portugal's historic ties with Britain facilitated development of Lisbon's tramway system, which dates to 1873, and was run by a British company for many years.

Of Lisbon's five tram lines, route 28E is among the most popular with visitors. Kin to San Francisco's Powell & Market cablecar line, this tram climbs up steep hills having panoramic vistas, runs through narrow alleys, and serves Lisbon's most colorful neighborhoods.

Lisbon's red tram tours are geared for visitors. They start at Praça do Comércio and make a loop around the hilliest portion of Lisbon's historic network. Although more expensive than regular yellow cars, red trams provide hop-on/hop-off accommodation.

Although still an impressive system of rolling antiques, it is vastly scaled back from the city's once-extensive network. By the 1990s, it seemed that Lisbon's old trams were on the road to extinction, but they survive on a handful of routes in daily service despite predictions of doom, the proliferation of rubber-tired road transport, and the expansion of the city's modern, largely underground metro. Age can be deceiving: Lisbon's tram bodies may be old; however, the cars have been skillfully renovated to retain the appearance of classic pre-World War II four-wheel trams, while being functionally improved with modern wheel sets and electrical gear.

In addition to the antique four-wheel cars assigned to popular tourist routes, Lisbon tram route 15 uses modern articulated trams. This line runs near the waterfront and shares trackage with historic trams in the comparatively level city center. Antique cars typically work lines 12, 25E, and 28E, while special red tourist trams make loops through the city. 28E is one of the most enjoyable routes, navigating the colorful historic Alfama and Graça districts, where photo opportunities flash by at every turn.

Entroncamento is a modern town by Portuguese standards; it flourished during the 19th and 20th centuries because of its strategic position on the railway. It makes for a pleasant place to wander around and is safe to explore after dark.

Here, you'll find some of the most extreme conventional electric tram trackage in the world, where the cars come precariously close to the walls of ancient buildings, turn around unusually tight corners, and drop down precipitously steep gradients through unusually narrow streets. Taking a spin on these cars as they squeal through lively alleys on a roller-coaster ride is one of the great thrills of Lisbon. Line 12 traverses some of the same tracks used by the other routes but instead plies a linear route making a complete loop through Lisbon's historic districts—a good means of transport for questing tourists.

Lisbon to Porto

Portugal's premier intercity corridor connects its two largest cities, Lisbon and Porto. Alfa Pendular express trains make the 209-mile (337km) run under 2 hours, 45 minutes with infrequent intermediate stops.

Settle into your seat in Lisbon. After departing Santa Apolónia, you pass urban sprawl as the railway follows the broad Tagus valley and passes a variety

Suburban trains serving São Bento Station in central Porto negotiate a narrow shelf on the north side of Douro, and views of the valley from the south side of the train are brief but captivating.

---

of smaller towns. Smaller stations along the way hark back to earlier times. The countryside is rolling and pastoral. Entroncamento, an hour north of Lisbon, is one of Portugal's most significant railway towns and is situated at the junction between the line north to Porto and an eastward route. CP maintains freight yards and locomotive servicing facilities here. Railway enthusiasts will be interested in the Museu Nacional Ferroviário (National Railway Museum).

In contrast with the open rolling landscape to the south, north of Entroncamento, the line passes through lush woodlands and deep cuttings. Approaching Porto, the railway spans the Douro River on an immense steel bridge. Long-distance trains serve Porto's Campanhã Station. Connections to the city center are available via a suburban train service destined to Porto's São Bento Station using a cliffside line above the Douro and then through a tunnel with its west portal within the confines of São Bento's historic 19th century train shed.

Among the railway museum's attractions are American-built Alco diesels, such as that pictured in the classic livery with a silver body and green stripe.

National Railway Museum

Portugal's Museu Nacional Ferroviário (National Railway Museum) at Entroncamento is adjacent to the railway station on the north side of the tracks. Its professionally designed exhibits include a roundhouse with an array of historic locomotives and rolling stock and railway memorabilia spanning a century and a half.

Among historic equipment of national interest are carriages used on royal and presidential trains. American visitors will be interested in the restored Alco-built, diesel-electric road switchers (adapted from Alco's domestic RS-series but built for Portuguese broad gauge track. These attractive 1950s locomotives wear their as-built silver and green livery.

There's no need to get up early, as the museum is open afternoons (2–6 p.m.) Tuesday to Sunday. Visitors arriving by train are afforded a 50 percent admission discount, and it is possible to buy combination rail fare/museum tickets at many CP stations. (See **fmnf.pt/museu**.)

Porto

Porto is a stunningly beautiful historic city located along the Douro River. Its urban verticality is attractive but difficult to navigate on foot. The city has two completely separate tram systems. Vestiges of the old network are maintained as a tourist ride and make a few loops through the city center on routes 1, 18, and 22. The old Massarelos tram depot is west of the center along the river and is now a museum. There's some urban street running. The cars are largely early 20th century, including

Porto's historic tram network is entirely separate from the modern system. Historic trams, including some American-designed four-wheel Brills, operate seasonally on three lines. Routes 19 and 22 converge near the Igreja dos Carmelitas Descalços (church) seen in this view.

some vintage Brills similar to those sold to many American street railways. You can purchase tickets when you board the vintage tram.

Porto's other network opened in 2002. This modern light rail metro system features sleek modern trams operating on six routes (A through F) that intersect in the city center via subways at Trindade Station. Route E serves the Porto airport. Part of the network is built on an old narrow gauge suburban system that famously operated steam locomotives into the 1970s. Metro tickets are purchased from automated vending machines at stations and must be validated onboard the trams. The Metro do Porto interactive website offers information and a map and has an English option (**metro-porto.pt**).

Designed by architect Marques da Silva and constructed in the early 20th century, São Bento is one of Portugal's most significant railway stations and tourist attractions. Many Portuguese stations are known for their elaborate blue-painted tile decorations, but none is more elaborate than São Bento. Inside the main hall, allegorical tile murals by Jorge Colaço depict the history of transportation and

Electric suburban trains reach Porto's São Bento Station by running along the River Douro and through a cavernous tunnel that exits a cliff side into this classic early 20th century train shed.

events in Portuguese history. Trains arrive via a tunnel and park beneath a classic old train shed.

Among Porto's other historically significant railway infrastructure are two majestic iron-lattice arch bridges designed by Gustave Eiffel, best known for his Parisian iron tower which shares the same style of construction with Porto's bridges. Historically, the Maria Pia Bridge carried the main line from Lisbon over the Douro, but it has been supplanted by a modern span. Eiffel's other Douro span is located farther west. It carries city streets on two levels and is now used by Porto's modern tram network. A funicular railway is located at the north end of the bridge.

DOURO VALLEY

Among the most spectacular railway routes in northern Portugal is CP's line east through the Douro valley, running from Porto via Caide and Pesoda Régua to Pocinho. The valley is famed for great natural beauty and is a historic wine-producing area designated a UNESCO World Heritage Site. Five trains travel daily

Gustave Eiffel's impressive Ponte Luís I spans the River Douro near central Porto, carrying the Avenida da República and Metro do Porto's line D on the level atop the arch and local city streets on the bottom level.

in each direction, plying the length of the line: they depart Porto eastbound at 7:15 a.m., 9:15 a.m., 1:15 p.m., 3:15 p.m., and 5:15 p.m., and they return westbound from Pocinho at 7:17 a.m., 11:11 a.m., 1:21 p.m., 7:21 p.m., and 7:07 p.m. Additional runs provide more frequent service between Porto and Régua. A seasonal historic train led by a 1925 Henschel steam locomotive operates on select days June through October.

Trains to Algarve

Portugal's most popular tourist destination is the scenically sublime Algarve region on the south coast. It is renowned for its miles of luscious golden beaches, wonderful climate, and historic cities that offer a dynamic mix of architectural treasures and a thriving nightlife.

The Algarve's largest city and principal railway hub is Faro, which is centrally located on the south coast. This is a holiday mecca famous for its historic harbor that offers visitors a mix of beach and surf attractions and old world charm with

Trains between Lisbon and the Algarve pass through rolling agricultural lands populated by vineyards, cork trees, and fields of cattle such as seen here near Ermidas Sado.

plenty of hotels, lively restaurants, pubs, and dance clubs. Trains run east, west, and north from here, and local fares are affordable.

Faro is served by a pair of direct Alfa Pendolino express services that run directly from Porto Campanhã to Faro, serving Lisbon Oriente and Lisbon Entrecampos but none of the main Lisbon terminals. These have a 5-hour, 36-minute running time from Porto, and a 3-hour running time from Lisbon Oriente. An additional three Intercidades round trips connect Faro and Lisbon Oriente. Travelers to and from central Lisbon can take connecting suburban trains between Lisbon's Rossio Station and either Oriente or Entrecampos.

In the Algarve region, nine daily trains connect Faro and Lagos; passengers traveling from the north can change trains at Tunes. Additional trains connect Lagos and Vila Real de Santo António (a historic town in the extreme southeastern corner of the country near the Spanish border). There are no longer cross-border rail services between southern Portugal and Spain.

Spain

Since the 1990s, Spain has had some of the fastest trains in Europe, both in terms of top-operating speed and end-to-end average speed. Here, a Madrid-bound AVE train races along at 186 mph.

Spain operates some of finest and fastest long-distance trains in Europe on track that is among the most perfectly engineered in the world. And state railway Renfe (Red Nacional de los Ferrocarriles Españoles) has remarkably tight timekeeping.

Historically, Spanish railways have shared broad Iberian track width with Portugal, and today Renfe's well-developed broad gauge network serves as the core of its rail services. In addition, there are narrow gauge systems in the north of Spain and around Barcelona, plus modern high-speed lines built to the Continental standard track width.

Renfe

In 1992, Renfe introduced its first all-new line, using French high-speed railway technology, between Madrid, Cordoba, and Seville. This service is marketed as Alta Velocidad Española (AVE). Since then, Renfe's invested in a nationwide network

The Spanish national railway, known as Renfe, operates a variety of fast, modern trains, such as this Italian-designed Pendolino.

of high-speed lines radiating from Madrid. This is now the third most extensive purpose-built high-speed network in the world, covering more than 1,678 miles (2,700km). In 2007, the Madrid-Valladolid (Campo Grande) high-speed route opened, and the fastest express trains cut travel time to one hour.

Some trains on this line continue northward to León (a 3-hour express journey). Madrid-Barcelona high-speed service via Zaragoza began in 2008, featuring 2-hour, 30-minute express trains. Madrid-València high-speed trains take about 1 hour, 45 minutes, and Madrid-Alicante between 2 hour, 15 minutes and 2 hour, 30 minutes. Madrid-Malaga expresses range from 2 hours, 20 minutes to 2 hours, 45 minutes.

On the Madrid-Seville, Madrid-Barcelona, and Madrid-Valladolid routes, high-speed trains run hourly, with greater frequencies at peak times. Madrid-Malaga through trains are largely hourly with a midday gap. Through high-speed trains to peripheral outlying destinations are less frequent but may be augmented with slower speed connecting trains.

Renfe's original AVE trains were adapted from Alstom's TGV design but feature smoother styling. Among the modern Spanish high-speed trains are the Talgo-Bombardier Pato (*duck* in Spanish) sets, so named because of their pronounced duck-billed nose. Service with the fastest trains are augmented with specially designed TALGO gauge-changing trains that operate at moderately high-speed on standard gauge fast lines and allow faster through services on Iberian gauge lines to cities beyond the reach of the high-speed tracks.

In 2010, following years of discussion, planning, and construction, the French and Spanish high-speed railway networks were linked at Barcelona, allowing for a variety of trans-European, high-speed railway journeys with a change of trains here from Spanish AVE to the French TGV and Euromed.

Renfe's broad gauge long-distance services are marketed under a variety of names and employ some very comfortable trains including TALGO or Pendolino tilting trains that provide greater comfort on curved track at speed. Its Euromed service runs along the Mediterranean coast from Barcelona França Station to Valencia, with some trains continuing to Alicante. Euromed consists of a stylish adaptation of the French TGV design and features a distinctive pearly cream livery. Renfe's many long-distance trains carry café/bar facilities that serve drinks and snacks.

Seville features this impressive modern terminus for Spain's original AVE high-speed line.

Renfe local trains pause at the Mediterranean coastal town of Garraf southwest of Barcelona. Spanish main lines are largely electrified.

RENFE also offers frequent local and suburban services to many Spanish cities. Unlike its long-distance trains, suburban trains do not require compulsory reservations and benefit from inexpensive ticketing options. In total, Renfe carries an estimated 410 million passengers annually.

Tickets and travel

Most Renfe long-distance trains offer first class (*preferente*) and second class (*turista*) seating. However, AVE long-distance high-speed trains also feature turista plus, which is only nominally more expensive and offers larger seats but without all the perks of high-speed first class such as complimentary in-seat meals.

For visitors living outside Spain looking to make several trips over a sequence of days, Renfe's Spain Pass may offer the best value. This allows for a fixed number of one-way journeys (4, 6, 8, or 10) to be completed in the course of one month. Purchase requires identification and proof that you are not a Spanish resident. Renfe's extensive website is largely in Spanish but offers a limited English language option. (Click on "Welcome" at the top of the site's home page: **renfe.com**.)

The original AVE trains built for the Madrid-Seville run were adapted from the French TGV design but with nominally different styling. Top speed was 186 mph (300 km/h).

Feve and Transcantábrico

In contrast to Spain's broad gauge network, the north Spanish Atlantic coastal region features an extensive narrow gauge system. Although state-run since 1965, Ferrocarriles de Viá Estreche (Feve) was finally melded into the national Renfe system in 2012. The narrow gauge railway retains its independent image and even features its own pages on the Renfe website (**renfe.com/viajeros/feve**).

Popular with tourists and railway enthusiasts, Feve is among the most scenic Iberian railways and features track that winds through canyons and mountains with numerous tunnels and high bridges. Among the most interesting routes is the picturesque Gijón-El Ferrol Line at the western reaches of its network.

At Gijón, there's a notable railway museum that is home to 150 pieces of historic railway rolling stock, many coming from the Asturias region. Among the collections of steam locomotives is a tank engine that had operated as late as 1991.

Other highlights of the region served by Feve include Bilbao's famous Guggenheim Museum, which offers an eclectic modern art display including the international works of Willem de Kooning, Andy Warhol, and Jeff Koons, as well as

Renfe's broad gauge Euromed train provides comfortable fast service between Barcelona, Valencia, and Alicante. A sleek Euromed glides through the station at Sitges on the Mediterranean coast.

numerous Spanish artists. (See **guggenheim-bilbao.eus/en**.) Consider visiting the historic northern Spanish port at Santander, which is scenically located on a harbor encircled by towering snow-crested mountains.

CRUISE-TRAIN SERVICE

Feve hosts El Transcantábrico cruise-train services that consist of a dozen deluxe vintage Pullman cars pulled by a diesel engine. Deemed to be among the best luxury sleeper trains in Europe, it contrasts with utilitarian functionality offered by Feve's own local and regional passenger services. While maintaining the appearance of a historic train, some of the sleeping cars offer deluxe accommodation with just two compartments per carriage with a sauna, onboard shower, wide screen television sets, and WiFi connections. El Transcantábrico operates seasonal itineraries where the El Transcantábrico Pullmans make 3–5 trips per month from June though early October.

One of the most popular destinations in Spain, Barcelona is famous for its ideal climate and stunning scenic setting and features wonderful culture, architecture, museums, and cuisine.

Barcelona

The Catalonian capital is one of Europe's greatest cities and a playground for visitors and residents. Home to more than 3 million people, the city has ancient origins as evidenced by bits of Roman walls woven into an urban tapestry that reaches from its Mediterranean harbor high into the hills to the north.

Barcelona has several railway stations: Barcelona Sants Station (Sants Estació) is the main intercity terminal and hosts domestic AVE high-speed services and TGV trains to France. Estació de França (Barcelona França) is a secondary long-distance station serving Euromed high-speed trains to Sagunto and Valencia and regional trains. Local trains serve smaller stations including the FGC (Ferrocarrilis de la Generalitat de Catalunya) station at Plaça d'Espanya, Plaça de Catalunya, and Passeig de Gràcia.

The city has a five-line metro system of which line 3 connects most of the railway stations, except Barcelona França. Urban transport also includes a funicular railway, an aerial tramway (cable car), and a historic tram.

Many popular attractions are centered in the old town, a compact walkable area with winding stone alleys and pockets of eclecticism. Beyond are more modern areas with broad avenues. Most famous is the La Rambla, an artery running from harborside to Plaça de Catalunya, deemed as the heart of Barcelona. This is flanked by narrow medieval alleys, known for their curio shops and cafés but also for adept petty thieves.

The city is famous for eccentric architect, Antoni Gaudí, whose organic flowing style defied established conventions and produced a host of colorful structures including his pioneering Casa Vicens, Parc Güell (**parkguell.cat/en/park-gueell**), and the epic Sagrada Família. As the symbol of Barcelona, and Gaudí's most famous structure, Sagrada Família is a monumental basilica that began construction in the architect's lifetime and is expected to continue until 2026, having spanned more than 140 years from inception.

Visitors with limited time intent on enjoying the wonders of Gaudi may consider purchasing the Barcelona Pass that offers priority access to Parc Güell and Sagrada Família among other discounts and benefits. (For details on the Barcelona Pass, see **barcelona.com/barcelona_tickets/barcelona_city_pass.**)

Among Barcelona's attractions are the architectural works of its famous eccentric architect Antoni Gaudi, who produced a unique organic style. The Gaudi House is located on Carrer de Sant Antoni Maria Clare and offers stunning views from its roof.

Czech Republic

Czech Republic has many wonderful towns and cities. Olomouc's baroque town squares are magical places on misty winter evenings.

Czech Republic's complicated history is a product of centuries of political machinations and intrigue that shifted national boundaries and changed the European map. For centuries, the Austrian Habsburg dynasty shaped the regions of Bohemia and Moravia that are now the Czech Republic. Czech cities' iconic and eclectic architecture stem from this imperial period.

The role and geography of the Austro-Hungarian Empire was crucial during the 19th century railway-building years when Bohemian industrialization fueled rapid railway growth linking Prague with cities across the expansive Habsburg Empire.

World War I and its aftermath resulted in complex changes for railways and nations in this region. After the war, Czechoslovakia was among the modern nations created from remnants of the old Austro-Hungarian Empire. Yet because the Austrian railway network had been built to fulfill imperial transport and its main

---

A ČD diesel leads an ALEX privately operated passenger service from Prague to Munich. Czech Republic enjoys excellent rail services including several private operators in addition to state-run trains.

Pictured is the baroque Samson's Fountain at Přemysl Otakar II Square in České Budějovice—an attractive southern Czech city famous for its beer, Budweiser Budvar, the original Budweiser.

lines connected provincial centers with Vienna, and to a lesser degree Budapest, once the empire was separated, some routes no longer fulfilled the roles for which they were created. Before the breakup, the Czech areas of Bohemia and Moravia were in Austrian territory, while Slovak areas were largely in Hungarian territory. Following the Czecho-Slovak union, railway connections between sections of the new country needed development.

During its relatively short existence, Czechoslovakia faced complex politics: with German occupation during World War II and then after the war with Soviet-backed Communist control. In 1968, the Prague Spring, which aimed at easing totalitarian repression, was brutally crushed by the Soviets and the Warsaw Pact. Yet core democratic ideals were manifested two decades later when Czechoslovakia regained its independence and democratic control was restored between 1989 and 1992. Then in 1993, Czechoslovakia was peacefully dissolved and divided along ethnic lines to become the Czech Republic in the west and the Slovak Republic in the east. Consistent with this political change, the Československé státné dráhy (Czechoslovak state railways) was divided along national lines. New national railway

A nocturnal view on one of ČD's traditional locomotive-hauled trains departing Praha Hlavní nádraží. The station's classic iron shed looms in the distance.

companies were created. Subsequently, both nations joined the European Union, and to comply with European Union transport predicates, the railways were separated into separate infrastructure and operating companies to facilitate introduction of open-access competition.

The historic commonality between Czech and Slovak networks, combined with a desire to maintain through services, has resulted in a high degree of cooperation between railways. Through passenger trains from Prague to Slovak cities routinely mix equipment from respective national railways. In the Czech Republic, the national railway České dráhy (ČD) operates most local and intercity passenger trains, while open-access operators RegioJet and LEO Express also compete for traffic on key trunk routes.

Prague

Prague is one of Europe's most beautiful and interesting cities. Famed for its elaborate and ornate baroque architecture, Bohemian culture, and a stunning setting in the Vltava River valley, Prague was among the first cities of the Eastern

Trams cross the Vltava River on Prague's Palackého Most, one of several bridges that link areas of the Czech capital on opposite banks.

Bloc to see a surge of tourism after the fall of the Berlin Wall. Its center is best explored by tram and on foot. You can wander the alleys of Old Town, visit Prague Castle, Wenceslas Square, and Charles Bridge. You can also take in a concert, enjoy a Pilsner, and feel the lively energy of this vibrant central European cultural center.

Prague is a great city for trams, with lines weaving through the city center from every direction. What should impress visitors is the speed and frequency of the trams. Rarely a minute goes by between the squealing of tram cars through city streets. They glide by majestic churches, beneath stone archways, and across the Vltava. In addition to trams, there are buses, a three-line underground Soviet-designed metro with superfast escalators, and a funicular.

Paper tickets may be purchased from automated machines at select tram platforms and in metro stations. The tariff system can be a little confusing. There are individual short-term tickets (good for 30 minutes travel after validation), basic tickets (good for 90 minutes), 1-day tickets, and 3-days tickets. Different fares apply to adults, children (6–15), students, and seniors (65–70, while Czechs over 70 may travel free). Children and senior fares may require proof of age. Large pieces of luggage and bulky items

Praha Hlavní nádraží (Prague's main passenger station) is a beehive of activity, with trains connecting all corners of the Czech Republic and beyond to neighboring countries.

such as baby carriages require a separate ticket. Most tourists will focus on the city center (covered by trams and metro); however, be aware that transport beyond the center on surface buses involves multi-zone tickets. (For fare details, journey planners, and up-to-date information on Prague transport see **dpp.cz/en**.)

PRAHA HLAVNÍ NÁDRAŽÍ

Railway lines radiate from the Czech capital like spokes from a wagon wheel. The main railway station, Praha Hlavní nádraží, is busy with numerous daily departures. Direct ČD trains run hourly to Plzeň and take about 1 hour, 35 minutes; every 2 hours, they run to Cheb and take between 2 hours, 35 minutes to just over 3 hours depending on the type of train (SC Pendolinos are the fastest); direct trains to České Budějovice run every 1–2 hours and take 2–3 hours depending on train type.

The original railway station building dates to 1871 (when it was known as Prague Kaiser-Franz-Joseph-Bahnhof/Emperor Franz Joseph Station). Between 1901 and 1909, the station was substantially remodeled by Czech architect Josef Fanta, who was among leading proponents of the Czech art nouveau movement.

The station is located east of the historic city center along Wilsonova (the divided highway named for American President Woodrow Wilson) and is just a 10-minute walk from Wenceslas Square. It is well connected by public transport with trams 6, 9, 26, 55, and 58 stopping nearby, and situated on metro line C, which connects directly with Praha Holešovice (Prague's charmless international station located north of the city center, which hosts several through EuroCity trains that bypass the city center).

While Praha Hlavni handles a variety of intercity and regional services, numerous local and suburban trains instead serve the nearby Praha Masarykovo nádraži, a 10-minute walk north.

In the last decade, Hlavni has undergone a dramatic transformation, as the dreary communist-era trappings were swept away and the whole station was substantially cleaned and modernized, and new platforms and electronic train indicator displays were installed. Today, on the lower floors below track level is a well-lit shopping mall with a range of shops and fast food outlets, as well as ticket counters and reservation desks. The station has coin-operated luggage lockers open 24 hours daily.

Czech trains

ČD operates several types of passenger trains. The fastest and most expensive are Pendolino tilting trains marketed as SuperCity (SC) services that require an extra fare with compulsory reservations. Like other premium fast services, these modern trains offer an airplane-like experience and feature WiFi, but they are only nominally faster than other trains. For a comfortable but more traditional central European railway experience, consider choosing InterCity/EuroCity (IC/EC) express trains, which tend to feature conventional heavy carriages hauled by locomotives. Some ČD railway carriages still have traditional compartments, while others have open seating. EC/IC trains carry both first and second class carriages. Slower regional trains operate on most lines and stop often at smaller stations. Czech fares are generally very reasonable, so when trains are busy, it is certainly worth paying extra for the greater comfort of first class.

The historic interior of Praha Hlavní nádraží is one of the most lushly decorated of any European station, yet many passengers never notice the artwork within as they proceed directly from platforms to public transport or streets.

In the beer-brewing center of Plzeň, you can get this view from the Americka Bridge over the Radbuza River located west of the main railway station.

PRAGUE TO OLOMOUC AND BOHUMIN

One of Czech Republic's busiest lines is the east-west trunk that connects the Austrian, Slovak, and Polish frontiers. Czech state railways (ČD) is the largest carrier, with hourly express trains to most points on this route, as well as regular through international services to cities in Austria, Hungary, and Slovakia. But this route is also served by open-access private rail operators LEO Express and RegioJet.

Traveling east of Prague's heavily populated and industrialized areas, the main line crosses rolling agricultural lands with enclaves of local industry and mid-sized towns. Kolin is the junction with a diverting line that runs north of Prague and is largely used as a bypass by through freight traffic to and from Germany. Farther east is Česká Třebová, the junction with the route toward Vienna and Bratislava, which diverges in a southeasterly direction running via Brno and Břeclav.

Continuing east, the main line toward Olomouc winds through rugged scenery while skirting mountains to the south. In recent years, ČD has invested in this route

One of ČD's modern Skoda-built class 380 electrics in a special nostalgic paint livery at Břeclav, Czech Republic, works EuroCity 103 Polonia from Warsaw to Vienna.

by building short line relocations to ease curves and speed running while shortening the line with tunnels and rock cuts to avoid older circuitous alignments that followed river valleys.

Olomouc has a big station with connecting services for points in every direction. Recently, the station has been overhauled, but unfortunately, it still presents a dreary welcome compared with Prague. But don't be fooled by its drab railway platforms—Olomouc is a Czech gem worth exploring.

East of Olomouc, many through trains use a line around the busy railway junction at Přerov. Most local trains serve Přerov, where you can make connections south toward Břeclav and Vienna.

Farther east at Hranice is a junction between ČD's lines to the east and those to northwestern Slovakia.

Most long-distance intercity trains travel via a northerly route that serves the industrialized cities of Ostrava, Bohumín, and Český Těšín. The southerly route is more scenic but mostly served by regional trains.

A ČD local train operating with new double-deck City Elefant electric multiple units crosses the famed Jezernice Viadukty (viaduct) on the busy line between Přerov and Ostrava.

OLOMOUC

The Czech city of Olomouc was historically the capital of Moravia. While the industrialized area around the railway station features communist-era concrete architecture, the old city resembles a compact version of Prague. With winding well-worn cobblestone alleys, eclectic detailed architecture, and two beautifully ornate squares paved with cobblestones and exuding old world charm, this is a great city to explore. (For Olomouc sights, attractions, and events, see **tourism. olomouc.eu**.)

Check out Olomouc's curious astronomical clock at Horní náměstí (Main Square), modified during the communist period, which features 20th century socialist themes. Nearby is the elaborately decorated Holy Trinity Column. Olomouc's St. Wenceslas Cathedral is the city's most prominent building, and it features the

Don't miss Olomouc's Horní náměstí (Upper Square). It is paved with cobblestones, ringed by shops and restaurants, and is the location of the town hall and its astronomical clock and several elaborate fountains.

At dusk, a modernized Tatra tram grinds westward along Olomouc's cobblestone streets toward the city center.

second tallest spire in Czech Moravia. The city has several museums, an atmospheric city park along vestiges of the old city walls, and a zoo.

For a relatively small city, Olomouc is a tram enthusiast's delight. Its compact urban rail system features several routes that converge at the railway station with direct connections to the city center. Riding through cobblestone streets in the old city on a tram is a great way to see Olomouc for the first time. You can purchase time-based or day pass paper tickets from vending machines outside the station and other public stations or buy tickets using your smart phone. Keep in mind that large pieces of luggage and items such as baby carriages require a special ticket. (See Olomouc transport's website at **dpmo.cz/en**.)

ELBE OR LABE? CONTINUING THE JOURNEY FROM DRESDEN TO PRAGUE

The Elbe River in Germany becomes the Labe in the Czech Republic. The railway line running from Dresden to Prague crosses into the Czech Republic immediately south of Schöna in Germany, opposite Hřensko. (For the German portion of this journey see page 130.) You'll find that the best scenic views are on the left-hand side of the train,

RegioJet's colorfully painted locomotive-hauled express trains are a contrast to the drab colors characteristic of older Czech trains.

RegioJet

RegioJet is the marketing name for a private operator of trains and buses in the Czech Republic and Slovakia. RegioJet has been running bright yellow locomotive-hauled trains since 2011, and today, it connects several major cities across Czech Republic and Slovakia.

It offers a low-cost transport option with three classes of travel: standard, relax, and business. Modern WiFi portal entertainment is available as are complimentary newspapers, magazines, coffee, mint tea, and bottled water. Some trains feature specially equipped Astra quiet cars. (See **regiojet.com/en**.)

where you can gaze across the gorge. Near Děčín, there is a spectacular junction that carries another railway across a bridge and almost immediately into a tunnel.

Děčín Castle sits atop a rocky promenade on the east side of the Labe. This picturesque Bohemian landmark has off-white walls rising to meet its steeply pitched cherry-red terra cotta roof, which is punctuated by a narrow gold crested tower. Its baroque interior has been restored, and tours are available year-round (**zamekdecin.cz**). Make sure to see the highlights of the castle grounds including its rose garden.

Děčín Hlavní nádraži (main station) is located across the river from the town and serves as a junction with secondary lines. Through EuroCity trains continue toward Prague on the left bank via Ústí nad Labem, but an alternate route used by local

An eastward Leo Express Stadler-built electric railcar passes Drahotuse on its way toward Ostrava and Bohumín.

LEO Express

LEO Express is a private Czech-owned bus and railway transport company founded in 2010 by Leoš Novotný. Since 2012, it has run trains consisting of modern Stadler Flirt electric railcars focusing on the Prague-Olomouc-Ostrava-Bohumín market. In addition, two pairs of trains continue to Košice, Slovakia. LEO Express offers three classes of travel: economy, business, and premium. Trains are equipped with WiFi and feature a food service. Premium class passengers are afforded spacious, fully reclining leather seats in a quiet section of the train, plus complimentary food and drinks, and free parking for Prague passengers. (For timetables, fares, and other information see **le.cz**.)

trains diverges to follow the right bank. The route east via Česká Lípa to Liberec also diverges here.

If you simply want to get to Prague while gazing at the passing scenery from the window, consider taking the more expensive EuroCity trains that operate at 2-hour intervals. They are faster and offer greater comfort, have better windows, and tend to carry dining cars. Remember that some EC services continue beyond the Czech capital, so check the schedule to see which Prague stations your train serves, especially if you are planning to make connections. Running time from Dresden to Prague Hlavní nádraži is about 2 hours, 45 minutes.

A locomotive-hauled ČD regional train works the secondary line on the east side of the Labe valley.

A ČD branch train crosses the Labe against the backdrop of Děčín Castle. Light four-wheel railbuses such as this one are used on many Czech branch lines.

Slovakia

Among Bratislava's charms is its 19th century neo-Renaissance opera house that was designed by a prominent Viennese architectural firm.

Železnice Slovenskej republiky (Railways of the Slovak Republic, abbreviated ŽSR) is in charge of the national railway network. Most trains are operated by the state-run Železničná spoločnosť' Slovensko (ŽSSK). The railway network handles nearly 50 million passenger journeys annually for a national population of just 5.4 million people.

Bratislava

Slovakia's capital Bratislava is a charming colorful city on the Danube located about an hour from Vienna by train. Two main railway lines connect these two former Habsburg cities. One runs from the Vienna Main Station (Wien Hbf) on a northerly route via Marchegg that takes about 1 hour, 10 minutes to reach Bratislava's main station, Bratislava Hlavná (located north of the city center). The other route follows

Slovakia's main lines are largely electrified with frequent intercity and local passenger trains connecting the capital at Bratislava with outlying cities and town. *Denis McCabe*

The Slovakian capital Bratislava straddles the Danube, making it a popular stopover for river cruises.

a southerly course and runs from Wien Hbf via Bruck an der Leitha to Bratislava-Petržalka, a smaller suburban station on the south side of the Danube. A handful of intercity trains using the southern route continue on to the main station.

Bratislava's attractions include its main square, where antique buildings, the famous Roland Fountain, and lively activity make for a pleasant place to walk around. (For Bratislava tourist information see **bratislavaguide.com** and **bratislava.com**.) St. Martin's Cathedral is an impressive Gothic church in the city center. You can't miss Bratislava Castle, which looms impressively on a hill overlooking the Danube and the city. Its panoramic views alone are worth the visit; the castle also houses Slovak National Museum, which also operates the Museum of History. These are open daily except Monday, but hours vary seasonally. (For information on Slovak National Museum, see **snm.sk**.)

Visit the Museum of Transport located at Bratislavský Kraj, just a short walk from Bratislava Hlavná. It exhibits a variety of old railway rolling stock and artifacts as well as a selection of automobiles. Be aware that in addition to an admission charge, there is a separate fee for photography and video. Other Bratislava area activities

404

Bratislava is well served by public transport including several tram lines (streetcars) and a host of bus and trolley bus routes.

include Danube boat tours and a Soviet-era and post-communist road tour in a vintage 1970s Škoda automobile.

PUBLIC TRANSPORT

Public transport is provided by the Bratislava Transport Company, which runs an elaborate network of tram, bus, and trolley-bus routes connecting points within the city and running to outlying areas. Tram routes are numbered 1 to 9 (there is no number 7); routes 1 and 2 serve Bratislava Hlavná, with route 1 running from the station to the city center.

A variety of tickets are available from automatic ticket machines at transit stops and from newsstands or kiosks; some tickets may be used on suburban trains as well as city transport. Options include timed single (one-way) tickets ranging from 15 minutes to 3 hours (limited by the number of zones traveled as well as time; for example, a 15-minute ticket is only valid for two zones and a 150-minute ticket for 10 zones). Day tickets are available from 24 to 168 hours, and flexible multiple-journey tickets (called Carnet tickets) are designed for long journeys. As on other eastern European transit systems, passengers bringing luggage, bicycles, or pets on public transport are required to purchase special tickets in advance (typically a 15-minute ticket). Reduced fares are available for children, students, and seniors. (For general information in English on tickets and transport, see **dpb.sk/en** or **imhd.sk/ba**.)

Bratislava transit tickets must be immediately validated upon entering a transit vehicle. (Machines will cease validating shortly after the doors close, so don't hesitate to stamp your ticket in the mechanical box near the door.) Unfortunately for visitors, using Bratislava transport can be an intimidating prospect because of the unusually complicated fare structure combined with a great variety of ticket options and the potential for difficulties with vigilant (and reportedly unsympathetic) ticket inspectors. The best way around this is to buy the Bratislava Card.

You should consider purchasing the Bratislava Card, which is available for durations of 1–3 days. Among the principal benefits is unlimited travel on public transport in the city and surrounding areas that includes one piece of luggage per cardholder. The card also offers free admission to 12 museums and galleries plus more than 120 discounts at shops, restaurants, cafés, and other attractions. A free hour-long walking tour is also included. Cards are sold at various locations including tourist information centers at Bratislava Airport, at Klobučnícka 2 (in the city center), at the ŽSSK Customer Center at the Bratislava Hlavná, and at various city hotels and major border crossing points. (For details on the Bratislava card, see **visitbratislava.com**.)

BRATISLAVA HLAVNÁ

Slovakia's complicated history includes its one-time role as an important city in the Hungarian region of the Habsburg Empire. At that time, the city was known in Hungarian as Pozsony. In the 19th century, Hungary's first railway tunnel was bored immediately west of Bratislava Hlavná (then known as Pozsony Station). Today the railway, the station, and tunnel serve the Slovakian capital.

Trains connect Bratislava Hlavná with numerous regional cities to the east: EuroCity trains run to Budapest Keleti every 2 hours, taking about 2 hours, 45 minutes. More than a dozen regional and InterCity trains run to Košice (schedules vary from 4 hours, 45 minutes to 6 hours), every 2 hours to Břeclav (1 hour or less), Žilina (2 hours, 45 minutes), and to Zvolen (3 hours). While trains

A modern double-deck electric multiple unit makes a station stop in rural Slovakia. Although Slovakian trains are frequent and inexpensive to ride, rural stations often offer sparse accommodation. *Denis McCabe*

departing on the western side of the station exit via the tunnel, those departing the curving terminal on the east end follow the old main line that runs toward Budapest on an elevated alignment around central Bratislava.

Slovakian railway journeys

One of the busiest and most interesting Slovakian main lines is the trunk route that runs from the capitol at Bratislava northeast to Žilina, where it joins a main line from the Czech Republic. This continues east through river valleys and then over the Tatra Mountains to Košice. This heavily traveled double-track route is completely electrified with excellent track structure. In addition to local and express passenger trains, you'll pass numerous freight trains, many of which serve the massive steel works near Košice.

Traveling east from Žilina is a scenic journey. The line initially clings to the Váh River through narrow rocky passes. West of Bešeňová, the railway loops around a dam and reservoir, and farther east, you'll span the Belá River at Liptovský and

Hrádok and then begin the ascent of the Tatras. This west slope is largely forested. The railway's summit at Štrba is a low pass in the mountains, located 2,789 feet (850 meters) above sea level. Here the railway line passes a deep cutting immediately west of the station. A connecting rack railway run by the Štrbske Pleso-Štrba rack railway runs from Štrba 4.75km up a steep line to Tatra mountain resorts. Additional connections are available via a mountain tram network operated by the Tatras Electric Railway.

East of Štrba, the double-track main line descends through mountain meadows with wonderful views of snow-crested peaks on the left side of the train. Poprad is an industrialized town and a jumping-off point to winter sport resorts via alternative connections to Tatras Electric Railway. The station features Soviet-styled architecture with the tram station on the upper level. The main line descends along the Hornád River valley toward Košice.

On the Žilina-Košice main line, the junction station at Vrútky allows transfer to nonelectrified secondary routes. If time allows, consider taking a diesel train that wanders south through the mountains. This route transits tunnels and horseshoe curves in a heavily forested landscape running toward Banská Bystrica, and beyond to Zvolen, where you can make further connections to Bratislava and other points in southern Slovakia.

KOŠICE

Located in the broad Hornád River valley, Košice is Slovakia's second largest city and the 2013 European Capital of Culture. This is an important industrial city and a regional railway hub that benefits from good intercity and local rail service. In addition to domestic services are international connections south to Hungary and east into the Ukraine; however, there are no longer through services into Poland.

The main railway station is a convenient 10-minute walk from the classic old town. Leave the station and walk compass west via Mestský Park past historic Jakab's Palace. Attractions include the compact medieval city center, which is well suited for exploration on foot. St. Elizabeth's is a well-preserved 14th century Gothic cathedral, and nearby is St. Urbain's Tower, a classic stone clock tower. A seven-line tram network connects the city and railway station with outlying suburbs.

Located in eastern Slovakia, Košice is a gem of a city, yet rarely visited by Western tourists. Take in the quaint old world architecture and explore railway lines on the edge of Europe.

Hungary

Budapest Keleti is a gateway to eastern European railway travel. Board here for railway adventures to Romania, Bulgaria, Serbia, and beyond!

Hungary's state railway is managed by the MÁV Group (MÁV stands for Magyar Államvasutak), and passenger services are operated by a subsidiary called MÁV Start. In addition, lines from Győr via Csorna to Sopron and Szombathely are operated by a separate company called GySEV (Győr-Sopron Ebenfurthi Vasút), which runs attractively painted green and yellow trains.

MÁV Start's extensive passenger network radiates from Budapest and connects the capital with cities and towns across the country. In addition to its intensive domestic services are international connections with Hungary's neighbors. Through international long-distance trains operate from Budapest to most adjacent capital cities. Trains to Vienna and Bratislava run every 2 hours and take about 2 hours, 4 minutes to either city. To Ljubljana, travel time is 8 hours, to Zagreb 6 hours, to Belgrade 8 hours, to Bucharest 8 hours, and to Berlin 11 hours, 32 minutes.

GySEV (Győr-Sopron Ebenfurthi Vasút) is a joint Hungarian-Austrian railway operating lines and trains in western Hungary, including cross-border services via Sopron. GySEV trains use this attractive green-and-yellow livery.

MÁV's website features timetables, a journey planner, and online ticket purchases (**mavcsoport.hu/en**). Tickets booked on the website may be transmitted as E-tickets or designated for local collection. Most domestic long-distance InterCity and InterPici express trains, as well as international trains, require payment of a supplement in addition to the cost of the ticket. The price of supplements varies depending on the distance traveled; however, the supplement is not locked to a specific train nor does it constitute a seat reservation (which may be arranged in addition to the supplement).

Hungary offers numerous fascinating destinations including Sopron (located just over the border with Austria and an easy day trip from Vienna), Győr, and resorts on Lake Balaton in the southwest part of the country. Debrecen is a moderately sized city in eastern Hungary that operates a short tram network. Owing to its many neighbors, Hungary is an excellent jumping-off point for international railway adventures, especially those further east. Consider a trip onward to Romania, the Balkans, or the former Soviet state of Ukraine.

Budapest

Budapest is the capital of modern Hungary and historically was the second city of the Habsburg Empire. It remains one of the most beautiful capitals in eastern Europe. Historically it was once two cities: Buda on the west bank of the Danube and Pest on the east bank. It is a cultural melting pot and a vast, fascinating urban environment to explore with amazing architecture, fine restaurants, museums, and colorful neighborhoods.

There are many choices: Take a Danube boat tour. Walk across the mid-19th century Chain Bridge—Budapest's first bridge over the Danube. Relax in the popular Széchenyi thermal baths. Take the funicular railway to Buda Castle to enjoy stunning views of the Danube and the city. (For Budapest tourism, see **budapest.com**.) Visit the Urban Transport Museum, which features historic vehicles (**bkv.hu/en/museums/urban_public_transport_museum_szentendre**) and the Millennium Underground Museum, which presents the history of the underground railway.

The Hungarian Parliament occupies impressive Gothic-style buildings on the east bank of the Danube. The best views are in the afternoon and evening when they catch the light from the west.

Of Budapest's three main railway terminals, Keleti (Eastern Station) is the most impressive, highlighted by its distinctive fan-shaped window on its main façade.

BUDAPEST STATIONS

The Hungarian capital has three main terminals. Keleti Station is the main international terminal and, by far, the most useful and most interesting. It features a 19th century building and train shed with an enormous fan-shaped window facing the street. Nyugati Station also is a fine old building and is the closest terminal to the city center. Déli Station is a characterless modern facility located on the western side of the Danube, primarily serving local and other domestic services. Kelenföld is an important junction station to the south of the city center and one of the busiest stations in Hungary.

BUDAPEST TRANSPORT

Budapest enjoys a comprehensive public transportation system. In addition to MÁV suburban trains and four suburban routes operated by HÉV (Budapest Local Railway), Budapest Transport Company (BKV) provides a wide range of transport with four metro lines, more than 30 tram routes, dozens of bus routes, plus seasonal Danube ferries and boat tours, the Buda Castle funicular railway, and a cog railway. In addition, BKV operates historic trams.

One of the most satisfying ways to explore Budapest is by riding the trams as they make their way through city streets. To avoid the hassle of buying individual tickets, get the Budapest Card, which is good on most public transport.

Visitors may consider buying the Budapest Card, which among other benefits covers public transportation and alleviates the hassle of having to purchase tickets for individual journeys. The cards are sold for durations of 24, 48, and 72 hours, and they are valid for the designated period from the moment of validation. (For details on Budapest transport by BKV, see **bkv.hu/en**.)